Three Medieval Greek Romances

Three Medieval Greek Romances

Velthandros and Chrysandza,
Kallimachos and Chrysorroi,
Livistros and Rodamni

Translated by
Gavin Betts

Routledge
Taylor & Francis Group

First published in 1995 by Garland Publishing, Inc.

This edition first published in 2018 by Routledge
2 Park Square, Milton Park, Abingdon, Oxon, OX14 4RN
and by Routledge
52 Vanderbilt Avenue, New York, NY 10017

Routledge is an imprint of the Taylor & Francis Group, an informa business

© 1995 by Gavin Betts

Publisher's Note
The publisher has gone to great lengths to ensure the quality of this reprint but points out that some imperfections in the original copies may be apparent.

Disclaimer
The publisher has made every effort to trace copyright holders and welcomes correspondence from those they have been unable to contact.

A Library of Congress record exists under ISBN:

ISBN 13: 978-0-367-14994-9 (hbk)
ISBN 13: 978-0-367-14995-6 (pbk)
ISBN 13: 978-0-429-05436-5 (ebk)

GARLAND LIBRARY OF MEDIEVAL LITERATURE
VOL. 98, SERIES B

THREE MEDIEVAL GREEK ROMANCES

The Garland Library
of Medieval Literature

THREE MEDIEVAL GREEK ROMANCES

*Velthandros
and Chrysandza,
Kallimachos
and Chrysorroi,
Livistros
and Rodamni*

translated by

Gavin Betts

GARLAND PUBLISHING, INC.
New York & London / 1995

Library of Congress Cataloging-in-Publication Data

Three medieval Greek romances / translated by Gavin
Betts.
    p.   cm. — (Garland library of medieval litera-
ture : vol. 98. Series B)
    Includes bibliographical references.
    Contents: Velthandros and Chrysandza—Kalli-
machos and Chrysorroi—Livistros and Rodamni.
    ISBN 0-8153-1279-2
    1. Romanes, Byzantine—Translations into English.
I. Betts, Gavin. II. Belthandros kai Chrysantza.
English. III. Kallimachos kai Chrysorroë. English.
IV. Libistros kai Rhodamnē. English. V. Series:
Garland library of medieval literature ; v. 98.
PA5173.T47 1995
883'.0208—dc20   94-32655
                                      CIP

Printed on acid-free, 250-year-life paper
Manufactured in the United States of America

To Katharine

Κρεῖττόν μοι βρῶσις, ἔλεγεν, νὰ γένω τῶν θηρίων
καὶ τῆς ζωῆς νὰ στερηθῶ παρὸ τῆς κόρης ταύτης.

Kallimachos and Chrysorroi ll.1001f.

Preface of the General Editors

The Garland Library of Medieval Literature was established to make available to the general reader modern translations of texts in editions that conform to the highest academic standards. All of the translations are originals, and were created especially for this series. The translations usually attempt to render the foreign works in a natural idiom that remains faithful to the originals, although in certain cases we have published more poetic versions.

The Library is divided into two sections: Series A, texts and translations; and Series B, translations alone. Those volumes containing texts have been prepared after consultation of the major previous editions and manuscripts. The aim in the edition has been to offer a reliable text with a minimum of editorial intervention. Significant variants accompany the original, and important problems are discussed in the Textual Notes. Volumes without texts contain translations based on the most scholarly texts available, which have been updated in terms of recent scholarship.

Most volumes contain Introductions with the following features: (1) a biography of the author or a discussion of the problem of authorship, with any pertinent historical or legendary information; (2) an objective discussion of the literary style of the original, emphasizing any individual features; (3) a consideration of sources for the work and its influence; and (4) a statement of the editorial policy for each edition and translation. There is also a Select Bibliography, which emphasizes recent criticism on the works. Critical writings are often accompanied by brief descriptions of their importance. Selective glossaries, indices, and footnotes are included where appropriate.

The Library covers a broad range of linguistic areas, including all of the major European languages. All of the important literary forms and genres are considered, sometimes in anthologies or selections.

The General Editors hope that these volumes will bring the general reader a closer awareness of a richly diversified area that has for too long been closed to everyone except those with precise academic training, an area that is well worth study and reflection.

James J. Wilhelm
Rutgers University

Lowry Nelson, Jr.
Yale University

Contents

General Introduction

Her mouth was small and lovely—enough to suffice for the kiss of a loving heart. Her lips were red and thin, like a rose when it opens at dawn to receive the dew. . . Such a countenance, I swear by my soul's pain and my woe, will never be seen again in the whole world.

For all her charms Rodamni, the heroine of the medieval Greek romance *Livistros and Rodamni* to whom the above lines refer, has not previously attracted an English translator, and this is also true of the other two romances presented here, *Velthandros and Chrysandza* and *Kallimachos and Chrysorroi.* The three form part of a curious niche of literature which has, until recently, been unjustly neglected. The genre to which they belong contains eleven stories, all in verse, and all with the theme of romantic love. Information about the circumstances in which the poems were produced and the audience to which they were addressed is scanty, but on the basis of what evidence there is they can be dated to the fourteenth century.

It seems likely that the poems were popular at the time of their composition in the late medieval Greek world. This, however, would not have recommended them to the scholars of the Renaissance when Greek and Roman studies were seriously taken up in the West. These men were laboring to produce editions of the great literary works of ancient Greece and Rome and they idealized the societies which produced them. They had little respect for the civilization of the very recent Greek past and only valued contemporary Greek culture inasmuch as it preserved a knowledge of the ancient language. The language of the romances, which was based—how closely it is now difficult to tell—on the spoken language of the fourteenth century, would have been held in contempt by scholars and one actually characterized it by the damning epithet *barbarograecum* (*barbarous Greek*).[1] Consequently, it is not surprising that references to our poems in the scholarly literature of the Renaissance are few.

Subsequently, although manuscripts were acquired by some of the great libraries of Europe, no scholar of the seventeenth or eighteenth centuries thought it worthwhile to produce an edition of any sort.

It was not until the second half of the nineteenth century that attitudes started to change. The romances were recognized as being among the first examples of modern Greek literature and some appeared, for the first time, in print. But even so, they were not studied solely for their own merits. Nineteenth century scholars began to investigate the form and immediate antecedents of modern Greek and realized that the language of these poetical texts provided evidence for the spoken language of the late middle ages. Because of this the poems provided ammunition for a particularly vicious controversy waged in Greece itself over the form that written modern Greek should take. The possibility that they might have literary merit was usually ignored.

Recent decades have seen a quickening of interest in medieval Greek literature, particularly the romances. The three poems presented here are now seen as complex works and have been subjected to studies of various sorts. But it will be some time before past neglect has been remedied. Much work is still required in the all-important matter of establishing satisfactory texts. The situation is particularly serious in the case of *Livistros*.

For Renaissance scholars the poems were the degenerate offspring of a great tradition. A hundred years ago they were seen as quarries providing raw material for linguistic battles. But to achieve an understanding of them we must examine their background and character; to do this a summary of their plots is necessary.

Velthandros and Chrysandza

Velthandros, the second son of a mighty Greek king, Rodofilos, is dissatisfied with the treatment accorded to him by his father. Despite the desperate attempt of his elder brother, Filarmos, to dissuade him, he goes abroad with three squires. After an adventure at Turk's Hill he comes to the city of Tarsus. In the vicinity he discovers a stream which contains a band of fire within its current. He is intrigued by this and sets out to find the stream's source. Finally, he comes to a mighty castle from which the stream issues forth. An inscription on the gate declares it to be Love's Castle and warns against entering. However, leaving his squires outside, Velthandros goes in. He follows the stream through a beautiful garden and comes to a building containing a dining hall. In front of the building is a statue from which the water pours although, as we later learn, its true source is inside the building.

Velthandros goes into the hall and on the wall he sees two bands of reliefs; a lower one shows men and women being tortured by cupids, and an upper one displays a group in a state of happiness. The men and women represented are labelled with their names and some details of their history. At the end of the hall Velthandros notices a sapphire statue of unspecified gender holding a peacock. The statue is in an advanced state of misery. Its tears are the source of the stream's water while its constant sighs provide the stream's band of fire.[2] When Velthandros reads a message on the statue declaring that he himself suffers a passion for Chrysandza, the daughter of the prince of Antioch, he is very distressed. Further inspection reveals another statue, this time designated as male, with an arrow in its heart. It too bears an inscription, which states that Love has determined the destinies of both Chrysandza and Velthandros. In a state of disarray, the hero continues his tour. When he ventures out of the building he sees a terrace on which stands Love's throne.

At this point a cupid appears before Velthandros and summons him to Love's presence. After Velthandros explains to Love how he happens to be there, Love announces that he wants Velthandros to judge who is the fairest of forty noble women. Velthandros is then left to do this and the meticulous approach he adopts leads him to make some very sharp comments on the first thirty-nine participants, whom he rejects. The fortieth he pronounces to be without flaw and he presents her with a wand of victory. He then reports back to Love on the lady's beauty in glowing terms. When he has finished Love disappears and there is nothing left for Velthandros to do but collect his squires at the castle's entrance and set out for Antioch to find his predestined love. He does not at this stage know that she is in fact the woman he selected as the beauty queen.

On arriving at the plains of Antioch Velthandros meets the city's prince, who is hunting. Velthandros joins in the hunt and impresses the prince with his archery. The prince takes him back to the palace and installs him in the royal retinue. On a later occasion Velthandros goes to see the prince when he is with his wife and his daughter, Chrysandza. Velthandros realizes that Chrysandza is his love and the woman he selected as winner of the beauty contest, and Chrysandza recognizes him as the judge. Velthandros does not press his suit, however, and things stay as they are.

One evening, after two years and two months have elapsed, Chrysandza is beside herself with frustration. She goes into her garden and gives vent to her feelings but is overheard by Velthandros. He decides to take the initiative and approach her. With little by way of preamble they embrace and before the night is over they have made love. But when Velthandros leaves at dawn he is apprehended by the guards. Immediately afterwards, Chrysandza hears of this and sends her faithful maid, Fedrokaza, to her lover. The maid tells him that he must say that *she* was the object of his attentions, not her mistress. Chrysandza then goes to see her father, the prince, and in a feigned rage complains that Velthandros has trespassed in her garden.

The prince becomes angry and immediately arranges a trial. However, when he hears of Velthandros's (pretended) love for Fedrokaza he softens and suggests that they marry. This happens, and their unconsummated marriage serves to conceal Velthandros's relationship with Chrysandza.

After ten months Velthandros becomes afraid. The lovers decide to escape together with Fedrokaza and the three squires. Unfortunately, the night on which they abscond is wild in the extreme. They try to cross a river but are separated by the current. Velthandros reaches the opposite bank, destitute and clad only in his underpants. Chrysandza, completely naked, is tossed back to the bank from which they started. Ignorant of each other's survival, they wander along the opposite sides of the river. After Velthandros finds the corpse of Fedrokaza, and Chrysandza that of one of the squires, they are reunited. A search reveals the two remaining bodies and they then follow the river to the coast. A ship appears and they make contact. It transpires that the captain has been dispatched by Velthandros's father, Rodofilos, to find him. After a recognition scene Velthandros learns the sad news that his elder brother, Filarmos, is dead. Velthandros and Chrysandza embark. They return to Velthandros's native land and receive a rapturous welcome. The story ends with their marriage and Velthandros being declared king.

Kallimachos and Chrysorroi

A mighty king sends his three sons out into the world to seek adventure and determine by their exploits who is the most valiant and most worthy of his father's throne. The youngest is called Kallimachos. When the three come to a castle guarded by supernatural creatures the elder brothers abandon the venture and return home. Kallimachos enters the castle, which is owned by a dragon who has conceived a passion for a young maiden, at present his prisoner. Kallimachos kills the dragon and rescues the lady, who has been suffering from the dragon's somewhat unconventional method of courting. The two fall in love. After exchanging vows they take a bath in the castle pool and consummate their relationship. They then live together happily in Dragon's Castle as man and wife.

But their idyll is not destined to last. A powerful king, as yet unmarried, is wandering about with his army and happens to come near Dragon's Castle. When he sees Chrysorroi looking over the castle wall he falls hopelessly in love. Before taking further action he returns to his kingdom, where a witch offers her services. An expedition to the castle is mounted and Chrysorroi is abducted by a trick of magic devised by the witch. The king takes her home but she resolutely rejects his offer of marriage and he is forced to delay the fulfilment of his desire.

Though the witch left Kallimachos in a death-like coma, he is revived by the timely (and unexpected) intervention of his brothers. He immediately sets out to look for his beloved. After some time he discovers her. He finds that she is in mourning for him and that the king is absent on a military campaign. Kallimachos takes up employment as a gardener to gain access to her. Recognition follows and the lovers enjoy secret trysts. Finally they are discovered and Kallimachos is thrown into prison. The king returns to sit in judgement on them both but after Chrysorroi's spirited defence of herself and her true lover the king grudgingly releases them and they return to their former happiness in Dragon's Castle.

Livistros and Rodamni

Livistros and Rodamni has a more complicated narrative structure than the other poems. Here two stories are brought together through a character, Klitovon,[3] who is the protagonist in one story (the subsidiary one) and the friend of the protagonist in the other. The romance is given a further degree of complexity by the fact that it is Klitovon who tells both stories.

Klitovon is addressing an audience consisting of a noble lady, Myrtani, and a mixed group of inhabitants of the land of Litavia. These others are not named and we subsequently learn that Myrtani is their queen. The romance concerns a man, Livistros, and his love for Rodamni.

Klitovon begins his tale in this way. He has left his native land because of an unhappy love affair and is riding through a beautiful meadow when he is intrigued to see a Latin knight utterly absorbed in grief. After a little coaxing, the stranger, whose name is Livistros, tells his story, but on the condition that they become friends and never separate.

Livistros explains that he had been the ruling prince of a country called Livandros and that, although he had reached manhood, he had been completely unfamiliar with romantic love. When a striking example of such love was brought to his notice he was profoundly troubled. He then had a dream in which he was taken to Love's court, where, after being upbraided for his neglect of love, he swore to become Love's servant. Love then informed him that he was destined to marry Rodamni, the daughter of the king of Silver Castle. Later, in another dream, he actually saw his fated spouse and, on waking, was impelled to go off in search of her. After two years he found Silver Castle and solved the initial problem of establishing contact by writing a message on an arrow and shooting it onto the lady's balcony. Subsequently, Livistros improved his technique by tying messages to the arrows. He used this means of communication to dispatch many letters. Although Rodamni showed a good deal of contrariness during this courtship by post she finally fell in love with him. A meeting was arranged and proved wholly successful, apart from Rodamni's disturbing news that her father had already arranged for her to marry Verderichos, the king of Egypt, who was about to arrive. But, excellent heroine that she is, she had a solution. She would suggest to her father that the two suitors joust and that she would accept the winner as her husband. In the event, her father was happy with this arrangement and in the ensuing fight Livistros was an easy victor. He then not only married his beloved but became ruler of Silver Castle. However, Verderichos was not easily put off. Two years later, he immobilized Livistros with the aid of a witch, kidnapped Rodamni and carried her off to Egypt. When Livistros returned to his senses he set out to find his beloved. He was still searching when he met Klitovon and his narrative ends at this point.

Klitovon now tells Livistros about his own unhappy love affair. But we can ignore his story for the moment as Klitovon gives up his own concerns completely and lends his full support to Livistros. The two set off for Egypt. They arrive at a strait separating them from their goal and appear to be at an impasse. But they find the witch who had helped Verderichos, only to be abandoned at this very spot. She tells them that Rodamni has so far resisted her abductor's importunities and has managed to persuade him to set her up as an innkeeper. She will keep the inn for four years and only after that time will she submit to his will. In her adopted profession Rodamni hopes to learn something about Livistros from travellers. The witch then gives the two friends magic horses to cross the strait to Egypt and tells them how to find and rescue Rodamni.

They follow her advice successfully. But on the return journey they call on the witch and Rodamni is so seized by hatred that she demands that Livistros kill the woman immediately. This is done and the three then return to Silver Castle where Klitovon marries Rodamni's sister and becomes co-regent.

So much for the main story. Klitovon's story is much simpler. He was born in Armenia, the nephew of the ruling prince. He had fallen in love with Myrtani, his cousin and the prince's daughter, while her husband was abroad. He was accepted by the lady but the prince learnt of their affair and threw him into prison. The situation was not improved by the return of Myrtani's husband. However, the resourceful lady bribed the guards and enabled her lover to escape. Not long after this he met Livistros and joined forces with him.

We learn Klitovon's story slightly after the middle of the romance but it is not until the end that it is concluded. We are told that after some years of marital happiness Rodamni's sister dies and the disconsolate Klitovon decides to return to his home. There he finds Myrtani, now a widow. She is the person whom we met in the opening lines and to whom he has told the whole story. He ends by announcing his intention to spend his remaining years with her.

The background

The background of the medieval Greek romances is complicated. It is made up of three strands, historical, linguistic and literary, which come from antiquity and after frequently intertwining, provide the fabric for the canvas on which the poems were composed.

The Byzantine empire, from the time of its inception in late antiquity, was centred on Constantinople. It had waxed and waned over the years until, at the beginning of the thirteenth century, it consisted of about half of Asia Minor and the greater part of the Balkan peninsula (considerably more territory than is occupied by Greece today). These territories represented a decline from the great days of the sixth century after Justinian had reconquered a large part of the old Roman world. But the empire could still boast of a cultural and intellectual tradition that went back in an unbroken line to antiquity. In 1200 A.D. Constantinople, alone of all the ancient centres of civilization and culture, had never been conquered or subjected to foreign control. And its society was essentially static. The long centuries during which the empire had survived numerous emergencies confirmed a general belief in the excellence of its traditional institutions. The Byzantines had little interest in progress or change, and nowhere was this attitude more in evidence than in matters of language. But to understand this conservatism we must go back to the period before Constantine, in 324 A.D., founded Constantinople, the new Rome and capital of the Eastern Empire.

In the second century A.D., when the Greek world had long been taken over by Rome, we see the beginnings of an educational movement which is called the Second Sophistic. Its missionaries were teachers of rhetoric. As a result of their activities rhetoric came to be an important part of higher education and its practitioners were regarded as upholding an aspect of Greek culture, the art of public speaking as it had been practised in the glorious days of the long dead city-states. The rhetoricians of the Second Sophistic turned to the great Athenian orators of the fourth century B.C. for models and this, combined with the prestige of Attic (i.e. Athenian) literature generally, led them to attempt a revival of the form of Greek used at Athens in its political and cultural prime, the period between 450 and 340 B.C.

This bizarre attempt to resurrect an old form of the language was destined to be the linguistic strand of the fabric of the background to our romances. The enthusiasm which it generated among the educated classes of the second century A.D. seems attributable to a mixture of cultural chauvinism and nostalgia. The Greek language had changed considerably over the previous four centuries, rather more than has been the case with English since Elizabethan times. It would have been no easy task to speak and write in an idiom that might have been acceptable to Demosthenes or Plato. Despite this difficulty, Attic Greek was taught to a greater degree than had happened previously and was given a very rhetorical flavor. Teachers, famous and otherwise, re-enforced this element by delivering set-piece speeches in which every trick of eloquence was exploited. With this skill they acquired both fame and wealth, and the practice of this type of oratory became popular by the end of the second century A.D.

As a result of this, Attic Greek, with at least a tinge of rhetoric, became obligatory, not just for speeches, but for many works of literature that claimed serious attention.[4] Several centuries later this idiom replaced Latin as the official medium of communication in the Byzantine court and its bureaucracy. As far as literature is concerned, the practice persisted up to the end of the Middle Ages (the romances are among the few exceptions). We have no means of judging to what extent and with what competence the classical tongue was spoken at different times, but it dominated the written word. Indeed it remained the vehicle used by the Greek intelligentsia for history and ecclesiastical matters even after the fall of Constantinople to the Turks in 1453.

This linguistic conservatism is reflected in the third strand of the fabric, which concerns a literary genre, the ancient novel.

By the time the Second Sophistic movement was under way in the second and third centuries A.D. the novel had long since established itself as a popular literary genre. Its origins were bound up with the new form of Greek culture which had developed from the end of the fourth century B.C. in Egypt and the countries fringing the eastern Mediterranean as a result of the conquests of Alexander the Great. These conquests had brought an end to the power and influence of the old city-states in Greece itself and elsewhere but had also placed vast new areas under Greek control and influence. After Alexander's death in 323 B.C. his enormous empire broke up into a number of independent states which lasted for several centuries. The elements which these states had in common were Greek rulers and an upper and middle class which, though by no means always of Greek origin, used the Greek language and saw themselves as the heirs of previous Greek cultural achievements. This period (late fourth century to middle first century B.C.), to which the term *Hellenistic* is given, witnessed the rise of various elite literary schools which gave new directions to Greek literature but which had little or no appeal beyond their dedicated initiates. However, with the geographical expansion of the Greek world literacy in Greek was increasing. A new reading class was created which needed some form of contemporary literature less sophisticated than that offered by the intellectuals with their high-brow productions.

It was for this new type of reader that the novel was created. In essence, it was a prose work of some length which told the story of a young man and woman in love who, after separation and many tribulations, are finally united. The heroine was given the same importance as the hero because the novel was intended to have an appeal for female audiences—literacy among women had also increased. The basic plot was mandatory. But this was not a disadvantage. Like many a stereotyped television drama the ancient novel was primarily meant to provide its readers (mainly city dwellers) with a means of escape from the banality of city life to a world of excitement, adventure, and, above all, romantic love. The ways in which this escape from reality was achieved reflected the anxieties and preoccupations of the day. They also stamped the novel with characteristics which it bore until the end of the Middle Ages and beyond.

For many people of the Hellenistic period the eastern Mediterranean was a dangerous place. The rival Greek states were more interested in furthering their own ends than in policing the seas and this, combined with the haven provided by the many clusters of small islands, gave ample scope for pirates, whose main activity, kidnapping, was intimately connected with the slave trade. As the basic theme in the novel was the triumph of true love over adversity it was little wonder that most ancient novels involved the hero or heroine, or both, being abducted by pirates and sold into slavery. This also involved them, albeit unwillingly, in foreign travel, a motif which has always been important in escapist literature. (We can see the abduction motif recurring in *Kallimachos* and *Livistros*, as well as journeys into unknown countries; the latter is also a feature in *Velthandros*.)

The Hellenistic period brought changes in religion. In previous centuries the civic organization of a city state and the lives of its citizens had been intimately bound up with the city's own variety of traditional religious beliefs. Under the new political conditions, where autocracy was the rule rather than the exception, the old divinities were often seen as irrelevant to the individual and as remote as the monarch to whom the individual's allegiance was due. Loss of political rights helped to stimulate a fatalism which saw events as irrational or pre-ordained, or both. One form which this fatalism took was a belief in Fortune (Τύχη *Tyche*), who was conceived of as an unpredictable goddess capable of taking a malign delight in her perverse treatment of mortals. She became so fixed a part of the novel that she was not subsequently banished by Christianity.

When in 30 B.C. Cleopatra was defeated and Egypt, the last surviving independent Greek state, was incorporated into the Roman empire the Hellenistic age came to an end. The Romans saw themselves as the inheritors of Greek civilization and now that all the old Greek states were under their control they began a policy of benign paternalism. Under their rule the Greek world fell into a state of peace and tranquillity previously unknown. But although pirates and other paraphernalia of the previous age no longer existed in real life, they were still part of the novel, which continued to present the same picture of the world as it had previously done.[5] In the Christian era its popularity continued and it became the literary form which had the broadest appeal in the Greek world.

Five ancient novels have survived complete and their authors are Chariton, Xenophon of Ephesus, Longus, Achilles Tatius and Heliodorus. Exact dating is difficult, but Chariton and Xenophon of Ephesus were probably writing in the first century A.D. or earlier as they do not show the influence of the Second Sophistic. But although, in fact, the novel was not considered as a sophisticated literary form, the other three are written in the revived form of Attic Greek. They must, therefore, belong to the second century or later. These three continued to be much read in Byzantine times, and this, it seems, was in no small part because of the language which their authors used.

In the twelfth century A.D. the genre was revived and we possess novels from four authors: Prodromos, Eugenianos, Manasses (fragmentary), and Makrembolites; the first three are in verse. These works continued to be written in the same artificial Attic Greek and were very much in imitation of their ancient prototypes. Each is set in the ancient world against a pagan background where Christianity is ignored. The old techniques and themes are continued. Apart from the switch to verse in three cases there is little that is new. There is also little that has reference to the contemporary world.

We have now traced our three strands of history, language and literature up to the end of the twelfth century. During the next hundred years the Greek world was thrown into confusion. The strands change their texture. Under influences from the non-Greek world old traditions were challenged. The type of romantic narrative that emerged from this period of change was different in setting, language and tone.

The continuity which the Byzantines had so long enjoyed was not destined to last. In 1204 they were jolted out of their age-old complacency when the Fourth Crusade, which had been diverted from its journey to the Holy Land by the Venetians, captured and pillaged the Byzantine capital. The invaders, who were known as Franks or Latins, were mainly French or Italian. After taking Constantinople the crusaders showed no inclination to resume their journey to the Holy Land. On the contrary, they appear to have thought that residence in the Greek world suited them very well.

A Latin kingdom was set up with Constantinople as its centre. This only lasted to 1261, but the Latin states established elsewhere in the Greek world survived, in some cases, for several centuries. These areas (in mainland Greece and on the islands) were subject to the undiluted influence of Western culture, and one of the most tangible manifestations of this can still be seen in the form of castles scattered over the Greek landscape. But it was not simply by strongholds that the Franks exercised their power over their Greek subjects. As was to be expected, they had no interest in maintaining Byzantine institutions and they replaced the old bureaucracy with their own. In this new administration the spoken Greek of the day was used, not the artificially maintained Attic Greek. By making this change the Franks eliminated one of the main supports of the literary culture based on the classical language. A Greek born in an area under Western control not only had to go to what remained of the Byzantine state to acquire a traditional education but also had to stay there to profit from it.

The choice of the vernacular language for official purposes in the Frankish territories would have conferred on it a new and unaccustomed prestige. But there was a serious complication. A language that had not previously been put to sophisticated uses would have lacked the many specialized words required for administration and other purposes. These were supplied from the native languages of the Frankish administrators, and they formed part of the flood of words that came into Greek at this time from Western European languages, mainly Italian and French. The recognition (and enlargement) of the popular tongue proved to be an important step towards its use in literature. Once the Greek world had settled after the invasion of the Fourth Crusade—this seems to have taken the greater part of the thirteenth century—it was inevitable that the position of the vernacular language in the new Frankish territories would affect literature.

Before the thirteenth century the spoken language had only been used for works of literature in an extremely limited way. The novels of the previous century (see above) were written in an uncompromising form of the traditional literary language. The genre of the novel had been regarded as still existing within the framework of its ancient prototypes, and consequently it had to be written in the ancient idiom if its authors were to be taken seriously.

But when the Frankish influence was established we see the beginnings of a literature written in a language that was relatively close to everyday speech. One of the first of these works is a long poem, *The Chronicle of the Morea*, which describes the Frankish invasion and occupation of the Peloponnese (called *Morea* in medieval Greek). Whether it was originally written in Greek or whether it was translated from one of the three existing versions in western European languages we do not know, but its anti-Greek bias marks it as a product of the occupied territory. Its narrative stops at 1292 and as it is unlikely to have been written very much later than the events it describes, the poem may be dated to c.1300. Its language is close to normal speech though we cannot say that it wholly reflects the vernacular because some traces of the learned language remain. No doubt the weight of tradition was such that even an opponent of the old regime, as we can imagine the author of the *Chronicle* to have been, could not escape it completely.

The character of the romances

The eleven extant romances, which present stories of courtly love and chivalry, seem to have been produced within the next hundred years. We know of two others which are now lost, and it is possible that still more once existed. The manuscripts of the surviving poems give no hint of author or date of composition, nor has any direct information about the genre survived elsewhere[6] and for this reason we are forced to be vague. Virtually all evidence we have is from the poems themselves and our knowledge of the period in which they were written.

Of the surviving poems six are derived from French and Italian sources. Fidelity to the original varies from what may be called translation to what must be termed adaptation. We have an account of the Trojan war (*The War of Troy*; the original is French), two Western romances (*Florios and Platzia-Flora* from an Italian original; *Imberios and Margarona* from a French original), a story derived from late antiquity (*Apollonius of Tyre* from an Italian original), Boccaccio's *Theseid* in Greek dress, and an Arthurian tale (*The Old Knight* from a French original).

The remaining five romances are original compositions. In addition to the three poems translated here, this group contains *The Tale of Achilles* and *The Tale of Troy*.

Like the *Chronicle of the Morea*, all eleven are written in a language which must have been fairly close to normal speech. This in itself indicates that the genre had its origin in Frankish occupied territory. Also, the fact that six of the eleven depend on known originals from the West, where romances of chivalry had been popular for over a century, is a clear indication that the genre was a Western import. But we may reinforce this argument.

In the Greek territories that remained under the control of the Franks after their loss of Constantinople in 1261 any Western-style literature in Greek dress could only have been the result of a fusion of cultures. It is easy to see how this blend took place. To administer their possessions the Franks were obliged to associate with the local population, or at least the local aristocracy, and to assimilate themselves, to some extent, to it. (The situation was not the same as occurred later under Turkish rule when the enormous gap between Christianity and Islam produced a dichotomy which made any cultural amalgam difficult.) Sometimes Franks took Greek women as wives, the children of such unions being called *gasmules*. By the end of the thirteenth century this mixed society, which controlled Frankish Greece, would have stabilized. It was within this context that *The Chronicle of the Morea* (and two other similar works) were written. Both authors and audience could only have come from a Franco-Greek background as the subject itself and the way it is handled would have been thoroughly repugnant in any Byzantine circles. And it is from this same blended society that we would most naturally expect people with the linguistic skills (and also, possibly, the interest) to adapt works of literature from French and Italian into Greek.

The adapted and original romances have language, style and subject matter in common, and these common features oblige us to classify both types of romances together. But what distinguishes the originals from the adaptations is the pronounced Greek element in the former. This is strong in *Velthandros, Kallimachos* and *Livistros*; we can be confident that they do not depend on some Western source now lost or yet to be discovered. The three may in fact have been written in the reconstituted Byzantine Empire.

However, even in our three poems there are Western elements, particularly in *Livistros*. When the hero, Livistros, is introduced he is described as a Latin (i.e. a Frank or Westerner)[7] and he is following the very Western practice of carrying a hawk for fowling and of having a hunting dog on a lead. His hair style is Latin. At Love's court he swears to become a liege to Love in good Western feudal style (the word used is derived from the Western term).[8] When Livistros describes his first meeting with his beloved, Rodamni, he tells us that her clothes are Latin[9] and we later learn that she belongs to the Latin race. Further, when she tells Livistros that she has another suitor and that she will ask her father to arrange a contest between them, what she suggests is a Latin joust. She goes on to emphasize that this will be highly acceptable to the inhabitants of her city, Silver Castle. *'I shall take,'* she says, *'the one who conquers by arms. The Latin race loves the brave and especially those who fight for love or fortune.'* [10] But, curiously enough, the contest shows a clear mixture of East and West. When the two joust and Livistros is victorious he is given a very Byzantine reception—he is raised on a hollow shield, and the cheers raised for the hero and his future father-in-law reproduce the standard Greek formula.

It has been argued that some of the Western practices mentioned above
(e.g. jousting, fowling) were known and practiced at Constantinople
before the Latin conquest of 1204; and because they were not introduced
by the Fourth Crusade they cannot be taken as evidence of Western
influence on the romances.[11] This criticism seems to miss the point.
Even though such practices may have been known in the Greek world
before 1204 they would certainly still have been recognized as Western in
the Byzantine world of the fourteenth century. After the Byzantines had
been given a forced lesson in things Western over the previous hundred
years it is inconceivable that they would have assimilated various Western
habits to such an extent as to have forgotten the origin of such
quintessentially Western practices as jousting. These could not fail to give
a Western flavor to a poem written in the fourteenth century, especially
when the hero and heroine are themselves designated as Latins. It would
also have been appropriate for a Greek author to introduce such features
when he was writing in a genre whose Western origins were in any case
clear from the translations and adaptations it contained.

Minor details of Western origin are very much less in evidence in
Velthandros[12] and are wholly lacking in *Kallimachos*. Neither romance
contains any mention of Latins. In the former the hero is stated to be
Greek and his father the ruler of the entire land of the Greeks.[13] In the
latter no ethnic affinities are given. There are, however, two broader
features common to all three poems to which a Western origin can be
assigned.

The first of these is the setting. The romances have a contemporary
background. Livistros comes from an imaginary land, Livandros;
Velthandros and Kallimachos come from unnamed kingdoms but no hint
is given that we are meant to see their stories as having happened in the
distant past. Livistros and Velthandros visit real places (Egypt and
Antioch respectively) which are not depicted as existing anywhere but in
the present. The magical and supernatural elements of the romances are
presented as part of everyday life. This type of setting was typical of
Western romance, but it was not part of the tradition of the Greek novel
as its twelfth century exponents had received it. Their works are still set
in a period remote from the present, in exciting and turbulent conditions
such as had characterized the eastern Mediterranean in the Hellenistic age.
The whole paraphernalia of paganism, pirates, kidnappings and so forth is
used to provide a setting which was considered an integral part of the
genre.

The second general feature coming from the West is the castle motif. In the rhetorical tradition as established by the Second Sophistic movement the place (normally a garden) where the lovers first meet is the subject of an elaborate description (ekphrasis—see below). This continues in the original romances, but the venue has changed. It is now a castle, or a place associated with a castle, which is important both in the story and as a symbol.[14] In *Kallimachos* the hero enters Dragon's Castle and there finds the heroine, whom he rescues after killing the dragon. The place, which had previously been perceived as fearsome and hostile, then becomes the lovers' home and symbolizes their happiness. It is to there that they return when they regain their liberty at the end of the romance. The symbolism is taken a stage further in *Velthandros*. The hero is led by Love's river with its band of fire to Love's very castle, which he enters and, in so doing, submits himself to Love's power. Inevitably, it is his destined love whom he chooses in Love's beauty contest when he sees her for the first time.

With *Livistros* the castle motif is treated differently. It is the heroine, not Love, who has a castle. Love has a camp which Livistros visits in a dream; he swears his allegiance and is rewarded with the prospect of Rodamni's love. When he finally reaches her home, Silver Castle, he finds that her bedroom is on the side of the castle which is decorated with the Twelve Cupids, personifications of different aspects of love. But he is not allowed to come into contact with her immediately, or even to enter the castle. He must camp outside the section of the castle wall in front of her room. The symbolism becomes even clearer when he starts to communicate with her by messages tied to arrows which he fires onto her balcony. Silver Castle is Rodamni's heart, which Livistros must win by laying siege.

Castles are a medieval concept. They did not exist when the ancient novels were written and they were not used in the twelfth century Greek novel, which, as we have seen, took over the ancient setting in its entirety. But by the fourteenth century Western romances had long since taken up the castle motif and associated it with chivalry and adventure, and with various forms of erotic symbolism; the most striking of these was the castle of Love himself. When this motif was taken over into a Greek context it opened up possibilities that had not existed in gardens, which were the novel's preferred meeting place for the lovers.

But the Greek elements in our three romances are considerable. They can be conveniently considered under two headings: echoes of Byzantine institutions and practices, and features derived from the tradition of the Greek novel.

As an example of the former we may take the concept of king. Kings who are given a status comparable with a Byzantine emperor are called by the various imperial titles normal at the Byzantine court[15] (Rodofilos in *Velthandros*; Kallimachos's father, Chrysorroi's father and also her kidnapper; Rodamni's father, King Chrysos, and Verderichos, king of Egypt; and, of course, the supreme monarch, Love himself). But these rulers also show, or are called upon to show, qualities which the Byzantines required of a good king. A king was expected to uphold justice and show humanity, as Chrysorroi's kidnapper does, albeit reluctantly, when he releases her and Kallimachos at their trial. Truth and Justice are attendants on King Love. A true king should not plunder and oppress his people; when Rodamni accuses Verderichos of doing this she calls him Egypt's executioner, its tyrant. And for the Byzantines the king stood at the top of a rigidly stratified society. Even the dragon in *Kallimachos* is aware of this; when he sets about eating the entire population of Chrysorroi's country, with the sole exception of the lady herself, his social conscience is in evidence when he consumes the king and queen separately from the rest.

The beauty contest which Velthandros conducts with considerable aplomb is in itself an echo of a former Byzantine practice. It reflects in considerable detail the manner in which the wife of the crown prince was chosen in eighth and ninth century Byzantium. At that time a number of candidates were assembled and were judged according to the same principles of beauty as Velthandros uses. When a girl was dismissed she was told the grounds for her rejection and the final choice was made from a field of three; Velthandros's procedure is much the same. The main difference between the historical reality and our romance was that the crown prince's mate was chosen by his mother, not by himself.[16]

The many other echoes of Byzantine court etiquette and life found in the poems include titles, modes of address, royal acclamations, the style of royal letters and the employment of eunuchs.

Finally, we may note the artificial birds which sing on the branches of equally artificial plants in *Velthandros* (*ll.*468ff.) and *Livistros* (S1368). These seem to be a recollection of similar automata on a tree made of precious metals with mechanical birds which was a feature of the Byzantine court of the tenth century.[17]

Our romances stand within the tradition of the Greek novel inasmuch as they reproduce certain themes and literary techniques. We can also detect some borrowings from the earlier works.

The chief theme which they continue is, of course, that of the ultimate triumph of true love. This needs no illustration. It is because Western romance had the same subject that an amalgam of the two traditions was possible.

But there are two features common to our romances which are peculiar to the Greek tradition. The first is the concept of Fortune, which, as we have seen above, had developed during Hellenistic times and had been taken into the ancient novel, where it provided a point of contact with everyday beliefs. The idea of Fortune was subsequently used by the twelfth century authors, for whom it was part of the pagan background which they adopted. Our romances, despite their contemporary setting, continue with this concept. Although they were written in a society where considerable importance was attached to religion, it is remarkable that Christianity is virtually absent. What references are made to it are trivial or irrelevant to the story.[18] Apart from Love himself, Fortune and Destiny are the gods of the romances but they are merged into one, so that Velthandros can say, *In this world it is completely impossible for a man to escape Destiny and Fortune's thread (ll.738f.)*. This twofold power acts in a completely irrational and arbitrary way and may, at any time, send good or evil to individual people. Appeals to it are often made but are always conceived as futile gestures because each person's fate is fixed. The notion is strongest in *Kallimachos*, and we find Chrysorroi complaining of her own individual Fortune, which has been assigned to her like an odd perversion of a Christian guardian angel and which she sees as taking a strong interest in increasing her misery.

There is an obvious reason why the authors of the romances kept this particular feature of the novel. All our poems show a frank attitude to, not to say an enthusiasm for, the sexual side of romantic love. In *Velthandros* and *Livistros* the god of Love actually appears as a character. In *Kallimachos* he is only mentioned as presiding over the lovers' oaths but the unabashed sensuality of the pool scene leaves us in no doubt about the author's views. Such attitudes are, of course, completely incompatible with the teachings of the Church. It would have been inconceivable for the Christian God or any of his minions to become associated with such excesses, which conventional belief could only associate with the Devil. What more natural than for the authors to ignore Christianity and take over the traditional divine machinery?

The other important debt which the romances owe to the tradition of the novel is rhetoric in its many manifestations. Some of its more superficial tricks are obvious even in translation. We may note the practice in *Livistros* of beginning a series of sentences, usually short, with the same word or phrase (anaphora; see, e.g., p.128, pp.168f.); or the way in which the author establishes direct contact with his reader. This sometimes takes the form of rhetorical questions such as *What did she do next?* (*Velth. l.*1189); *So what happened?* (*Kall. l.*1026). In one of the most striking examples the author describes his own reaction to Chrysorroi's circumstances when we first see her:

In the middle (grievous to tell) a solitary girl was hanging by the hair. (My senses reel, my heart quivers!) ... By the hair! (Perverse invention of Fortune!) ... She was hanging by the hair! (Words fail me. I am speechless. I write this with a heavy heart.) (*Kall. ll.*449-454)

But the most prominent feature taken from rhetoric is the ekphrasis, or lengthy and elaborate descriptive piece. The subject can be anything that arouses the author's admiration and enthusiasm; this could be a building, a garden, a work of art, a human being—all find examples in the romances. The technique for such descriptions had been developed with the Second Sophistic and became a stock-in-trade for writers generally. The subject matter of our poems with its emphasis on the remarkable and strange obviously provides scope in this direction. We may take the description of Chrysorroi at the pool:

The lady was completely alluring. She inspired love. Her charms were beyond compare, her beauty beyond description, and her graces outdid those of the Graces themselves. Her hair flowed down in rivers of lovely curls and shone on her head with a gleam which surpassed the golden rays of the sun. Her body, which was whiter than crystal, beguiled the sight with its beauty as it seemed to blend the charm of roses with its color. Just the sight of her face alone shook your entire soul, your entire heart. Indeed, the lady seemed to be the image of Aphrodite and of every other beauty that the mind can conceive. But why prattle on? Why describe at length the beauty of her body? A few words suffice to define it. All the women that the world has produced, whether before or after her—or her contemporaries—can only be compared to her charms as one might compare a monkey to Aphrodite. (*Kall. ll.*807-826)

The romances often deal with the superlative and we are not surprised to learn that Chrysorroi is supremely beautiful. But to press this home within the ekphrasis the author resorts to various figures of speech which include: metaphor (*Her hair flowed down in rivers of lovely curls*); hyperbole (*Her graces outdid those of the Graces*); authorial interruption (*But why prattle on?*); hypophora (a question which is immediately answered, *Why describe at length the beauty of her body? A few words suffice to define it.*) But most of all we should note the way in which the author uses these figures to work up to a superbly audacious hyperbole (all other women are to Chrysorroi as a monkey is to Aphrodite). In true Byzantine fashion the ekphrasis is treated as an art form in its own right.

A good deal of energy and emotion has been expended by scholars on showing that *Velthandros*, *Kallimachos* and *Livistros* are either more Greek than Western or more Western than Greek. Unfortunately, we have no external evidence to help us decide. But on the basis of the poems themselves and the literary and historical context in which they were written the most plausible conclusion seems to be that their authors took over a Western genre and were so successful in adapting it that its foreign origin was obscured. Frankish and Greek elements are brought together so well that the result shows no joins.

The circumstances of the romances' composition

We are primarily concerned here with *Velthandros, Kallimachos* and *Livistros* and only indirect reference need be made to the other romances. What follows, however, has relevance to both the other two original poems, *The Tale of Achilles* and *The Tale of Troy* and the group of translations and adaptations.

The text of *Velthandros* starts with an exhortation to young people to hear the story which is about to be told:

> Come! Attend a moment, all you young people. I wish to tell you the fairest tale, a beautiful and unusual story. Whoever wants to taste of its sadness and joy will also wonder at its account of daring and bravery. (*Velth. ll.*1-5)

The beginning of *Livistros* shows something similar happening within the dramatic context of the poem. Klitovon is represented as telling the story of Livistros to an assembled group:

All sensitive people schooled in love, who have been reared and instructed by the noble Graces; who have been subjected to exquisite torments; and all you of low degree; every soul of goodwill who is versed in love, every heart of noble grace which is devoted to virtue—come now and hear with me of love's passion in the fair story which I shall tell. (*Liv.* N1-9)

If we were able to take this as more than just a literary convention and as representing the way in which the poems were actually presented we might suspect that the eleven surviving romances existed within some sort of tradition of recited poetry. This is an attractive idea but here too we have no external evidence. What evidence there is comes from the poems themselves and the manuscripts in which they survive.

Velthandros has survived in a single manuscript, and this is also the case with *Kallimachos*. But where we have more than one manuscript of a particular romance we are often presented with textual differences between the manuscripts which are so great as to make it impossible to reconstruct a now lost original. In some cases these differences are of such a magnitude that we are entitled to speak of versions. An example of this is provided by *Livistros,* which survives in five manuscripts.[19] Four make up a group which give one version of the poem; of these four only one is even approximately complete, but using the evidence of all four we have a work of about 4400 lines. The fifth, which is virtually complete, gives a version of the poem which comes to slightly over 3800 lines. This condensation by almost 600 lines is not the result of omitting episodes or anything of importance. Brevity is achieved by dropping unessential lines or by a different wording. Other romances from the eleven also exist in different versions and in some cases these versions do show significant differences in the narrative.

This suggests that the original text of a romance, as it came from the author's pen, was regarded as something which could be changed at will and did not merit careful preservation. Again, a passage in *Livistros* gives a hint of this. At the end of the poem Klitovon, after wondering whether his own story will find a narrator, answers himself:

But a man whose soul is so inclined will pity those who suffer, will learn from their sorrow, and will tell their story to other sufferers. If someone, after inquiry and scrutiny, writes down <my story> in detail, even though he cannot tell everything, he will compose an account of most of what I say. But if perchance some

lover wishes to describe it, he will refashion it according to his
wish and fancy. (*Liv.* S3255-3262)

The existence of versions of this nature is normally associated with oral
poetry, where illiterate bards recite long poems which, because of the
technique involved, vary, sometimes considerably, from one performance
to the next. But while the language of the romances has some
characteristics of oral poetry these are by no means sufficient to justify
any classification under this heading. We are left with the conclusion that
in preparing a new copy of a particular text a scribe was free to make
alterations for any of a number of reasons that today we can only guess at.
It does not seem implausible that one of the reasons may have been the
effect which a scribe thought a particular word, or phrase, or passage may
have had on an audience before whom the poem was to be recited.
Certainly, the fact that some romances exist in different versions
corroborates the hypothesis that they were intended for recitation.[20]

Artistic achievement

Byzantine literature has never lacked detractors in modern times. We may
well wonder how, if this criticism is deserved, it happened that the
Byzantines were not able to attain the same heights in letters as they did
in other fields.

Byzantine authors wrote under the shadow of their mighty predecessors of
antiquity. This sense of their heritage had a dampening effect at the time
and the heritage continues to obscure our judgements of their literary
achievements. In art and architecture Christianity had created a break with
the pagan world which allowed the Byzantines to develop styles and
traditions of their own. Direct imitation of earlier works was ruled out. A
Byzantine church of the tenth century A.D. and a Greek temple of the fifth
century B.C. have so little in common from an architectural point of view
that comparison becomes pointless. But with literature, which exists in a
different artistic dimension, a similar break did not occur because the
Byzantines continued the traditions established in late antiquity. Even
when change came it was natural that much from the past was kept.

The romances have much in common with the ancient novel and its
twelfth century successor but their distinctive character puts them in a
different literary genre. They are still escapist literature but the escape they
provide is no longer one into the distant past of pagan Hellenism. It is
into the world of chivalry and romantic love as it had developed in the
West. Against this basic structure two elements are blended.

Firstly we have the world of fairytale. This is strongest in *Kallimachos* with its dragon and magic castle. Very appropriately, the abduction of the heroine is effected by a witch. In *Velthandros* we have Love's castle with its own magical effects; but what could be more appropriate to the world of fairytale than Love's stream with its band of fire which draws the young hero to its source? For *Livistros* it is again a witch that organizes the abduction of Rodamni; the witch also plays a vital part in the rescue of the heroine.

The second element is the Byzantine world. Imperial practice, groveling courtiers, scheming eunuchs and other aspects of contemporary court life find their place beside the occasional resurrection of some feature of royal life from the past (mechanical birds, the bride competition). Sometimes a touch of humor peeps through. In *Velthandros*, when Chrysandza is deceiving her royal father about her lover and disingenuously refuses to let her maid marry, the unfortunate parent is putty in her hands:

But when Chrysandza heard [about the decision of her father, the prince, to let Velthandros marry her maid] she was greatly distressed. Quickly she turned and said to the prince, 'I am not giving my Fedrokaza to a husband.'

The prince in turn replied, 'I shall allow you to speak, but my wishes will be carried out!' (*Velth. ll.*973-977)

Again, in *Kallimachos* when the itinerant king who has fallen hopelessly in love with Chrysorroi returns home and after taking to his bed, must be aroused from his torpor, we have an amusing picture of court etiquette:

The page went off, leaving the old woman alone. He ran quickly and, on coming to the king's room (his bedroom), he hastily went inside. He did not act discourteously but he stood back a little and touched the head of the bed, shaking it gently—once, twice, three times. The king, who was mentally turning over his troubles and had his mind weighed down by anxiety, took some time to realize that his bed was being shaken. However, after the third shaking he got up, opened his eyes and asked what was wrong and why his bed was being shaken. (*Kall. ll.*1095-1106)

Both elements help create an atmosphere different from that of the Greek novel. This difference is re-enforced by the use of a close approximation of the vernacular in preference to the learned and artificially preserved official language.

The authors of our romances were writing after a period of great change. Neither the upheavals of the past century nor the present state of the Greek world could be ignored. Old traditions had to be re-interpreted, new influences had to be assimilated. In order to create a form of light entertainment for the educated classes they did not try to resurrect the ancient novel yet another time. Instead, they set about adapting a foreign genre. The result was narrative poems which were not slavish copies but which successfully blended East and West. We can still read them with pleasure.

Editorial policy for this translation

Less than a century and a half has elapsed since the appearance of the first printed versions of the three romances presented here. It is not, therefore, surprising that the amount of scholarly attention devoted to them has been small when compared with that lavished on even minor ancient works which first appeared in printed form during the Renaissance. This deficiency is particularly serious in the all-important matter of reliable editions. Texts of *Velthandros* and *Kallimachos* have been produced which, if not wholly satisfactory, can at least be termed readable. For *Livistros*, as will be explained later, the most recent text is not an edition at all but a slightly modified transcript of certain manuscripts. Unfortunately, it is improbable that we shall, in the near future, see texts which will be generally accepted by scholars as adequate. For this reason it seems better to present a translation now, rather than to wait for a surer foundation on which to base it.

Textual problems relevant to the translation will be mentioned in the introduction to each romance. It would not have been desirable to dispense wholly with end-notes on textual matters in the translations themselves, but these have been kept to a minimum. For the text of all three poems I have consulted the work of Hatziyiakoumis (see *Select Bibliography*) and I have adopted the greater number of his textual suggestions, as recorded in the notes.

The two guiding principles of translation which I have tried to follow are: to use normal, intelligible English in rendering the meaning of the Greek, and to keep as close as possible to the original syntax. I have often been obliged to sacrifice the second to the first. However literal a particular rendering may be, it is a mistranslation if it is unintelligible. This simple truth is often ignored by scholars. The old word-for-word translation of school cribs is not a model to be used for either an expert audience or a broader one, as the following versions of two passages from *Kallimachos* (taken from a study of the romances) show:

> But often did a body become so overwhelmingly pleasing in that bath because of the bath's graces; if only you could see another great and wonderful pleasantness then: for even a most noble body and a crystal-white flesh increase their grace and pleasantness because of this bath. (*Kall. ll.*792-796)

> The daylaborer went as daylaborer to the garden, as if tending the plants and planting the trees; as mistress he left the mistress on the mattress, that royal mattress and the splendid pavilion, which the morning star laid out with all the graces and so became the leader-beautifier of lovemaking. (*Kall. ll.*1985-1990)

The style of the originals is characterized by loose syntax and strings of synonyms. These features have a charm in the Greek which is often difficult to reproduce in readable English. Occasionally a synonym has been suppressed when the object or action involved is mentioned for the third time and a close rendering would offend against English style.

The translation of a few particular words deserves separate mention:

In ancient Greek ἔρως means *(sexual) love* (there are other words for different varieties). Because of a tendency to create divinities from concepts, a god, Ἔρως *(Sexual) Love*, became part of the Greek pantheon at a very early date and was made the son of Aphrodite. Later, during the Hellenistic period, the name was used in the plural, Ἔρωτες *(cupids)*, to designate Love's helpers (akin to the *putti* of Italian Renaissance painting). The three forms of the word (ἔρως, Ἔρως, Ἔρωτες) were taken over into medieval Greek and occur constantly in the romances. They are translated by *love, Love, cupids/Cupids* (the singular *cupid* also occurs). It is, however, often impossible to distinguish between *love* and *Love*.

In dictionaries the word κόρη is given the meaning of *girl*, or *daughter*. In its first sense it is regularly used in the romances to designate the heroines, and in this context the English *lady* seems more appropriate than *girl*, which might conjure up a childish image whereas an expression such as *young woman* would be clumsy. Only occasionally has *girl* been preferred.

The English equivalent of λουτρόν is normally given as *bath*. The word is used in our poems to designate the type of pool which the Byzantines used for bathing, as the Romans had done before them. It is here translated as *pool* because for us today the word *bath* normally conjures up a picture of a bathtub.

The word στρατιώτης means *soldier* in Classical Greek and it must be so taken in some places in the romances. However, its more common meaning is *knight*. This semantic development may have been influenced by the medieval use of the Latin *miles*, which is parallel.[21]

In official Byzantine terminology the word βασιλεύς (*king*) was reserved for the Byzantine emperor. All other temporal rulers were seen as inferior and were described by other words, the most important of which for our purposes is ρήγας. This word, which is derived from the Latin *rex* (*king*), and βασιλεύς both occur in the romances, the latter being applied to rulers who, presumably, were considered to be comparable with the Byzantine emperor (the prime example is the god Love himself). To make a distinction between the two for purposes of translation it seems preferable to use *king* for βασιλεύς and *prince* for ρήγας rather than *emperor* for βασιλεύς and *king* for ρήγας because in modern usage a prince is more clearly inferior to a king than a king is to an emperor.

Greek proper names present a problem. Should they be transliterated according to the system used for ancient Greek or should we try to represent them as they were pronounced when the romances were written? I have opted for the latter and have written *Velthandros* (not *Belthandros*), *Livistros* (not *Libistros*), *Chrysorroi* (not *Chrysorrhoe*) and so on. Names occurring in the notes or in the introductions which have reference to an earlier period are transliterated in the conventional way.

Because of the unsatisfactory nature of the text of the romances, particularly that of *Livistros*, a number of conjectures have been suggested in the notes and followed in the translation. These should be regarded as provisional.

Pointed brackets (< >) are used for words, usually of a supplementary nature, which have no equivalent in the Greek original. Not all such words are treated in this way.

In conclusion I wish to thank Mrs. Nina Mills for her proof-reading; Dr. Tina Lendari for transcripts of manuscripts E, N, P, and S of *Livistros*; Professor Vincenzo Rotolo and Professor Fabrizio Conca for Italian translations of *Livistros* and *Velthandros* respectively; Professor Roderick Beaton and Professor Alan Henry for general advice and help; and, above all, Damos Amanatides who, in his kindness, first introduced me to the romances.

Notes

Where an author and page number are given without further details please consult the Select Bibliography.

1   Quoted by Lambert p.28.

2   On whether the statue rather than the peacock is supplying the sighs and tears see p.3.

3   This is the form of his name which is always used in the best ms. (S). The form *Klitovos* is found, but not exclusively, in the other mss.

4   Some works such as chronicles and the lives of saints were written in the Greek of the New Testament (the Koine [Κοινή]) but this was also a dead language.

5   Somewhat different is the novel of Longus, which has a pastoral setting.

6   The attribution of *Kallimachos and Chrysorroi* to Andronikos Komninos is, in my opinion, mistaken (see pp.33f.).

7   P13 (Λατίνος ἦταν εὐγενής *he was a noble Latin*). This reading occurs in only one ms. (P) but, given the general attitudes to Westerners, it is more likely that scribes would have changed Λατίνος to something else than that they would have introduced the word here. In any case, Livistros is described as *prince of a Latin land* at S202 (emending χώρας to ρῆγας) and at the corresponding places of the other mss.

8   λιζιώνομαι P549 (βουλώνομαι εἰς...); the word λίζιος *liege* occurs elsewhere, e.g. N327.

9   S1072; the same phrase occurs in N1906, P1742 (λατινικὰ τὰ ροῦχα της...).

10 S1131ff.

11 As, e.g. by Beck p.126.

12 The word λίζιος *liege* occurs once (*Velth. l.*789) and ρῆγας *prince* several times.

13 *Velth. l.*385.

14 See in particular Cupane's article.

15 As, e.g., αὐτοκράτωρ, δεσπότης, αὐθέντης.

16 See Hunger.

17 Details will be found in G. Brett 'The Automata in the Byzantine "Throne of Solomon" ' *Speculum* XXIX (1954), pp.477-487.

18   In *Velthandros* the two marriages have Christian trappings; and
     Chrysandza says she and Velthandros will *give an account to before
     the impartial judge who is fearsome and great* for the deaths of their
     companions (*Velth. ll.*1214ff.). In *Kallimachos* there is a religious
     tailpiece which forms no part of the story and is probably a later
     addition. In *Livistros* the word *Christian* occurs with the meanings
     caring person such as a Christian should be (S702, S1455, S2402)
     and *poor wretch* (S932).
19   There is a fragment of a sixth; see the introduction to *Livistros.*
20   For a different point of view see the articles of M. and E. Jeffreys.
21   See J.F. Niermeyer *Mediae Latinatis Lexicon Minus* Brill, Leiden
     1976, *s.v.*

Select Bibliography

I. EDITIONS

The following editions are those used for the translations:

Kriaras, E. Βυζαντινὰ ἱπποτικὰ μυθιστορήματα (Βασικὴ Βιβλιοθήκη 2), Athens 1955 (contains an edition of *Velthandros and Chrysandza* on pp.85-130).

Lambert, J.A. *Le Roman de Libistros et Rhodamné publié d'après les manuscrits de Leyde et Madrid avec une introduction, des observations grammaticales et un glossaire,* Verhandelingen der koninklijke Akademie van Wetenschappen Afteeling Letterkunde N.R. XXXV Amsterdam 1935.

Pichard, M. *Le roman de Callimaque et de Chrysorrhoé,* Paris 1956.

II. TRANSLATIONS

There are no English translations of the romances. The following are in German or Italian. A French translation of Kallimachos and Chrysorroi is included in Pichard's edition (see above).

Conca, F. *Il Romanzo di Beltandro e Crisanza,* Milan 1982.

Ellissen, A. *Analekten der mittel- und neugriechischen Literatur,* Leipzig 1862 (contains a German translation of *Velthandros and Chrysandza*).

Rotolo, V. *Libistro e Rodamne, Romanzo cavalleresco bizantino, Introduzione e versione italiana* (Κείμενα καὶ μελέται νεοελληνικῆς φιλολογίας 22), Athens 1965.

III. WORKS OF CRITICISM

Agapitos, P.A. *Narrative structure in the Byzantine Vernacular Romances*, Munich 1991.

Beaton, R. *The Medieval Greek Romances* (Cambridge Studies in Medieval Literature, 6), Cambridge 1989.

Beck, H. *Geschichte der byzantinischen Volksliteratur*, München 1971.

Browing, R. *Medieval and Modern Greek*, Cambridge 1983.

Bury, J.B. *Romances of Chivalry on Greek Soil*, Oxford 1911.

Cupane, C. 'Il motivo del castello nella narrativa tardo-bizantina. Evoluzione di un' allegoria,' *Jahrbuch der Österreichen Byzantinistik* 27 (1978), pp.229-267.

Hägg, T. *The Novel in Antiquity*, Berkeley and Los Angeles 1983.

Hatzis, D. Τὰ ἑλληνικὰ στοιχεῖα στὸ μυθιστόρημα 'Διήγησις ἐξαιρετικὸς Βελθάνδρου καὶ Χρυσάντζας' pp. 93-111 in vol. 3 of J. Irmscher, H.Ditten, M. Minsemi (edd.) *Probleme der neugriechischen Literatur* Berlin 1959-1960.

Hatziyiakoumis, M.K. Τὰ μεσαιωνικὰ δημώδη κείμενα, Athens 1977.

Hunger, H. 'Die Schönheitskonkurrenz in "Belthandros und Chrysantza" und die Brautschau am byzantinischen Kaiserhof,' *Byzantion* 35 (1965), pp.150-158.

Hunger, H. 'Un roman byzantin et son atmosphère: Callimaque et Chrysorrhoé' in id. *Byzantinische Grundlagenforschung*, London 1973, pp.405-422.

Jeffreys, E.M. 'The popular Byzantine verse romances of chivalry,' *Mantatoforos 14* (1979), pp.20-34.

Jeffreys, E.M., 'The later Greek verse romances: a survey,' in E. and M. Jeffreys and A. Moffatt (edd.), *Byzantine papers* Canberra, 1981, pp.116-127.

Jeffreys, E.M. and M.J., 'The oral background of Byzantine popular poetry,' *Oral Tradition 1* (1986), pp.504-547.

Jeffreys, M.J., 'The literary emergence of vernacular Greek,' *Mosaic* 8 (1975), pp.171-193.

Knös, B. 'Qui est l'auteur du roman de Callimache et Chrysorrhoe?' Ἑλληνικὰ 17 (1962), pp.274-295.

Kriaras. E. Review of Pichard's edition of *Kallimachos*, Ἑλληνικὰ 16 (1958-9), pp.253-264.

Kahane, H. and R. 'The hidden Narcissus in the Byzantine romance of Belthandros and Chrysandza,' *Jahrbuch der Österreichen Byzantinistik* 33 (1983), pp.199-219.

Manousakas, M. 'Les romans byzantins de chevalerie et l'état présent des études les concernant,' *Revue des Etudes Byzantines* 10 (1952), pp.70-83.

Pieler, P. 'Recht, Gesellschaft und Staat im byzantinischen Roman der Palaeologenzeit' *Jahrbuch der Österreichen Byzantinistik* 20 (1971), pp.189-221.

Schissel, O. *Der byzantinische Garten, Seine Darstellung im gleichzeitigen Romane,* Sitzungsberichte der Akademie der Wissenschaften in Wien, Philosophisch-historische Klasse, 221 Band, 2 Abhandlung, 1942.

IV. WORKS OF REFERENCE

Kazhdan, A.P. (ed.) *The Oxford Dictionary of Byzantium,* New York 1991.

Kriaras, E. Λεξικὸ τῆς μεσαιωνικῆς ἑλληνικῆς δημώδους γραμματείας Thessaloniki 1968-.

Lampe, G.W.H. *A Patristic Greek Dictionary,* Oxford 1961.

Liddel, H.G., R. Scott, E. Stuart Jones *A Greek-English Dictionary,* 9th ed., Oxford 1940.

Introduction
to
Velthandros and Chrysandza

In *Kallimachos* the only place given a name is Dragon's Castle. In *Livistros* the hero comes from the fictitious country of Livandros and the heroine from the equally imaginary Silver City; only two real places enter into the narrative, Egypt and Armenia. But *Velthandros* is largely set in the real world.

Velthandros himself is described as Greek, although we are not told the name of his country. His father, Rodofilos, is presented as holding an office similar to that of the Byzantine emperor. He is a βασιλεύς *king* (see p. xxxiv) and he *wears the crown of the entire land of the Greeks* (*l.*385) (the word used for Greek is Ῥωμαῖος *Romaios*, the term employed by the Byzantines for themselves; the expression *the entire land of the Greeks* may refer to the area controlled by the Byzantines before the Fourth Crusade).

Velthandros wanders around the countries of the East (no doubt western Asia Minor) and of Turkey (which only refers to the eastern part of present day Turkey) and goes close to Armenia. He then arrives at Tarsus, a city close to the coast on the south-east corner of Asia Minor. After his adventures in Love's castle he journeys to Antioch in northern Syria where he finds his true love. At the end of the story he departs from somewhere on the nearby coast and arrives back at his (unspecified) home in five days. It has been noticed that a voyage of this length could take him back to Constantinople.[1] This is in keeping with the representation of his father as having imperial status.

Antioch had been an important centre of Hellenism for the first five centuries of the Christian era but suffered several conquests in the early Middle Ages. Finally, it was taken from the Seljuk Turks by the Crusaders in 1098 and remained under a Latin ruler until 1268 when it was captured by the Mamluks of Egypt. This Christian interlude seems to be the historical period which *Velthandros* reflects; the fact that its ruler is a ῥῆγας *prince* and not a βασιλεύς *king* (see p. xxxiv) corroborates this hypothesis. However, the author does not take the

1

opportunity of giving the romance a historical setting after the manner of
the ancient novel. Nothing, for example, is said to indicate that the
ambience of the courts at Antioch and in Velthandros's native land is any
different from the courts portrayed in the other romances; the details
provided about them give both a definite Byzantine tinge.[2]

But part of *Velthandros's* narrative steps beyond the bounds of normal
geography and it is here that we meet problems of interpretation. When
Velthandros enters the confines of the lord of Love, we encounter a
setting where elements of fairytale are blended with symbolism. Some of
the symbols have a fairly obvious meaning. Love's stream with its fiery
band represents 'the paradoxical nature of love, which . . . both refreshes
like water and burns or consumes the sufferer like fire.'[3] The bedroom in
Love's castle with walls which *had no foundation and did not stand on the
ground but were floating* (*ll.*451f.) is meant to evoke the ecstatic
consummation of romantic love. But we face serious trouble in Love's
hall, where Velthandros sees two statues which are obviously meant to
be charged with symbolism. The first is the source of Love's stream, the
stream which has led him to the building (*ll.*369-388):

He . . . saw a figure carved out of sapphire and it was from this
that the flaming river came. The sight was exceeding fair but sad.
Above sat a carved peacock resting its knee on the middle of one
hand of the statue which held the seated bird with the palm of its
<other> hand. Skilfully represented, the figure was sighing and
kept its gaze fixed on the ground. It was very distressed and
serious as it stood there sadly. The spring of the flaming river ran
from the eyes of this statue, and also from its mouth; but it was
only[(380)] its sighs, blazing like raging fire, that brought on the
flame. Carved skilfully into the stone were letters which said:

'Velthandros, the second son of his father, Rodofilos, who wears
the crown of the entire land of the Greeks, is suffering from a
passion for a <princess> of great Antioch, Chrysandza by name,
the daughter of its mighty prince, supremely beautiful, glorious
and born to the purple.'

A little further on he sees the other statue (*ll.*401-425):

With difficulty he then regained his senses and threw a cursory
glance to the other part. There he noticed huge chiseled blocks and
a statue of a standing man of fearsome appearance and terrible
aspect, without cloak and naked to the navel. Velthandros looked.

He carefully examined the striking and beautiful figure and saw, fixed in its heart, an arrow which had been shot through the air by Love. From this wound in the statue's heart, a blazing flame streamed out amidst no little smoke and mingled with the tears of the stone figure. Women are by nature easily moved and always have a ready flood of tears and sighs, just as men are by nature the ones who bear arms. Yet what was it that fired the arrow at the statue and caused such grief? Surely it was the passion for a woman!

Velthandros found another inscription cut into the stone. The letters ran as follows: 'The daughter of the mighty prince of great Antioch, Chrysandza, whom Fortune that ordains mortal destinies decreed to be noble, fair, and born to the purple; Velthandros, of the Greek land, the son of Rodofilos—Love has determined the destinies of both.'

The salient facts are:

1. The gender of the first statue is not specified and it is holding a seated peacock. The second statue is of a half-naked man and it has an arrow fixed in its heart.

2. While the Greek is not absolutely clear it seems more natural to understand the stream with its band of fire as coming from the eyes and mouth of the first figure, not from the peacock which it is holding.[4] The second figure, in contrast to the sadness of the first, has a *fearsome and terrible aspect*. His semi-nudity allows Velthandros to see the arrow in his heart. From the wound comes a blazing flame which mingles with his tears. We are not told that this mixture contributes to the stream.

3. The inscription on the first statue says that Velthandros is suffering from a passion for Chrysandza. The inscription on the second tells us that Love has fixed the destinies of both.

The significance of the statues is obscure and in the absence of parallels elsewhere we are necessarily driven to guesswork.

It has been suggested that the first is female and represents Chrysandza, and that the second is Velthandros.[5] In this case the first inscription would gain in relevance, but why should Chrysandza be shown as sad? And why should she be holding a peacock? And, more important, why should she be represented as the origin of Love's stream? Again, if the second statue represents Velthandros, why should he have *a fearsome appearance and terrible aspect*?

A more fruitful approach may be to regard both statues as representing aspects of Love. Velthandros has been drawn into tracking Love's stream and his quest clearly symbolizes the awakening of desire in the young. The first statue, whose sighs and tears feed the stream, represents the tribulations of love as yet unfulfilled; this accounts for its sad appearance. The concept of love in the romances is bound up with suffering before the lasting attainment of one's desires, as Velthandros is to learn when he meets Chrysandza. The statue's gender is not indicated because Love's woes come to both sexes. The peacock it is holding symbolizes the paradise which mortals attain through love.[6] And when Velthandros finds the statue which is the source of Love's stream and which symbolizes what he is to suffer it is appropriate that he should also learn the name of his predestined love; hence the first inscription.

The second statue represents Love's power, from which Velthandros cannot now escape. The implication of the sentence beginning *women are by nature easily moved* is that while women can be expected to fall in love it is surprising in the case of the sex *who bear arms*. And yet precisely this has happened to the figure despite his *fearsome and terrible aspect*. His tears and the flame from his wound do not feed into Love's stream, presumably because we are meant to keep the imagery of the two statues separate. The inscription re-enforces the idea of Love's strength. It is Love who *has determined the destinies* of the daughter of a prince and the son of a king.

Text

The romance survives in only one manuscript which is dated to the early sixteenth century. The edition followed here is that of E. Kriaras, Βυζαντινὰ ἱπποτικὰ μυθιστορήματα (Βασικὴ Βιβλιοθήκη 2), Athens 1955, pp. 85-130. Changes are recorded in the endnotes.

At the beginning of the translation the words in italics are the title and prose summary as given in the manuscript. The initial 24 lines of the poem itself provide another summary but we can be reasonably certain that neither are original. The first summary calls Rodofilos a prince (ῥῆγας) whereas everywhere else he is called a king (βασιλεύς); the second purports to give more details but omits the turning point in the romance, Velthandros's visit to Love's castle.

Velthandros and Chrysandza

The excellent story of Velthandros the Greek

who, because of sorrow caused by his father, left his native land and went into exile. He returned back with Chrysandza, the daughter of the prince of mighty Antioch—although without the knowledge of her father and mother.

Come! Attend a moment all you young people. I wish to tell you the fairest tale, a beautiful and unusual story. Whoever wants to taste of its sadness and joy will also wonder at its account of daring and bravery:

There was a king, a certain Rodofilos who had two sons, Filarmos and Velthandros, remarkable, glorious, and born to the purple.[7] Velthandros was the second born of Rodofilos, this mighty king.[(10)] Well, Velthandros suffered a terrible grief. He was persecuted by his father and scorned beyond limit. He even went into exile from his home. <Hear> how he left his native land, how he suffered woes with Chrysandza too, and how, after much time had passed, he attained his father's rank. Though previously hated he came to be loved and gained[8] the crown and diadem of the kingdom. He became king[(20)] and had as his fair wife the lady Chrysandza, the daughter of the mighty prince of great Antioch. So attend; hear the story and marvel much. I shall not be proved a liar.

A certain king, Rodofilos, (the name is Greek) was sovereign of countless lands. As their rightful master, he governed them in a lordly way and also kept the neighbouring rulers under control. He had two, fair, much loved children. The first was called Filarmos by all.[(30)] The second had the Greek name of Velthandros. He was an exceptional hunter and a bowman always on target. He was handsome, well-built and brave, blond and curly-haired, bright-eyed and fair. His chest was as white as cold marble.[9] But when (alas!—the madness of Fortune and ill-starred Destiny!) his father began to persecute him and load him with scorn, he yearned to go abroad and depart for distant exile, wherever Fortune might take him.[(40)]

He asked his father for permission to go to foreign parts and the king said to him, 'Velthandros, if you wish to go into exile from my land, a curse upon me if I should keep you!' He immediately bade his father farewell. He went out and found Filarmos. He embraced him closely, kissed him with affection and told of the madness of his ill-starred Destiny.

'I, unfortunate one, am being exiled from the affection of my brother.' Then in turn, Filarmos held Velthandros, covered him with kisses[50] and said, 'If our father has ever vexed you, I can today win over his heart. But if it is through me that you suffer any sting of injury, I offer you my body—my whole self. Kill me, torture me foully, injure me in return. Though I must face death, insult, dishonor, I cannot hear of your exile. Even if I must abandon the kingdom, my privileges, and what we claim as our rightful crown, I shall regard this as nothing.[60] With you I shall go into exile and with you I shall walk as we visit foreign, pagan countries. With you I shall die and with you I shall go down to Hades. Only let me retain the sight of you.'

Much did Filarmos say to win Velthandros over but he could alter not the latter's resolve. As he considered the road to exile unavoidable, his brother's words did not move him or change what he had decided; not even a little. When once an idea comes to germinate[70] it cannot be held back by another's advice.

After they had finished all their talking they embraced tenderly and kissed like brothers. Both wept—wept over their separation. But Filarmos was unable to bear the grief he was suffering at his brother's departure and in his great pain he fainted and fell. Velthandros bent over, held his brother, and covered him with kisses. He then girt on his sword and departed, leaving Filarmos unconscious.[80] With only his three squires, Velthandros mounted and started out on the road to exile.

Meanwhile people drenched Filarmos (the fairest of young men) with rose-water, to bring him to his senses. And when he had regained consciousness and was fully recovered, he looked for his brother. He shouted for Velthandros. The latter, who had been impatient to leave, was nowhere to be seen as he had ridden off. Filarmos went hurriedly to the palace, found his father and spoke thus to him:[90]

'Learn, my lord,' he said, 'about Velthandros. You will receive much, much criticism from everyone and no little blame because today you have committed a great injustice. Turn this over, ponder on it, weigh it in your mind: if my brother goes to a pagan ruler and enrols as his vassal, he will belong there and the ruler will have an excellent man, a fine knight, in every way capable and good, utterly courageous, an outstanding hunter and a bowman always on target!*(100)* I swear by our separation, this is in no way a lie! The whole world does not have his equal in valor. If ever it should happen that war breaks out and like some mighty border-rider he chases and deposes you, proving himself a conqueror and mighty champion, what will Velthandros's then lord say?[10] Weigh this in your mind. Ponder upon it yourself.'

Filarmos spoke at length using many gentle words to his harsh and pitiless father. When finally he set his mind on a better course*(110)* the king turned and spoke to his own men. He gave orders to twenty-four knights (his relatives) with the words, 'All saddle your horses, ride quickly, catch up with my son. And if you succeed in catching him, first greet him and ask him courteously if he wishes to return. But if perchance you see that his purpose is inflexible and if he stubbornly refuses to return, take him up bodily and bring him back without delay.' Straightway they all mounted and rode off.*(120)* They rode swiftly and soon caught up with Velthandros.

Velthandros had found a pleasant spot. He had dismounted to camp there with his squires. The night was pleasant with a full moon and there was a fountain which watered a green meadow. He pitched his tent by himself and sat down. In this position he took his mousiki[11] and started to play. He sang a dirge laden with sighs:

'Hills, plains and mountains, glens and dales, lament with me in my unhappy fate.*(130)* Through boundless hate and no small reproach, I, unhappy one, am today separated from my country and my great name—ah, the fearsome horror!'

And suddenly the knights dismounted too and spoke gentle words to him, 'In truth, Velthandros, have you now renounced your feelings as a brother and taken the road to foreign lands? In truth, do you renounce the company of us, your own people? In truth, have you renounced your friends and all those who know you? Do you want to become an exile?*(140)* Have you renounced both your relatives and the country that bore you and will you seek out other lands—lands you do not know? You have royal rank, you live as a lord, and you are honored by all, great and small. Tell us now, to where are you travelling. And how far? Do you wish to become the servant of the other kings? Are you—child of the purple and offspring of the Graces—are you completely renouncing your relatives—renouncing our company, the crown, diadem, royal rank and everything else? Do you who have never known servitude—do you really prefer[150] to become a servant? Do you love those much abused foreign lands? Life abroad is miserable, bad, and dangerous. We at any rate who know your intelligence are astonished that you should be doing this. Free us of our bewilderment. Come, let us return.' The knights said this and more to the brave and handsome Velthandros but they did not succeed in changing his purpose in the least.

That night the knights all remained around Velthandros in the meadow and kept watch over him.[160] When the dawn leaped up from the ridges over the mountain peaks and tree tops, they rose and addressed him, 'Arise, my lord, so that we may go quickly. Do not distress your brother.'

Velthandros got up, put on his boots and fastened his sword. He jumped onto his horse in a valiant fashion and said to them, 'My lords, I take my leave of you. And now farewell! Behold! I shall now go on the road to exile.'

One of the lords said,[170] 'Velthandros, child of the crown and heir to the sceptre, we beseech you to abandon what your evil spirit has put into you. We beseech you to choose what is right and to act upon it. But attend; ponder on this, weigh it in your mind: even if you go out to those of pagan blood, enter into their service, and for this receive payment to cover your needs, and find honors, fame and wealth, you will not be preferred to another once you choose servitude.[12] But you are free; you are not a servant;[180] no, you are a royal child, the son of our king. Others should be serving you, not you serving others. Because of this I do not understand your thoughts or what is on your mind. So abandon these futile ideas. Come! Let us return.'

Velthandros heard this and replied, 'Not even foreign lands will wipe out all the many sorrows which I have suffered at my father's hands.'

In response the other said, 'Take our pledge that you will never endure grief. From now on you will have no sorrow.[190] We shall arrange with your father that he treat you as his beloved and true son. As for us, why should we hide something and not tell you? (Be assured of it and weigh it in your mind.)—If by your own will and choice you turn and come back we shall say no more. But if by chance you resist and are not willing to follow us, we shall take you up bodily and bring you back without delay. The king, your father, gave us this order.'

Velthandros quickly replied to them,[200] 'Know this, my lords! All believe what I say. Your wives, who are my relatives, had expected to enjoy my respect. And now today—do you wish me to make them all widows?'

When they saw that his purpose was completely unchanged the knights rushed to seize him then and there. Velthandros quickly flourished his mace and killed ten.[13] He shouted to the rest, 'I am not to blame. You have committed this slaughter.[210] But now I have escaped from you as I desired. Tell my father what your company has suffered. I take my leave of you. And now farewell! Behold! I shall go on the road to exile.'

So Velthandros went on his way to foreign parts. He wandered through many lands, kingdoms, and cities. No place pleased him enough to make him stay. He roamed over the countries of the East and of Turkey. He wandered and traveled over lands and cities. He came to a particular defile, the pass at Turks' Hill,[220] which bandits were guarding with great daring. When they saw him they observed that he was armed, handsome, in bright clothes and with only three squires following him. They said, 'Let us allow him to enter the pass and when he is inside he will, without desiring it, fall into our hands.' They let him come up, approach, enter, and when he was a little way inside they fell upon him. Against this mighty and countless host[230] he drew his mace—I tell no lie—and they all went to below the earth.

So Velthandros and his squires came to the boundaries of Turkey, went at one point[14] close to Armenia, and finally arrived at the city of Tarsus. While he was wandering there with his squires he came upon a small river. Within its waters there seemed to be a moving star which remained within the water and ran along with it. In his desire to find the river's source and also from whence came the flame[15] in the water, Velthandros went upstream and searched.[240] For ten whole days he traveled and finally came to a mighty castle, vast in appearance, wonderfully constructed from chiseled sardonyx. On top of the shining edifice, placed together instead of battlements, were a lion and the heads of dragons made of variegated gold. An artist had constructed them with much skill, and if you looked you could see that from their mouths[250] there came a wild and terrible whistling. You would have said that they were possessed of movement like living things and they were talking and shouting together. Since the shining river was coming from the castle Velthandros went up to its entrance. He found a shining gate made of diamond and he saw letters chiseled into its middle part. These engraved letters proclaimed:

'The man never touched by the shafts of the cupids will straightway be subjected to ten million woes by them[260] when he sees Love's castle from the inside.'

He read these words and stood pensively for a long time wondering in his mind what he should do and how he should act. 'If I go up and advance on foot, how will the inscription on the door <affect me> since I have not seen the cupids' arrow at all? But how shall I go back without having seen the flame? I have spent ten days searching out and following this blazing river with its fire. I wish to discover its source[270] and how it is that the flame of fire runs inside it. Well, I should in truth much prefer to determine this as it is better to become food for birds than to retreat and go back down the river.'

To his three squires he immediately commanded: 'Dismount and wait for me. All the time I am away, no matter how long, even if I spend this whole day inside, even if perchance I take up the following day as well and the next, remain here waiting for me.[280] Do not enter Love's castle. This I order you.'

Velthandros immediately entered on his own. He saw both banks of the river variously set with white vines and red flowers of narcissus and with a covering of trees. He threw a glance up at them and saw their beauty, their pleasing symmetry and the graceful rise of their trunks. You would certainly have said that a carpenter had turned them smooth on a lathe, set them upright and planted them.[290] The form of their flowers and leaves was very beautiful. This Velthandros saw and was amazed. He marveled greatly but, wanting to see the flame, he kept on, following the river's banks upstream. He then came upon a remarkable fountain whose water was as cold as snow. The beauty which the fount of the cupids possessed in boundless measure, I am wholly at a loss to describe.

A carved griffin was standing there with extended wings and its back arched to a level with them.[300] Its tail was bent round to its head. In its front paws it held a beautiful round basin carved from a precious stone. Water came from its mouth and flowed into the basin without the smallest drop falling down to the ground. For some time Velthandros stood contemplating the griffin's construction and the strange property of the water. How was the water, which came from the griffin's mouth, held in the small basin, which had no aperture at all?[310] Or did the water change its direction to escape? But how could the water flow back from the basin's lips? He marveled at where the water went. Suddenly the griffin stamped away from where it was standing, crossed the river and stood there.

Once again Velthandros saw and wondered at the blazing river. He walked around examining everything carefully and wandered over the wonderful place. He saw remarkable palaces whose charms I cannot describe[320] in detail. With the outside of Love's castle built of chiseled sardonyx, imagine what was inside and how those palatial buildings were constructed! He saw a fair statuary in front of the dining hall. Wondrous it was, beautiful and huge, and from it the stream flowed. The hall was of large bright stones of sapphire, skilfully hewn. Who could describe the building's roof?[330] There was much ornamentation on the <door>[16] of the hall. It was bordered by three wondrous, beautiful and huge stones, artistically constructed and fitted together.

The interior was illuminated by lamps and a bright glow.[17] The floor was red and bathed in moonlight. Velthandros marveled greatly when he saw it. In the manner of an inspector, he closely examined the ornaments on the wall. He saw many figures carved in various ways. One was in the form of a woman tied by the neck[340] and being dragged by the tyrant who leads to love. Another was of a man with his feet in irons,[18] and Love, the executioner, was standing behind him. Another stood above, in the hands of cupids, waiting as a true friend for Love's affection. Others were shooting down arrows to show their despotic power. Everything was carved as though it were in movement. Some figures walked in front, others behind. Others were bound to the hands of their executioners. Tears poured from their eyes[350] and they breathed anguish from their mouths.[19] Those above who were in the hands of cupids seemed to be laughing loudly and to be always covered with broad smiles. On each you could find a message written. One man, it said, <loved> the daughter of a certain prince. Another, it said, was the son of a certain king and was a noble Greek. Because of his suffering, he had given up his land, his fame and his glory to be driven by passion to the place where Love marked him down as a slave.[360] Again, it recorded a noble woman whom refinement had nourished and whom grace had educated but who had never served Love's armies. Other women used excessive endearments as they held the mighty leader of the cupids by their hands.

Velthandros looked at everything from one end to the other. How can I list the other objects in the hall he saw and carefully examined? He glanced towards its end and saw a figure carved out of sapphire[370] and it was from this that the flaming river came. The sight was exceeding fair but sad. Above sat a carved peacock resting its knee on the middle of one

hand of the statue which held the seated bird with the palm of its <other>
hand. Skilfully represented, the figure was sighing and kept its gaze fixed
on the ground. It was very distressed and serious as it stood there sadly.
The spring of the flaming river ran from the eyes of this statue, and also
from its mouth; but it was only[380] its sighs, blazing like raging fire,
that brought on the flame.[20] Carved skilfully into the stone were letters
which said:

'Velthandros, the second son of his father, Rodofilos, who wears the
crown of the entire land of the Greeks, is suffering from a passion for a
<princess> of great Antioch,[21] Chrysandza by name, the daughter of its
mighty prince, supremely beautiful, glorious and born to the purple.'

He read the message and felt a great longing. A flood of passion came
over him, greater than I can convey.[390] He stood for some time looking
at it. He was engrossed in thought and greatly troubled. Again he looked
at it, surveyed and examined it. Many times he read the words. He saw the
figure standing in its distress and he too was distressed and seemed to feel
sympathy. He joined in its laments, he shared its passion, and his own
tears mingled with the tears of the river's source. Some time passed before
the lamentation and the sadness of his heart went away.[400]

With difficulty he then regained his senses and threw a cursory glance to
the other part. There he noticed huge chiseled blocks and a statue of a
standing man of fearsome appearance and terrible aspect, without cloak
and naked to the navel. Velthandros looked. He carefully examined the
striking and beautiful figure and saw, fixed in its heart, an arrow which
had been shot through the air by Love.[410] From this wound in the
statue's heart, a blazing flame streamed out amidst no little smoke[22] and
mingled with the tears of the stone figure. Women are by nature easily
moved and always have a ready flood of tears and sighs, just as men are by
nature the ones who bear arms.[23] Yet what was it that fired the arrow at
the statue and caused such grief? Surely it was the passion for a woman!

Velthandros found another inscription cut into the stone. The letters ran as
follows:[420] 'The daughter of the mighty prince of great Antioch,
Chrysandza, whom Fortune that ordains mortal destinies decreed to be
noble, fair, and born to the purple;[24] Velthandros, of the Greek land, the
son of Rodofilos—Love has determined the destinies of both.'

He read the message and sighed deeply. From the depths of his heart he
said, 'Would that I had never been born and that I had been without life on
the face of the earth! But since I chanced to live would that I had been

<without feelings>.[25] But since nature has fashioned me and given me feelings[430] would that I had not become acquainted with the world as I have done, and that I had never entered Love's castle! Since I have entered this hall, would that I had not looked at the carved figures! But since I have looked at them, would that I had not seen what is written there! Would that I had escaped this destiny, that I had exercised care, that I had looked and attended only to myself! Now that I have found my own destiny, what fate is in store for me! Let me make a close inspection, and attend to[440] the bitter-sweet charms of this castle of Love.'

He left the hall and entered the bedroom. This was made of diamonds. It was adorned with pearls and precious stones such as the world does not possess. The bedroom's construction was remarkable. Skilfully constructed, the vaulting rose and wound around a keystone like a snail. If mortals were to see it they would be lavish in their praise and admiration.[450] The bedroom's four walls had no foundation and did not stand on the ground but were floating. One would say that they resembled the heavenly spheres.

Velthandros marveled greatly at everything he saw, and his amazement was no less at the courtyard where he saw Leander[26] hewn from stone and an exquisite pool adorned with every charm. It was as no other, nor can my tongue begin to describe it. Beyond the pool lay a superb reservoir,[460] beautiful, and made wholly from stone. Round about were many statues, also of stone, which ingeniously supported the reservoir from below. From these statues under the reservoir there flowed a pure, very clear spring from which the pool was watered. Around the reservoir's rim there sat all sorts of small birds made of gold, each of them chirping as a bird does—you would say with its own natural voice.[470] The birds were sitting as though alive, some above, some below, some round about. Velthandros went on a little further and saw a very beautifully constructed terrace. The stone carvings that surrounded it, the bright columns, slender as reeds, the marble-clad walls, the leaves of ivy and the golden leaves of violets, lilies and roses—all perfectly formed from pure gold—made a fair scene, one object contrasting with another.[27] He also saw an exquisitely beautiful stone block[480] and on its top stood a golden throne. Around the throne was a large quantity of weapons pointing towards the ground.

At this point a moonless night succeeded the day and it was time to seek other attractions in Love's castle. A cupid came to Velthandros through the air on wings and, poised above him, said, 'Velthandros, hasten! The king summons you.'

On these words Velthandros immediately got up and followed the cupid who had addressed him.*(490)* He climbed the terrace and on the throne he saw the lord of the cupids sitting, wearing a royal crown and holding a mighty sceptre. In his hand he held a golden arrow. On seeing him Velthandros fell at his feet but straightway the lord of the cupids said, 'Arise, and tell me, your lord, about everything. Why did you leave the land of the Greeks and your native country to go into exile and come here? How did you enter Love's castle?*(500)* Arise now, speak, and tell me these things.'

Velthandros immediately got up from the ground, bowed his head again and fell at the king's feet. Then he arose and said:

'Lord of the cupids, do you desire to learn why I left my native place and my own land, and chose to become an exile in another country? Rodofilos showered me with countless woes, with many terrible outbursts of insatiable anger. This is, O king, why and how*(510)* I left my home—it was through the distress and scorn that I suffered at my father's hands. Because of this, in sorrow I went away and began my wanderings. I visited innumerable lands in my travels. Finally, I came to the city of Tarsus where I found a small river and in the middle of its waters there went a flame of fire. Because of this fire I followed the river upstream in my desire to see its origin. I wanted to discover its source and to learn how the fire in its waters flowed in unison with them.*(520)* Know, O king, that it was for this reason that I entered your castle. And what a castle! Remarkable and fair it is. Nowhere do I know of its like.'

Love then addressed these words to him: 'Learn this, Velthandros. Tomorrow I have forty noble women, all maidens of royal blood, the daughters of kings. Choice they are and fair in appearance and beauty. What I want from you is this: you will make your own judgement by yourself and select the fairest of them.'*(530)* Velthandros immediately replied, 'You require, O Love, my own judgement. You will, O lord, soon see the one who is superior to all.'

But Velthandros was frightened by the squadron of cupids and he had not gone far when he was seized by panic and said, 'I shall carry out your order now.'

Love gave him a wand woven from three strands; iron, gold, and the stone, topaz. 'There, Velthandros, I give you this wand. Present it to the one you judge to be fairer than the rest.*(540)* She will be queen of all.'

Velthandros reached out and took the wand from Love's hand. 'You order me to judge the beauty of these women. Nothing that the eye can see will escape me.'

All immediately left him and Velthandros remained completely on his own, and he continued examining the charms of Love's castle. Presently he glanced to one side and saw a group of forty beautiful women who were sitting around[28] the outside of the terrace.[(550)] On seeing them Velthandros said, 'Mighty Love has ordered me to compare you. Come then, noble ladies, and I shall judge you.'

One left the group and said to him, 'Forgive me, my lord, but do me no injustice.'

Velthandros said to her, 'In truth, madam, I judge you unsuitable and unworthy of the wand because you have red and bleary eyes.' She received his decision and went and stood apart.

Yet another left the group, came up[(560)] and stood facing Velthandros. He said to her, 'Madam, those big lips of yours! They are enormous and unshapely! They make you very ugly.'

She moved away in her shame, went over to the first woman and they stood together, and apart from the others. She too sighed deeply from the bottom of her heart.

The third walked up quite out of turn. She did obeisance to the arbitrator and he said to her, 'I judge you unworthy of the wand. You are not the chosen one. Nature, I think, made your skin dark[(570)] but, madam, she gave you a frigid mind.'[29]

The fourth came and he said to her, 'If your eyebrows didn't meet, as I see they do, you would certainly now obtain the wand.'

Yet another came up from the group and stood shamelessly before the mighty judge. He said to her, 'You are not the winner even if I were inclined to give you the wand. You are stooping towards the ground. Your body is not properly proportioned. How could I give it to you?' She sighed deeply and stood with the others.[(580)]

After them the sixth came in like manner and said, 'Take care, O judge, not to do me an injustice.'

He looked at her and replied, 'If you were without that flabby and superfluous flesh you would obtain the wand and hold it alone.' She received the decision and joined the others, her body drenched with much perspiration.

Yet another left the group of women out of turn and approached him. Immediately he said to her, 'You are not the winner[590] even if I were inclined to give you the wand. I note that your teeth, madam, are faulty. Some point inwards, some poke outwards. So, as I started by saying, you are not the winner.' She received the judgement and stood with the others.

The group of women who had not yet been judged came and faced Velthandros. Three, four and then another five stood before him and after he had justly found fault with them, received his judgement.

Finally, three women of the original forty remained standing together.[600] Velthandros said to the three beauties, 'Come over here together, the three of you! Come for me to judge you.' They came and stood facing him. He addressed them with his directions:

'I must exercise much subtlety and refinement in judging you if I am to avoid condemnation or blame for my decision on beauty. So, ladies, the three of you go in a group to the spot over there, come back to me, then go away, and turn back.[610] My orders and my wish are to judge carefully and, as is necessary, to examine the beauty of each one's face, her whole body, her gait, her movement, and manner of walking.'

They went and came back, twice, three times, four times, and they said to Velthandros, 'Compare and judge us.'

Velthandros looked at the three, made an inspection, and, with an artist's eye, examined them carefully. To one he said, 'Leave the other two. The hairs on your hands, fair one, condemn you.'[620]

Immediately on hearing this criticism of herself she sighed in her vexation and said to him, 'Just as you have ignited and scorched the roots of my heart, so may your heart burn with the pangs of love.' With these words she went and stood with the others.

To the next Velthandros said, 'I have determined, after going into the finest detail, that in beauty and shape of face, body, and figure you are like the first. Her fault was in the hair on her hands, yours is in your eyes.[30] I notice, lady, that they[630] are fighting to swim in the waters of Love.

They, fair one, seem to be in danger of drowning. Now they sink—I am completely unable to bring them back to the water's surface.'[31]

When she heard Velthandros's judgement, in her bitterness she fixed him with a bitter eye and said, 'O most unjust of judges, I hope in God's name that you fall to the depths of Love's passion and that you drown in the water's current and die since you have utterly seared my heart too.'[640] With these words uttered in her bitterness, she went to join the others.

Velthandros then turned his attention to the last lady and made a careful examination of everything about her, her figure, grace, facial beauty, movement, gestures and deportment. With his eyes on her he said in admiration, 'Nature sat in the court of the Graces and meticulously gathered and put together everything, all the charms and beauties in the world. To you, madam, she gave them for your adornment![650] On you she endowed them! Madam, rejoice! She made your noble body as straight as a wand and fashioned it to be as lithe as a cypress twig. Then she breathed on the whole and gave it life, creating every bodily charm and living grace. Here is the wand which the lord of cupids took pleasure in fashioning for you. I bid you, my lady, stretch out your hand and take it.'

She leaned over, took the wand from Velthandros's hand, and then went and stood apart from the others,[660] holding the wand in her hands as her prize.

When the contest was finished a winged cupid appeared and said, 'Come, Velthandros, the king calls you.' At these words Velthandros immediately followed him and entered the sapphire hall from whence descended the river of flame. There, sitting loftily on a seat carved from a single ruby, at the end of the chamber, he saw Love with his bow. Around him stood ranks of cupids.[670]

With much emotion he addressed Velthandros: 'Velthandros, tell me, how did you conduct the contest? To whom did you give the wand to be mistress over the others? Tell me, Velthandros, describe to me in detail the charms, the graces and beauties of the fairest woman. How is she superior to the rest?'

'You desire, O Love,' Velthandros replied, 'to learn of the woman to whom I gave the wand, and of her lovely beauty and the other charms which she has to a greater degree than the rest? That woman fell from the bosom of the moon[680] and she broke off its bright part and took it with her. Your royal highness richly adorned her figure, her frame and the limbs of her body and made of her whole being a throne for you to sit in glory. You took half of Beauty's self and fashioned her body. You have given her a form and shape beyond that of humans. Her hair is the color of gold and matches her figure. Its thickness is like that of the grass of Paradise or of celery in a garden.[690] All the graces of the world seem to sit upon her and make her their dwelling. Certainly, beyond any doubt, her forehead bears your imprint of mottled gold. If a man casts a glance at her eyes they immediately tear at the roots of his heart. In the depths of their[32] lake tiny cupids swim, shoot their arrows and sport. Art created her jet-black eyebrows and with consummate skill made them bridges.[700] The Graces forged the fair one's nose and to the Graces belong her mouth and her pearly teeth. Her cheeks are rose-red, her lips have the color of nature. Certainly, her mouth is perfumed. Her chin is round in shape, she is tall and her arms are white and delicate, her neck is as from a lathe. Her waist is slender and shows the great skill of the one who fashioned it like a thin reed. As for the angle of her neck and her litheness! Indeed, her body is so perfect in its composition[710] that the Graces seem to come from her.[33] Her bosom is a paradise of love. The apples <of her breasts> shine even on a casual glance. Her look and her gait are miraculous. When she walks with confidence and glances up and down she ravishes your senses and tears at discretion. O King, my words may be bold but if you chance to catch my meaning[34] you will make a winged descent from your throne!'

After Velthandros had spoken, Love immediately vanished.[720] When he realized this, Velthandros was much agitated. Love had disappeared, flown off, gone! The group of women had vanished completely and the scene he had witnessed had dissolved like a dream. He reflected upon this and said to himself, 'What does this mean? Life, how volatile and unstable you are!' Velthandros straightway went back and examined the hall. He entered the park and saw the superb flowers of the fair garden. He returned to where he first saw[730] the stone figures inscribed with his destiny. He read the message and cried copiously. All alone, he reflected in his mind: 'I saw, recognized, and found written Fate's decree of my own fortune. To me it assigned the daughter of the king of Antioch. Let me go to her. Her name is Chrysandza. In this world it is completely impossible for a man to escape Destiny and Fortune's thread.'

He went quickly out the castle's gate[740] and found his men just as he had commanded them. None of them had dared to enter the castle. Straightway Velthandros and his squires mounted their horses. Sighing deeply, Velthandros set out on the road to Antioch. How soon will he get there?

For five whole days Velthandros rode and when he came to the plains of Antioch he chanced to find the prince, who was hunting. He quickly dismounted and did obeisance. The prince saw him kneeling low[750] and shouted to the stranger from a distance, 'From here your appearance seems Greek. Tell me your name and your country.'

He in turn briefly addressed the prince, 'I am of high and proud birth and my name is Velthandros in the language of the Greeks. I have left my father's land and kingdom and have chosen to wander in foreign parts.'

The prince said to him with a smile, 'If today you choose to serve me[760] I shall give you glory, honors, and money such as you never had in your own land.'

Velthandros replied to the prince in turn, 'My lord, let your wish be effected today. Act quickly to bring it about. I shall, to my own honor, become your servant, faithful beyond all others in your service.'

Velthandros and his squires mounted and joined in the hunt behind the prince.

When they found a hare in a lofty place on a mountain they released a falcon.[770] A swift eagle appeared flying in the sky, swooped down and seized the falcon. The prince saw what had happened and was grieved and distressed but Velthandros quickly drew his bow. Taking good aim he hit the eagle's wing. In its pain it released the unscathed falcon—it was completely without harm or injury. The prince marveled at Velthandros's bowmanship and praised his great skill effusively.

They now turned back and gave up the hunt.[780] The prince returned to his city accompanied by Velthandros and his men. They set about dinner at once, the table was prepared and all types of food were brought in order for the large gathering of lords and nobles. Velthandros was there with them. The prince then began the story of Velthandros; how he had seen Velthandros coming with his squires, how he had made a compact to become the prince's liege, how they had found a hare in a lofty place on a mountain[790] and released a falcon; and how when an eagle had swooped and taken it, Velthandros had shot the eagle on the wing while the falcon remained unscathed and without injury. Velthandros received much praise from everyone, including the fair princess and Chrysandza.

After the account the prince addressed him: 'I invite you to take food from us.' Velthandros reached over and took food from the hands of the prince who said earnestly to him,[800] 'I hope, Velthandros, you will now stay with my own men and enter the service of my kingdom.'

Velthandros obtained a place of high honor. He used to go to see the prince without permission and at any time. He did not need the approval of another. One day, he entered the royal chamber and greeted the princess, the prince and their beautiful daughter, Chrysandza. When the lady looked closely at him she immediately realized that he was the one[810] from whose hands she had received the wand when the contest took place at Love's castle. She waited to hear his name. When she heard 'Velthandros' from the prince's mouth, the name tore the roots of her heart and she straightway became filled with love. He too looked and in turn recognized the lady who was regarding him closely. She saw and clearly recognized the traits of his face, which she had preserved in her mind. Everything was confirmed.[820] She also remembered the wand, and even more, the words which he had spoken to her and the other thirty-nine ladies at Love's castle.[35] Velthandros and Chrysandza then indicated their mutual recognition by using signs. No-one noticed their secret behavior. Two months passed and no-one suspected; and then a further period of two years. Velthandros and Chrysandza kept secret the woes of love.

On one occasion in the early evening as the sun was setting, Velthandros was sitting alone in the palace[830] when he glanced from a window. He noticed that Chrysandza, the prince's daughter and his beloved, had gone out and was walking towards the garden. There she lay down under a shady tree and gave a loud sigh which came from the depths of her heart. The lady's tears flowed like a river and amidst her tears and sighs she said, 'Learn now for certain, Velthandros, that it is for you I suffer. My heart and my mind are in torture. I am on fire. I burn. I find no end to my suffering.[840] The time that I have kept this love for you hidden in my bosom has grown to two years and two months. How long am I to be secretly enslaved by this woe? Would that I had never seen you! Would that I had never met you!'

Velthandros was standing outside and listening. When he heard what Chrysandza was saying about him he quickly jumped down and went into the garden. When the two turned and saw each other, both fell in a faint and their bodies lay there half-dead.[850] Some time passed before they recovered. When they did so and completely regained their reason, Velthandros turned and said to the lady, 'You carry the wand, my slender one, and you do not realize your beauty. Only the judge who gave you the prize knows it.'

She in turn said to him, ' Why, sir, are you concerned with looking for the wand?'

In reply he said to the lady, 'I, madam, your own true servant, am searching for it in order to guard my lord's[36] property.'[(860)] With this he turned towards her with a smile. He put his arm around her and the two fell. Even the trees, though without feelings, re-echoed their many kisses and embraces. Till midnight they lay there unconscious. Later, when they had gratified their desires and they saw the eyelids of dawn opening, they kissed tenderly and separated. The lady went quickly and entered the palace. Velthandros left as well and was going to his quarters[(870)] but four of Chrysandza's guards, the protectors of the fair lady, were watching and they arrested him, tying both his arms behind him.

After they secured Velthandros with bonds there was a mighty uproar in the palace. One of Chrysandza's maids went out and approached the guards in order to learn the password. There she saw Velthandros with bound arms and went and told Chrysandza. The lady was greatly distressed on learning this[(880)] and she called her maid Fedrokaza, whom she trusted most of all her servants. When they were alone, she said with much emotion, 'Do you have the same love for me as I do for you?'

Fedrokaza replied with a smile, 'Fair mistress, you know that I was brought up with you. Do you not realize the love I bear you? In any case, I am your slave, your complete slave. Give me the order and for you I shall drown myself.'

She made Fedrokaza swear an oath[(890)] that whatever Chrysandza told her would not leave her mouth before she died and that she would keep secret what was entrusted to her.

Chrysandza then began to tell her maid the story: 'Dear Fedrokaza, you should know that for two years and more I have been hopelessly in love with the Greek, Velthandros, and that he has an even greater passion for me. But I had never found an excuse to say a word to him. Last night he was in the garden. We were together till midnight and he left me when dawn was breaking.[(900)] My guards have caught him and bound his arms behind his back. I think it impossible that the prince should not find out and that he should not sit in council this morning to judge him. I entreat you, dear Fedrokaza, to say that it was for love of you that he came to the garden. If you do this and it is not detected I shall regard you as my other self.'

Fedrokaza then went immediately to the station of the guards where she found Velthandros lying with his arms tied and fetters on his legs and she began to mock him.*(910)* But when she found the opportunity she approached, spoke to him, and said furtively so that she would not be heard, 'Listen carefully, Velthandros, and pay attention to what I tell you. The words are not mine but those of my illustrious mistress, the fair princess Chrysandza. If the prince sits in council this morning to judge you and happens to ask why you came to the garden, give me as the reason. Say that you love me and that it was for love of me that you went there. But be careful not to panic and make them take further notice of you.*(920)* Say that I invited you and that you came to where I indicated. Perhaps if you say this all will be well for you. The shame will be mine and you will go innocent.'

With these words she left, went to her mistress and related what she had said and done. Chrysandza covered her servant with kisses. And what did Chrysandza set about doing next? She donned the arms of a man, girt herself with boldness, and before dawn, before the sun rose, she went by herself and found the prince.*(930)* She stood before him in this terrible array. Seeing her in a very agitated state the prince said to her with <concern>,[37] 'Is something wrong, dear Chrysandza? What terrible thing has happened to you?'

With bitterness she replied, 'How can I not appear serious and disturbed when Your Majesty's men shamelessly enter my own garden as they think fit? Last night Velthandros did precisely this.'

When the prince heard Chrysandza's words*(940)* he immediately jumped up in a great rage. He commanded that Velthandros be brought to him and ordered nobles, judges and lords to assemble in council in the great palace, as well as a countless number of the common people. Each class stood in its appointed position. The prince immediately sat down on his throne and all the lords and judges did the same according to rank.

He summoned Velthandros and when he came into their midst the prince saw him[38] and said,*(950)* 'Tell me, how did you dare to enter the garden belonging to my noble daughter who was born to the purple?'

To this Velthandros quickly replied, 'Know that I love Fedrokaza, my lord. The matter now depends on Your Majesty.'

The prince gave orders for Fedrokaza to be brought as well. He took her to one side and questioned her.

And she confessed, 'I loved Velthandros.'

The prince then said to those present, 'Speak, my lords, give me counsel in this.'(*960*) All were silent. No-one spoke a word. The prince spoke for a second time.

Then the lords replied and said, 'We do not have a single word to say in objection.'

The prince then addressed them: 'I need Velthandros. I want to keep him. I very much desire him as an excellent knight. Since he has become involved with my daughter's maid and fallen in love I shall now give him to her. I shall now make them man and wife and give them my blessing.(*970*) I shall allow him to live as he wishes and desires.'

All rose and praised the prince.

But when Chrysandza heard she was greatly distressed. Quickly she turned and said to the prince, 'I am not giving my Fedrokaza to a man.'

The prince in turn replied, 'I shall allow you to speak, but my wishes will be carried out!'

Chrysandza took Fedrokaza by the hand and led her to her bedchamber. They entered by themselves and locked themselves in.(*980*) 'I kiss you, I really kiss you for the favor you have done me. Even if it happens that the prince gives up the idea of marrying off my handsome Velthandros, be careful not to divulge the secrets I have entrusted to you, and see that you do not approach my lord.'

Fedrokaza said in reply, 'I, madam, shall have him in appearance only. He will be my husband in word but the right to him belongs to Your Highness. I shall not, madam, touch the man who is my master.'(*990*)

When Chrysandza saw that the heart and mind of her faithful and much beloved Fedrokaza were firm, she dressed her and sent her straight to the prince to attend to the arrangements for her marriage with Velthandros and to what the prince would give Velthandros by way of settlement.

The prince sent Fedrokaza back with the message: 'Ask your mistress how much she is giving you for a dowry.'

The hour for dinner had come and the table was set up. She laid the table-cloth and started to eat. Chrysandza ordered the maids to go$^{(1000)}$ but kept Fedrokaza to eat and drink with her. She summoned Velthandros who came quickly to the table and stood in front of her. The lady gave a faint laugh on seeing him and then, smiling sweetly, said, 'Since you have dared to come so abruptly into my room and you are going to take my own maid from me, I do not know what to say or how to rebuke you. Would you like me to give an order for the dogs to devour you immediately?' Velthandros listened but made no reply.$^{(1010)}$ But when they had eaten and the table was removed Chrysandza went into her quarters with Fedrokaza. They also kept Velthandros and went inside. Straightway Chrysandza and Velthandros embraced and fell down. When they had taken their fill of sweet kisses they went out again with Fedrokaza into the garden where they had first satisfied their love. Chrysandza immediately looked at Velthandros and said, 'Tell me how you dared come into my garden and how my guards caught you so quickly.'$^{(1020)}$

[*A short gap in which Velthandros's reply was probably followed by a discreet description of further love-making, perhaps in a similar vein to the account of their previous meeting.*]

When they had taken their joy as both desired Chrysandza quickly gave orders for a clerk who was a secretary to be summoned and he wrote out the contract for Fedrokaza's dowry. She then sent him to her father so that he too could see the dowry and the terms. It was to be conveyed to the prince with the message: 'This is what I am giving my servant as a dowry. Tell me, my lord, what you are giving Velthandros.'

When the prince learnt of his daughter's wish, he in turn gave Velthandros an even larger sum.$^{(1030)}$ The patriarch was summoned to perform the ceremony. When they came to the traditional rite of the crowns, the prince took the crown of Velthandros, and Chrysandza in turn took that of Fedrokaza.[39] Then they reveled, they sported, they danced.

After the wedding their cares were allayed. Fedrokaza left with Velthandros, the prince with the princess, Chrysandza went to her own accustomed bed, and Velthandros pretended to be sleeping with the bride.$^{(1040)}$ Early next morning Chrysandza went and gave Fedrokaza the garment which she had stained with the blood of her maidenhood at the time when Velthandros had first united with her in the garden. Fedrokaza took this and wore it to give the impression that Velthandros had slept with her and taken her maidenhood. The story spread and reached the prince.

After all this they returned to their duties; Velthandros served the prince as before, Fedrokaza served the lady Chrysandza.*(1050)* From then on Velthandros came to Chrysandza every time his passion was great. Often he came to the midday meal, but also to dinner. When all had gone to bed and were asleep, mistress and maid would go to Velthandros. Sometimes Velthandros came to her. This they did for ten months and no-one knew except only Velthandros's three squires and Fedrokaza with them. Only the four knew.

At this time Velthandros became afraid and his heart was troubled.*(1060)* His mind and his soul were alarmed. He confided his thoughts to Chrysandza, 'Listen, my dear, and take heed of my words. Ten months have passed since we were united and no-one knows what is between us except the three squires and Fedrokaza. Well, I fear her and I fear my squires. I am afraid that your maid may change her mind or alter her purpose and go and slander us, or that some enemy may trick my squires.*(1070)* Your father would learn of what has happened and immediately condemn me to a bitter death. And you, my dear, would incur shame and no light reproof. So come, let us leave completely without fuss; quietly, secretly, and unnoticed, so that no-one realizes. You are losing a kingdom, my slender one, but a kingdom you will find.'

When Chrysandza, and also Fedrokaza, heard this, they began to put the plan into operation. They looked for a chance to escape but they were afraid of being discovered and shamefully detained.*(1080)* After about a fortnight had passed an opportunity came when the prince decided to go abroad with the princess for a holiday. They invited Chrysandza to come and enjoy herself but she had the idea of pretending to be ill and so they left her behind to recover. Straightway that night Velthandros and Chrysandza, together with the squires and Fedrokaza, set out without anyone knowing.

The night was dark and without a moon.*(1090)* There was a windstorm with much thunder and lightning. From the violence of the terrible rain and flooding even birds lost their mates that evening. But as for Velthandros, he did not complain. He and his band kept persisting with everything. They took a hard and rocky road and for the whole of that night suffered many ills. Despite the great danger and violence of the waters they were quite unwilling to stop for rest because they suspected that they were being pursued from behind.*(1100)* Finally, at dawn, they came to a river. Velthandros crossed and got to the other bank and the rest of the company followed him. But alas! Woe! Woe! What happened? The river encircled them and carried them off. Fedrokaza drowned with her mule, as did the three squires with their horses. Velthandros went through it and crossed over, but was stripped of his clothing and came close to drowning. He reached land with difficulty, naked except for his drawers.*(1110)* He had lost everything, his horse and his clothes, and was thrown up like a corpse onto the right bank. He lay stretched out on the ground half-dead. Chrysandza was thrown up on the left bank of the river, half-dead, completely naked, and stretched out on the shore. Destiny's decree, which Velthandros had seen in Love's castle, was then fulfilled.

In the dangers of that day two turtle-doves had been separated by the terrible violence. The female approached Chrysandza and attached itself to her.*(1120)* The other, which was male, did the same to Velthandros. This proved a comfort to them. But Velthandros searched the river to find the body of any of his band. Again he went up and down. He ran along the banks and along their bends. He searched and he searched but found nothing. He cried like a bird at losing its feathers.

But why prattle on at length? He found the drowned Fedrokaza, lifeless and dead, lying stretched out and swollen.*(1130)* He wept and shed tears over her body. Then he stood up, dug a grave with his hands and buried her. Again he searched to find Chrysandza, whether drowned or alive, and his squires. The turtle-dove strutted everywhere with him and joined in his grief as though it were human.

So much for Velthandros, but what of Chrysandza? She searched and searched but discovered nothing. She went up and down the river but was able to find no solace*(1140)* except from the female turtle-dove, which bewailed her misfortune as one female for another. Again she returned and searched the lower reaches. Five times she went up and back. In one bend of the river she found the most valiant squire of Velthandros, utterly lifeless and dead. The features of his face were completely lost. She thought that the dead man was Velthandros because the latter's clothes and sword*(1150)* were where the corpse was lying. She took hold of the body, dragged it, looked at it, examined it closely. She believed it was Velthandros, as it appeared to be, and in her terrible grief she fainted. The anguish tore at the roots of her heart.

As soon as she recovered consciousness Chrysandza began to lament and sing a dirge:

'Velthandros, my light, my eyes, my soul, my heart, how is it that I see you dead, how is it that I see you without life? Instead of the bright coverlets and royal bed*(1160)* and mantles sewn with pearls which should cover you,[40] you lie here naked on the river's sands. Where is your father's lament, or that of your brother, of your noble relatives, of your lords? Will your servants and maids bewail and lament? And where are the prince and princess, my father and mother, to join in my grief and to comfort me? Where is the solace of all my own women? I am here alone of all my family, unfortunate, miserable, cursed by fate![(1170)] What shall I do, unhappy that I am? What will become of me in my misery? In my woe what path, what road shall I take? Behold the misfortune I have suffered, the ruin that has befallen me! O horror, what will happen to me? What shall I do, what shall I do? How is it possible for me not to feel your noble charms, my beloved, my rare Velthandros, my sweet lord? Let me kill my poor heart, let me bury it with you, let me join you in death and with you go down to Hades instead of spending my whole life in woes. Alas! Unhappy me! I do not know what will become of me![(1180)] Alas! Woe! Woe! What avails me my noble birth?'

With these words she fainted from her terrible pain. She fell and lay stretched out on the ground as though dead. The turtle-dove brought water on its wings and by drenching the lady, immediately brought her back to life. When she had with difficulty revived and recovered consciousness she grabbed the sword and dug in the sand. With her two hands she made a grave large enough for the two of them. What did she do next? First the lady put in the corpse, then she took the sword,[(1190)] placed it next to her heart and uttered the doleful words: 'Go, poor soul, go to your beloved.'[41]

Suddenly she heard a sound from across the river. 'Where are you, dear Chrysandza? I cannot find you.' Chrysandza heard the voice and straightway ran to whence it came. As the place was thickly wooded she was not able to see or catch a glimpse of anything. She returned again to the corpse[(1200)] and a second time she heard a loud voice calling out her name *Chrysandza!* Straightway she ran and saw Velthandros on the other bank. He saw her and his soul rejoiced. Immediately he came across the river. It was five days since they had seen each other. They were naked, without clothes and nourishment. Together they fell down senseless on the meadow. When both had recovered their wits the lady asked after Fedrokaza.[(1210)] On hearing that she had drowned, the fair one was distressed and tears poured from her eyes like a river. In the anguish of her soul she said to Velthandros, 'For my Fedrokaza and your three squires we shall give an account before the impartial judge who is fearsome and great. It was we two who drowned them.'

For a long time they searched the banks of the river to find the two drowned squires. And when they did discover their bloated, drowned bodies[1220] they took them and buried them with much grief. They then set off on their journey, naked as they were, and in this fashion ran along the river's bank. As they were approaching the sea they saw a ship coming and they waited for it. After a short while it arrived very close to them and moored. The captain launched a large dinghy into the sea and headed for the land. When he disembarked he saw Velthandros there, naked except for his drawers. Chrysandza too he noticed in the shadow of a rock.[1230] Velthandros recognized the captain immediately but the captain did not know him at all and started to hurl abuse at him.

'From your appearance,' he said, 'you seem Greek, and you have lawlessly kidnapped this woman from somewhere. You have snatched her from her parents and made off.'

Velthandros gave a faint laugh and said, 'You have not yet been caught in the thorns of Fortune and have not seen Love's images as I have. You say that I have carried off my wife against the will of her parents like some pirate cut-throat.[1240] I see that you are of the Greek race, as I am myself. If you wish it, permit me to talk to you and you can learn who I am and who my father is, and how it is that I am naked here with my wife.'

The captain heard Velthandros's words and said mildly, 'Since you are Greek, as appears from your speech, wait, noble stranger, for me to go to the ship and fetch the eunuch whom our king Rodofilos sent with us.[1250] The king had two beloved sons. The elder of the two died. The second had gone away in a rage and it is said that he went to the East. His father, no longer able to maintain his kingdom, has now sent us to the lands of Asia to search through regions where we may find this second son of the king so that he may rule over his lands and provinces.[1260] This is what I have to tell you, my lord. It is none other that we seek.'

Velthandros said, 'Let me see the eunuch.' Straightway the captain gave the order and the eunuch disembarked. Velthandros recognized him on sight but the eunuch did not know Velthandros at all, so much had suffering changed his appearance. They greeted each other briefly and Velthandros said, 'Has the son of Rodofilos really died?'

The eunuch immediately replied, 'How is it, stranger, that you knew Filarmos?'[1270]

Velthandros then mentioned the name of the eunuch, who immediately recognized him and fell to his feet and happily covered them with kisses.

'Arise,' he said, 'Give ear and tell me the truth. Is Filarmos, my dear brother, dead?'

When he learnt the details of his brother's death he groaned from the depths of his heart. Both Chrysandza and he wept in their grief. The rocks were shattered by their terrible laments.

When Velthandros recovered his wits and his reason[1280] he began to tell the eunuch about himself; how, because of the boundless grief caused by his father, he had gone into exile and left his home; how he had wandered through many lands—beyond counting, had traversed the regions of the East and of Turkey, how he had slain the robbers at the pass and how he had finally come to the city of Tarsus and seen the river with the flame; how, because of this river, he had traveled and come to the castle of Love;[1290] all the inscriptions and figures he had examined, what Fortune had in store for him, the union with Chrysandza, their nakedness as they fled, the fatal river. Of these and of other things he spoke to the eunuch and they both cried.

Next they set up a table and ate. They rose, went on board the ship, and put on royal clothes and crowns which Velthandros's father, Rodofilos, had sent. Velthandros dressed the royal lady in female attire with his own hands.[1300] She shone like the sun, the ship glistened, the glens danced, the hills reveled, misfortunes disappeared and joy spread abroad. The vessel weighed anchor and left. There was a favorable wind and in five days they arrived at their country. The ship moored and with a mighty shout they put out many flags. News which brought great joy to Rodofilos quickly reached the palace: he should run to his royal son;[1310] he should receive and embrace him; Velthandros had returned from foreign lands and he had come home on the ship which Rodofilos had sent to search for him; it had found him and brought him back with Chrysandza, the daughter of the mighty prince of great Antioch.

When the old man heard the wonderful news he jumped from his throne, assembled his lords and they made a great and splendid procession. In their joy all gave Velthandros a magnificent reception. When the father saw his son[1320] he embraced him joyfully and covered him with kisses. He also embraced the fair Chrysandza. Women escorted her. Great ladies of the court accompanied her in their splendor and formed an escort of honor. They paid their respects to her, extolled her and said, 'Long life to the king's son and his queen!' All the people, great and small, rejoiced. King Rodofilos frolicked and was happy. Many were the splendid performances of music.

The king called the archbishop and his priests[1330] and the archbishop put the crown of marriage and power on the two heads of Velthandros and Chrysandza. Velthandros was acclaimed bridegroom and emperor alike, and appointed ruler by senate and people; the lady Chrysandza was made queen. Music was played according to tradition and when the food was ready they sat and ate.

King Rodofilos then addressed the assembly: 'Know, all you lords and nobles, that I have found my hawk, which I had lost.[1340] The dead one has returned from the depths of Hades!'

Let this be the end of my tale. Let us attend to the words of the writer of proverbs.[42] 'If the beginning is good but the end is bad,' as the sage remarks, 'it makes the whole bad. But if there is good at the end of life, everything is good and the object of countless blessings.' And I say, 'Amen! Amen!' and end my tale.

Notes

1   Hatzis p.109.
2   Pieler pp.198-205.
3   Beaton p.120.
4   The main clue is the word ζῴδιον (translated by *figure*), which occurs twice in the first passage (in *ll*.370 and 378 in the Greek). When it is mentioned for the second time it is said to be the origin of the stream; if we suppose that this is the peacock then the first occurrence of ζῴδιον will have to refer to the statue and its peacock together. However, it seems unlikely that the word would be given two different connotations within a few lines. Also, the peacock is represented as sitting (*l*.375) but the figure from which the stream comes is standing (*l*.377 νὰ στέκῃ).
5   Kahane p.201.
6   On the association of peacocks with paradise see Oxford Dictionary of Byzantium *s.v.* peacock.
7   An allusion to the Byzantine custom that the Empress always gave birth to her children in a room decorated with purple (the royal color).
8   Kriaras's punctuation in *ll*.19f. has been changed, but *l*.20 is probably corrupt.
9   *l*.36 is corrupt and has been omitted.
10 The text of this sentence is corrupt. The sense seems to be that if Velthandros invades his father's kingdom in the service of a foreign ruler the latter will show Rodofilos scant consideration.
11 Type of stringed instrument resembling a lyre.
12 Following the text of Hatziyiakoumis (p.235) in *l*.179.
13 The first six words of *l*.208 are corrupt and have been omitted.
14 Emending καθόλου to κάποτε in *l*.234.
15 Emending κεῖνον to κείνη in *l*.242.
16 The word in the Greek (τρίτον *third*) is either corrupt or unexplained. Some word meaning *door* seems required. In *l*.334 ἃ εἴπομε is corrupt and has been omitted.
17 Reading παρεῖχον in *l*.335 but the line may be corrupt.
18 Following the text of Hatziyiakoumis (p.236) in *ll*.341, 342.
19 Following the text of Hatziyiakoumis (pp.236f.) in *l*.351.
20 The sense of this rather obscure passage appears to be: a human figure of unspecified gender is represented as holding a peacock; the figure is distressed and from its eyes and mouth comes the water of the river which Velthandros has been tracking; from its mouth also come sighs

which are so hot that they provide the flame which runs within the river. See also pp.2ff. and endnote 4 above.

21 The text of *l*.386 is corrupt.

22 Emending to σὺν καπνῷ οὐκ ὀλίγῳ in *l*.412.

23 Following the text of Hatziyiakoumis (p.237) in *l*.416.

24 Reading Χρυσάντζα in *l*.422 and emending the genitives of *l*.423 to accusatives.

25 The text is corrupt. The context requires some expression such as that given in brackets.

26 The young man who used to swim across the Hellespont to visit his love Hero. On one occasion, after inadvisedly setting out in bad weather, he was drowned.

27 Kriaras's punctuation has been changed. *l*.478 has been put in parenthesis with a colon at the end of *l*.479 and no stop at the end of *l*.480.

28 Following the text of Hatziyiakoumis (p.238) in *l*.550.

29 The point of Velthandros's comment is not obvious. Perhaps *frigid* may have reference to the woman's shamelessness in coming out of turn.

30 Following the text of Hatziyiakoumis (pp.238f.) in *l*.629.

31 Sense uncertain.

32 Emending σου to των in *l*.697.

33 *l*.712 is corrupt and has been omitted.

34 Sense uncertain.

35 Following the text of Hatziyiakoumis (p.239) in *l*.823.

36 Velthandros tells Chrysandza that he is searching for the wand because it belongs to his lord, i.e. Love.

37 The text is corrupt.

38 Following the text of Hatziyiakoumis (pp.239f.) in *l*.950.

39 The ceremony of the exchange of crowns is traditional in the Orthodox church. Both bride and groom wear crowns which, at one point in the ceremony, are exchanged. This is done by those assisting (here the king and Chrysandza), not by the bride and groom themselves.

40 Following the text of Hatziyiakoumis (p.240) in *l*.1161.

41 Emending τοῦ ποθητοῦ to ὁ ποθητός in *l*.1193.

42 The Greek παροιμιαστής *writer of proverbs* would most naturally be taken as referring to Solomon, the author of the Old Testament *Book of Proverbs*, where, however, nothing resembling the words quoted here is to be found. The closest parallel seems to be in the *Gesta Romanorum* 67: *si finis bonus est totum bonum est* (if the end is good all is good), which may give us the English *all's well that ends well*.

Introduction
to
Kallimachos and Chrysorroi

Kallimachos and Chrysorroi is the only work in the whole corpus of the late medieval Greek romance for which an author has been claimed. A poem of 161 lines survives from the hand of a fourteenth century Byzantine author, Manuel Filis, and bears the title *Epigram on a Book of Romance by the Emperor's Cousin*.[1] Filis is celebrating a romance written by a contemporary member of the royal family, Andronikos Palaeologos. This involves him in giving a summary of the plot of the romance and he follows this with an allegorical interpretation of the story. He does not give a title or the names of the hero and heroine.

The extent to which this summary matches the story of *Kallimachos* is remarkable and makes it likely that there is a connection between Andronikos's romance and our poem. But this does not mean that Andronikos is the author of *Kallimachos* as we have it. Several considerations are against this conclusion. Some incidents in Filis's account do not occur in *Kallimachos*; for example, the brothers capture towns at the beginning of their expedition, and the hero kills a lion before reaching Dragon's Castle. Filis also gives a different version for some incidents; for example, the ring with which Kallimachos makes his presence known to Chrysorroi is put on a tree in our poem but in Filis it is included with roses which the hero has plucked for the heroine. Further, Filis sees a religious allegory in Andronikos's poem and interprets it as a warning against sexual pleasures. Anything less in accordance with the spirit of our poem, which is devoid of religion and glories in erotic love, would be hard to imagine.

We do not know the motive Filis had for writing his verses. However, it seems unlikely that when praising, in the most fulsome terms, the literary efforts of a member of the royal family he would have made mistakes in something so elementary as a summary. Nor, one might imagine, would he have received much thanks for providing an interpretation so implausible that it would not withstand the most cursory reading of the text. We can readily admit that there may be a

33

connection between the narrative praised by Filis and our poem but its exact nature is difficult to determine.

There are, however, some aspects of *Kallimachos* which, while not conclusive evidence against the idea of it being written by a single person, do seem to indicate that it existed within some kind of tradition and that its text was in a state of flux. These are the loose ends and inconsistencies with which it abounds. We find similar lapses in *Velthandros* and *Livistros* but here they are much more frequent.

The most glaring examples are:

At the beginning of the poem Kallimachos and his brothers are dispatched by their father to determine who is the most suitable to succeed to the throne (*ll*.45-67). Although Kallimachos reiterates this at *ll*.2509f. the arrangement is completely forgotten in the final resolution of the plot.

At *ll*.261-265 the eldest brother gives Kallimachos a magic ring which, if placed in his mouth, will allow him to fly. When Kallimachos finally has a need for this we are told that it has been lost (*l*.1552) and also that its effect was obtained by wearing it on one's hand (*l*.1555).

When the ring is mentioned for the second time we are informed that Kallimachos has also encountered a gown with miraculous healing properties (*ll*.1556-1561). This appears nowhere else in the poem.

The inscription on the magic apple which annihilates Kallimachos is reported differently three times (*ll*.1210-1214, 1407f., 2553-2556). The versions of the inscription differ in both form and length.

Such inconsistencies are more in keeping with fairy tales than with a work of self-conscious art such as Filis seems to describe. An affiliation with fairy tales is also indicated by other features of the poem, particularly motifs such as the three rival brothers, the enchanted castle, the witch, the magic apple and so on. If *Kallimachos* in its present form is derived from Filis's romance it must have undergone a considerable reworking.

But despite the fairy-tale element it is curious that *Kallimachos* is the only one of the three romances which refers to its readers (*ll*.1005, 1061, 2393).

A problem of translation specific to *Kallimachos* is the word used for the villain who first captures Chrysorroi and tortures her in his castle. In the Greek he is described as a δράκων (dhrákon),[2] a word normally translated by *dragon*. Some aspects of his conduct, in particular his desire to marry Chrysorroi, might suggest, at least from a Western perspective, that we should think of him as a giant or ogre, and he is so described in some studies on the poem. The word, in a slightly different form (δράκος dhrákos), occurs in Greek folktales collected in modern times, where it has been translated as *ogre*.[3]

In *Kallimachos* we are not given any description which could help us decide on a particular English term, except that at *ll*.556f., 560, 654, 664 he is called a *wild beast* (θηρίον). The same word is used in *ll*.189ff. to describe one category of the castle's guards, the other two being serpents and, confusingly, dragons. But subsequently they are, as a group, referred to as serpents (e.g. *ll*.218, 1034, 2527), and perhaps no particular differentiation between the three types of guard is intended. In any case, in the Greek world no great distinction was made, either in antiquity or in the middle ages, between a δράκων and a snake.[4] This association is not in harmony with the normal idea of an ogre, which is defined by the OED as 'a man-eating monster usually represented as a hideous giant.'

We do, however, have a description of the creature in question in an earlier medieval Greek work, *Digenis Akritis*, which relates the exploits of a popular folk hero. When Digenis meets a δράκων we are told that the latter's *body was thick and brought together his (three) heads; behind, it was slender and contracted into a tail.*[5] This δράκων, a dragon beyond question, can transform himself into a handsome youth. A being of this sort is completely plausible as Chrysorroi's captor. Further, the ability of such a creature to switch between human and beast would explain why Chrysorroi is considered a dragoness (δρακαίνα) by the subjects of the king who has kidnapped her (*ll*.1515, 1539f., 1587).

For these reasons δράκων has been translated as *dragon*, not as *ogre*.

Text

Kallimachos, like *Velthandros*, survives in one manuscript of the early sixteenth century.

In addition to the poem itself the manuscript contains numerous short passages of one to five lines which are not part of the narrative but which either summarize the section which follows or make some comment on it. In manuscripts where such insertions occur the normal practice of scribes was to distinguish them from the text proper by using red ink (hence their name *rubric*) and this is the case here. The greater number of the rubrics in *Kallimachos* are in the same verse form as the poem itself. Similar rubrics occur in *Livistros* but are totally absent from *Velthandros*.

It is inconceivable that these rubrics come from the pen of the original author, if indeed we are justified in conceiving our present poem as written by a single person. Some interrupt the narrative, some make a trite comment, while others display an awkwardness which is quite out of keeping with the story (for example, the rubric at 2021f. where the rubric's author addresses the author of the romance). In no case are they necessary for a comprehension of the poem. It seems, however, from their presence here and in other romances, that they were regarded as an integral part of the written presentation of the text and perhaps served some function now lost to us; on this ground alone they deserved to be kept. They are included in editions of *Kallimachos* and have been incorporated into the numeration of the poem's lines. Accordingly they have been translated and presented here.

As, however, it would have been distracting to the reader to encounter rubrics in the body of the translation they have been given as boxed text in bold italics at the places where they are found in the manuscript. In most cases they stand at the beginning of a paragraph. Where they occur inside a paragraph they have been marked with an initial asterisk and the point in the translation to which they belong has been marked with a vertical line.

The text followed is that of M. Pichard *Le roman de Callimaque et de Chrysorrhoé* Budé, Paris 1956. Changes are recorded in the endnotes.

Kallimachos and Chrysorroi

The Romance of Kallimachos and Chrysorroi

Prologue on the ways of the world.
We begin the story of a man sorely tried, affectionate and capable, who was much loved.

Nothing that happens on this earth, no action, no exploit, does not partake of grief. Joy and grief are mixed, even blended together. Beauty and charm have their share of grief just as grief often has its share of joy. Fame, glory, honor, wealth, beauty, intelligence, learning, bravery,[10] love, charm, noble appearance; the qualities that give sweet joy and pleasure—joined with them you see danger and malice, infirmities and obstacles which cause grief, not to mention the loss itself of what we long for. Desire deprived of its object shuns patience, and shows, one might say, no concern for other things. Love instils its charm into everything except separation and there alone it is filled with great bitterness. If, however, you read this tale and learn the matter of its verses[20] you will see the workings of Love's bitter-sweet pangs. Such is the nature of Love, its sweetness is not without alloy. But we must turn to our story. . .

The beginning of the story.

A certain foreign king, a proud monarch, master of much wealth, lord of many lands, of insufferable pride and arrogant bearing, had three fair and very dearly loved sons who inspired Love with their handsome appearance and their bearing; they were wondrous in every other way, and of manly courage.[30] Their father, seeing them matched in bearing, in beauty, in build and every valor, divided his paternal affection equally among them. He wanted to see the first inherit his crown; the next he wanted as joint heir, and to the third he earnestly desired to hand over the rule of his empire. He judged each worthy of the crown and of power. His wish was not to prefer one before another. But he did not see it possible to transfer the empire to all three[40] nor did he judge this expedient since it would bring disorder and a mighty tempest.

So he sat in royal state, summoned his sons, and with much affection addressed them:

'My children, adornment of my soul, flesh of my flesh, I wish to transfer and hand over to you my crown, my authority, my fame and my power. But my love for the three of you is equal; my feeling for each is the same. I do not know whom I should, by my preference, place first[50] and make master of my crown. I do not want to transfer the empire to all of you; I want my crown and power not to be the subject of dispute but to last into the future and beyond. Sharing is bad and brings disorder.[6] Just as sharing has no place in love, so it has no place in ruling an empire.[7] Behold! Here is much money, here are troops in arms and whatever else is necessary for great deeds. Here are treasure, equipment and a mighty army. Depart, go, take much money[60] and everything else you need for support. The one who shows great military valor, strength, intelligence and proper wisdom, the one who acts in the most kingly way, and gains a great trophy with his mighty exploits, to him shall I give the command of the empire, him shall I crown and make king in my place.' No-one was dissatisfied with their father's words or with his wishes and orders. It was with cordiality, with much affection,[70] with goodwill and a good heart that the three immediately said farewell and set out together, with many battalions, with a mighty army, and with a vast array of arms and equipment.

And so the three set out They went over many vast and trackless
to leave. lands. Finally, to omit details, they
came to a deserted region where they
found a rugged and precipitous mountain which could not be scaled. The mountain reached beyond the clouds and afforded no way of ascent.[80] It was rough and stony, dark, wild and frightening. Immediately they took counsel as to how they should proceed and what they should do. The first said, ' The mountain affords no way of ascent, so far does its height reach. You would say that its peak even reaches the heavens and that its trees stretch their branches to the same extent. So let us withdraw from this place. Let us go to some level country. Come!'

Immediately on hearing this, the second said, 'I agree. I am departing from here.[90] A mountain higher than the clouds, a place full of rocks and stones, an unscaleable peak, trees as high as the heavens! Who could climb the height of such a peak with an army and all our baggage here, with a great host and innumerable camels? If there were people living near the mountain and this vast region, the forests here would show signs of destruction or disturbance;[8] or some trace at least of a hunter would be visible. But the mountain is deserted of human beings.'*(100)*

The third said, 'I consider such action not worthy of a man. Whatever happens to me, even if I face death itself, no mountain will prove me a coward. I shall not show fear of this place. If a mountain can defeat me, and a place is enough to make me retreat, how shall I stand in battle and play a hero's part? How shall I look our father in the eye, formidable as he is? How shall I see and confront him? Have I forgotten our father's orders and counsel, that wise counsel of his? Will a mountain and lifeless nature take away my father's royal inheritance and rob me of it?*(110)*[9] O father, royal father, you have cowardly sons if they retire before battle and flee before the fighting. Hand over your empire to another, to a man not of your race or blood, a foreigner, but at least someone who is brave. Dismiss us, sire, and do not call us your children. We have the nature of women as appears from these deeds; we are afraid of woods. I feel shame before our generals and the soldiers of our army;*(120)* I feel shame before their ancestral courage. And you, royal father, when you see us all in flight, escaping from I know not what, routed, defeated—to whom will you give the kingdom? Whom will you crown first? Whatever happens, I shall not look upon my father with a coward's heart, I shall not disgrace my race, nor shall I today lose the kingship from an unmanly will or from cowardice. But our army with its equipment, its battalions and troops,[10] our brave and costly expedition*(130)* cannot climb this difficult place with its hostile mountain and thick forest. So let the army with its generals, camels, yoked oxen, its equipment and everything else today come to a halt. But let us, alone, with those arms we have, with just our horses and our reserve mounts, climb up the mountain's rocky slope like men.'

All judge the advice of   The elder brothers were put to shame
the third preferable.   by the words of the third, gave in, and
                                   said, 'So be it!'*(140)* Immediately the entire force—the great army together with the other equipment brought for its support, the treasures, the guards and the troops, decamped and departed for home.

The three went up the mountain. They climbed for a long time and with great difficulty reached the top. It was after the space of about three months that they together got to the summit of the mountain and there they found a charming and pleasant spot, a wondrous meadow of quite exotic grace*(150)* divided by a river of crystalline water. Roses and lilies were mixed in profusion over the ground, with flowers of every plant which captivates the soul. They dismounted, sat and refreshed themselves a little. They unsaddled their horses in the middle of the meadow, marveled at the scene's beauty and charm, and bathed in the water.

Further words of advice Again the third brother spoke, | 'We
from Kallimachos to his must not stop our labors and our
two elder brothers. journey here.*(160)* What has this
meadow to do with our father's
command and deeds of courage? Or looking at flowers and plants, roses
and lilies? The beauty and charms of this country contribute nothing to
our father's orders, counsel and wishes, nor to our hopes of the most regal
of crowns.'

On these words of advice the brothers left the place with all its graces. They took up their arms and again set out. After a long journey they came to a region of cliffs*(170)* where no human had ever been, nor any wild animal, bird or beast. After passing this wide land as well, they came upon a great castle, fearsome and strange. Together the three went up and approached it—the terrible and mighty Dragon's Castle.

A superb description of The wall was high, all of gold on the
the castle of the dragon. outside. The purity of its metal and its
sparkling beauty quite outshone all the
rays of the sun.*(180)* The hammered cladding of its battlements blended
together gold, precious stones and pearls. Such was the wondrous castle.
Its gates were huge and fearsome, and possessed of a terrifying beauty.
Gold, precious stones and pearls (but of the most valuable, the fairest and
best) were fitted together to make up a pattern, but in no haphazard or
chance manner. Live serpents stood in front of the closed gates; huge and
terrifying serpents and supernatural animals;*(190)* who, ever-wakeful and
alert, guarded the mighty castle. Fearsome dragons were there, and wild
beasts as gatekeepers. A man would die from fear alone on seeing them.

When the brothers saw the magnificence of the castle and its ramparts
they marveled and were amazed. They saw the sparkling gold, the precious
stones and pearls and all the other beauties of the castle. But the wall was
high and afforded no entry. No man approached them, nor any beast or
bird, not even a sparrow. The place was wild.*(200)* They ran up and down
looking for a way in. The castle had lofty towers and walls that reached to
the heavens. They came to its shining gates, which were of great value,
they saw the serpents and they shuddered at the gate-keepers. They did not
know the master of this fearsome but wondrous city with its glittering

castle. So they turned and headed back lest they serve as food for its gate-keepers. The sight had stunned them and they turned in flight.

The three brothers, including Kallimachos, stop, talk and take counsel on what to do. The first said, 'Without doubt, this castle[212] is impregnable, unassailable, completely invincible. Who will begin battle? Who will start the fight? Who will enter the fray with wild beasts? I see that the castle is made wholly from gold, costly pearls and many precious stones. It is guarded by vigilant serpents—huge, fearsome, supernatural—who never sleep. My guess is that the ruler of all this,[220] its lord and king, is a man-eating dragon. Examine and consider the matter. Weigh it in your minds so that we are not dazzled by the gold and the pearls. If we want this gold with the precious stones and pearls, we shall surrender our lives for them. So let us go back and start on new journeys.'

To this advice given by the first brother, the second said, 'I too shall flee these serpents. Unnecessary fighting with wild beasts is forbidden by both convention and good strategy.'[230]

The third brother's firm counsel and remarkable spirit. The third took no notice of the advice of his elder brothers. He judged it cowardly and said, 'Even if I see death with my own eyes, even if the danger is clear and Charon[11] appears . . .[*A short gap*]. . . the great beauty of the castle, the great charm of the castle with its precious stones, its pearls, its gold, and the mighty gleam of its rubies. If the wall is so beautiful from the outside, whose mind will not in turn be amazed at its beauty from within? So whatever happens to me, whatever is in store,[240] I shall attempt to enter and I shall see its inner beauty. So farewell! I shall persist by myself. Alone I shall undergo the labors; alone I shall reap the pleasures. If I meet with danger, if I find a difficulty which possibly I must endure, as[12] happens to many, this will mean that the destiny I bear has turned and changed.'

The first brother's words of distress to the third. The first brother again addressed the third, saying, 'Destiny's decree and Fortune's turnings[250] no man has ever escaped, even though he might labor mightily. Now Fortune's wheel bears you off in your turn and takes you down to the very gates of death. Why willingly meet so great a danger and such a war, such a battle against the supernatural? If you do not win and have to flee, you will be killed. However, even if you do not flee, if you are not defeated and possibly even win, your advantage will be uncertain and there will be no-one to witness your good fortune.

So the first brother gives the third a magic ring of gold.

'But as some small relief and comfort[261] I give you this ring of mine. If you are in peril remember it and you will find solace. If you put it into your mouth it will give you wings and you will escape the danger.' Then, with lamentations and tears, they kissed, tore their cheeks and beat their breasts. Finally, they said farewell and the two elder brothers left the third.

The bitter farewell. The brothers part in grief and are separated with no little pain.[13]

*A superb description of the garden and castle which Kallimachos saw on going inside.

The third then went around the castle by himself[271] and discovered a small projecting hill. He planted his lance, resolutely sprang up, I and jumped manfully over the wall. He fell directly inside the castle's courtyard. He saw strange objects of charm, beauty, delight, all supernatural. What mind, what intelligence will count them all?[280] What tongue will be able to describe them in detail? The very first thing was a lovely garden laden with crops of fruit, with charms, with flowers, and leaves. Its fragrance gave a pleasure beyond[14] words, but its appearance provided an even greater delight. However, this large garden had no gardener and much of its charm was impaired from the absence of a human being. But why waste words on its unusual nature and its many charms? Rather I should describe it in detail.[290]

A superb description of the castle's pool as well.

Inside the enclosure with its lovely garden there was a delightful pool, completely and absolutely beautiful, extraordinary, quite remarkable, and full of charms. What shall I say first, what shall I write first about this pool? Its size, its radiance, its graceful beauty? Or its glittering splendor? Or its strange plants? A flower garden with fronds and plants, perfumed beyond nature, hung inside over the side of the pool. Its builder had, with great skill,[300] constructed windows with shutters. When these opened mechanically the leaves of sweet-smelling plants straightway lent inside.[15] Instead of costly marble cladding, the pool had jointed mirrors. Through another remarkable and skilful device the thick, cloudy steam of the warm pool did not fog these up at all, nor did it blur the gleam of the precious stones. The material of the mirrors was not affected by the mist,[310] which also did not dim the loveliness of the rubies. When you peered through the pool's door you looked into a mirror and saw the pool. In the mirrors you thought you were really seeing the leaves of the trees, the fruit,[16] the entire garden.

The dome was of gold set with precious stones and pearls. The artist had made a tree from gold and on it skilfully placed jewels for fruit. I The cornice of the pool was entwined in a wondrous band. I marvel at the hands of the artists and the nature of the gold[320] which had been made by the chisel to resemble a twisted vine and had become the complete slave of the artists' hands.

A description of the cornice.

If by chance you took your eyes from this you saw some other great marvel of beauty.

The pool was filled with rose-water which seemed to ripple. It bubbled and gave off an amazing mist which could make the heart quiver. The water came in a wondrous manner from the mouth of a human head in gold. On catching sight of it you would surely have said that the mouth was of a living person,[330] so skilfully had the goldsmith created this golden head.

A description of the doors.

The pool's doors were a remarkable and imposing combination. They were made of wood with a waving grain from India and the land of the Arabs and inlaid with musk. Their charm had an effect on the heart. I On the inner door, to match the pool, there hung a curtain which was made of the flowers of lilies and roses. The eye could not take in the wonder of its art.[340] But why talk at length and describe it in detail? Simply to see the pool I shall faint; I shall fall in a swoon and breathe in its beauty.

A description of the curtain.

In all this there was not a single human being. Kallimachos was puzzled by this absence of people. He wanted to make a search, to investigate and explore, and then reflect on the problem. 'At any rate,' he said, 'there must be somebody at this pool.'

A description of the furnace.

He then went and paused by the furnace. He looked to find the pool's furnace-attendant.*(350)* He went about, searched but saw no-one. He found the furnace burning of its own accord without any human assistance. It was filled with Indian aloes for fuel.

A description of the table.

After the beauty of the pool . . . [A gap, probably not long, in which other wonders of Dragon's Castle were described. The text resumes with Kallimachos in the dining hall.] And amid the other beauties and objects full of wonder there was a splendid board laden with wonderful food. The table was magnificent, the dishes were sumptuous. Speech does not suffice to describe it in detail nor to list its many foods and elaborate courses*(360)* nor to go through its charms or tell of its graces. The splendid table and its settings were of gold with many a wonderful work of art. You would certainly have been astounded at the goldsmith's skill. Amid all this beauty and luxury no-one was in attendance, not a single human being. No-one was guarding the table, no-one was guarding the entrance.[17] There was no servant for all the magnificent food. This brought much bewilderment and confusion, turmoil and agitation to Kallimachos's soul.*(370)*

An account of the shining couch.

There was a shining, rich couch of gold with pearls and the bright red stones called rubies. Kallimachos gazed at its magnificence and its pure gold covering—the covering too was of gold—and at the luxury of the food. He saw that amid all this splendor there was no-one and he was much worried and confused. 'From where,' he said, 'has all this gold been amassed? Who collected such precious stones, brought them here*(380)* and emptied them in a place where they serve no purpose? Gold, pearls, and precious stones are for human use. At any rate, it is no ordinary matter. It troubles and frightens me to see this limitless magnificence with no human being, without master or plausible explanation.[18] I am afraid that these supernatural wonders may hide something evil.' In his distress he said this to himself and sat down on the gleaming couch. He ate as much as a troubled man can*(390)* and got up. He then found a second table nearby with a different magnificence and different charms. Its service was made of precious stones. On it were all sorts of vessels carved from shining balas. From another stone—ruby—were carved all the water jugs, while the bright drinking cups of this table were beautifully made from the stone, hyacinth. *(398)*

All the many shining precious stones
An account of how they   ... [*A short gap*] The vessels placed
were expertly carved.   on the second table were filled with all
                               types of wines and delights.[19] Snow
                               and ice were there to refresh the heart of
all those troubled by the heat. But why speak at length about these
drinks? Kallimachos was affected by the heat, by the length of the journey
and particularly by the loneliness—the loneliness of this strange place
was great. He drank his fill of a cool drink and revived a little despite all
the distress he was suffering.*(410)* But his troubles and his cares started
again, and especially his horror of the solitude. However, he resumed his
walk, took a few steps and saw yet another splendor and yet another
charm.

And an account of how   He found a room of solid gold. Ah!
he found the dragon's   Who shall speak of its grace or count
room.   up all its beauties in words? The room
                               was charm itself and the house of the
Graces. It had (but how shall I describe it?) a ceiling made completely
with gold and pearls,*(420)* except that it was not simply gold and pearls,
nor was its decoration just of shining stones. The ceiling represented the
heavens and the paths of the stars (the heavens and the paths of the stars—
I marvel how!) with an extraordinary ingenuity and remarkable skill. This
golden ceiling represented Kronos holding the heavens in his hands, seated
on a lofty throne, and with grey hair. The white planet of Zeus was also
represented in the form of a mighty king, a proud monarch,*(430)* lord of all
empires and of all crowns. The bright star of Aphrodite glowed there with
its bright rays, charming and fair. Next, the artist represented Ares
amorously frolicking with Aphrodite. Athena was there, seated on a
throne, and the Graces who were adorning the heavens.[20] In the middle
there were constellations of many stars.

The suffering begins.   The most remarkable thing (and a real
                               wonder) was how skilfully the artist
had made the ceiling like another sky.*(440)* With great and remarkable art
he had introduced another star. But this sky contained distress, great pain,
much lamentation and evil. Who will describe this without anguish? Who
will not shed rivers of tears before beginning? Whose senses will not be
shattered? Whose heart will not melt?

Amid groans the author describes how the lady was hanging.

In the middle (grievous to tell) a solitary girl was hanging by the hair.[(450)] (My senses reel, my heart quivers!) ... By the hair! (Perverse invention of Fortune!) ... She was hanging by the hair! (Words fail me. I am speechless. I write this with a heavy heart.) The girl in all her charms was hanging by the hair. When Kallimachos, that third son of his father, the ornament of the cupids, with his bold, stout and mighty heart; when he set his eyes upon her, alone, he was immediately fixed to the spot like stone.[21] He simply set his eyes on her and he stood there looking.[(460)] He told himself that she too was one of the paintings. Such is the power of beauty to uproot the soul, to bewitch the tongue and voice, and to overwhelm the heart. Kallimachos stood gazing intently at the woman, at the many graces and great beauty of the maiden. His heart was wrenched. Saying nothing, he stood gazing at her with conflicting feelings. He was amazed at her beauty but he pitied her grief. In his shattered soul he could only groan. In a sad and grievous fashion[(470)] she addressed him. Her voice was despondent and her tongue feverish.

The very sorrowful address of the lady to the young man.

'Sir, who are you? Where are you from? If perhaps you are a ghost in human form, are you brave and wise or are you stupid and desperate? Who are you? Why are you silent? Tell me, why do you stand and simply stare? Has my Fortune brought you too to torment me? Do not spare me if you also are an instrument of her malice. My body, as you see, has been delivered to tortures. If you look upon this and feel pity, as your face[22] indicates,[(480)] if my envious Fortune is satiated with my many tortures over so long a time and has sent you today to relieve and free me of these many afflictions, I thank her. Slay me! Kill me! But if you have come for my comfort, (but the notion is groundless and utterly without reason!) say something! Why are you silent? Let me revive a little! This is the house, the abode of a man-eating dragon. Don't you hear the thunder? Don't you see the lightning?[(490)] He's coming! Why are you standing there? He's coming! Go now, hide yourself. He is a dragon and is strong. He is the offspring of a man-eater. If you conceal yourself in a hiding place and take care, with luck you will live. Look, you see the silver vessel lying there? Get down and crawl underneath it. Perhaps you may escape the dragon's boundless strength. Go! Get down! Hide and keep quiet! He's coming now!'

Kallimachos took the advice and heeded the lady's words as she hung there by her hair. He immediately covered himself with the basin and hid.[(500)]

The dragon comes into the room. The dragon arrived in no gentle mood.[23] Who with a steadfast mind and strong heart could tell of his cruel rage? Who will write of his iron soul, his pitiless heart? Who will describe in words his entrails of stone? He took a thin osier stick which was lying on the ground and spent much time flogging the hanging lady from head to foot, even to the ends of her toes. Eros, who was represented there seated[(510)]—he who inflames the passions and enslaves flinty hearts—was unable to ignite the dragon's heart or to soften his hard soul. His harshness eluded the flame of love. He feared neither torch nor bow of Eros. After this terrible flogging he cruelly placed a stool of solid gold under the lady's golden feet. With some trouble she was able to reach it, but not even then was her hair free.[(520)]

Observe the food which the dragon gives the fair lady! The dragon brought her a morsel of bread and a stone cup made of a real emerald with enough water for one gulp and no more. In reality he was keeping her for further torture. Burning with the pain of her flogging and from hanging by her hair, she drank the water. Immediately the dragon snatched away the stool from her feet and again the lady was hanging by the hair.[(529)]

The dragon issues a command and receives immediate and complete obedience. See, learn and be amazed at everything when you hear! A small bed of great value stood in the dragon's wondrous room, or rather the lady's torture chamber and prison—to call the room an instrument of torture would not be wrong. The small bed stood there, raised a little from the ground, low, and made of precious stones. The dragon sat by himself on the bed and gave an order. Immediately the table came of its own accord[(540)] with rich food for his insatiable mouth. Very much he ate, and as soon as he had his fill he lay down and went to sleep. He showed no pity for the hanging lady.

Learn how the dragon slept and was killed. His sleep was deep and fatal, as you will learn from the story.

*Chrysorroi's words to the man in hiding.

When Chrysorroi saw that the dragon was sleeping—in the pleasure of his deep drunkenness and repletion he was snoring and completely stretched out (sleep had come from food and much drink)*(550)*—when she saw him in the deepest slumber and utterly without consciousness, I she said to the hiding Kallimachos, 'Sir, are you still alive in your fear or are you dead? Do not be afraid! Show more courage! Come out. Abandon your fear if by chance you have survived the sight of my many tortures and the terror of the dragon. Come out now and quickly slay the beast.'

At these words the terrified Kallimachos emerged. The lady said to him, 'Show no cowardice. This is your chance to kill the beast while it sleeps*(560)* and, for a start, to save your body and soul. You are wearing a sword. Draw it and strike the man-eater. Slay in your turn the one who has slain many human lives. Slay the bane of my entire heart.'

Kallimachos stood up, sighed, and with a noble gesture valiantly raised his sword. He smote the sleeping dragon with all his might but the blow did not even wake him.

The maiden sighed and said, 'Throw away that wooden sword of yours or we'll be slaughtered.*(570)* Take the key on the pillow. You see the dragon's cupboard there? Open it. You'll find his sword. It has a magnificent ruby hilt. If you have the strength to draw it, if you do not tremble from fear but stand and strike with it, you will cut the monster in two.'

Kallimachos took the key from the pillow, opened the dragon's cupboard and removed the dragon's sword. He struck him with it and immediately cut him in two.*(580)* Then he freed the hanging lady. He released her persecuted body from its torture, and rescued her voluptuous beauty in all its splendid perfection from the miseries of her prison.

So the end of mis-fortune, the end of grief for the utterly charming Chrysorroi and the amorous Kallimachos.

In tears, she again asked him, 'Who are you? How did you come here into the mouths of dragons? I am afraid that you, too, are one of Fortune's creatures and have been sent by her to menace me again.*(590)* I cannot believe that she will ever be satiated.'

The lady enquires of Kallimachos's family. He speaks to her in reply. He then told of his ancestry, his family, and his country, the reason for his journey, the beginning of the expedition, and the departure of his brothers—everything in detail. In turn, he enquired after the lady's ancestry, her family, her upbringing,[24] her country, her forebears, and the terrible tortures of the dragon.[(599)]

Kallimachos in turn asks Chrysorroi about her birth, her country and her misfortune. She sighed bitterly from the depths of her heart. A river of tears, alas, flowed from her eyes, and she said, 'In vain, sir, you ask me of my country, my unhappy upbringing, and my unhappy family. You see me today a lifeless wretch, tortured like some slave bought for money. Why do you want to know the country of an unfortunate? Why do you want to know the country of a poor creature? It is sufficient for you to see me lifeless from this torture. Leave me alone. I shall myself clean all the wounds[(610)] which my spiteful Fortune has heaped upon me.'

Kallimachos replied, 'What are you saying? I alone shall clean your wounds. Today I shall serve your lovely body.'

She started to cry again and said with a deep sigh, 'I alone have suffered the woes of my unhappy and envious Fortune. I alone know what they are.'

Kallimachos felt sorry for the woman's pain, for her terrible grief and her distressed air. His speech was kind, his heart heavy, and his face distressed, as he spoke encouragingly to her.[(620)] 'Your body clearly proclaims your birth as most noble and fair, royal and great. I implore you once more. Tell me of your country and your upbringing. How is it that although from a mighty and royal family you were given into the hands of an inhuman dragon?'

Chrysorroi tells of her family and her upbringing. She addressed him in tears, choking on her words. 'You see my poor body naked. First bring some of the clothes[(630)] which the dragon hung up inside and kept after receiving them from my parents, and cover me with them. And carry out the greedy creature's body as I hate to see its corpse even in death.[25] Light a fire, burn it, turn it into fine ash, and then you will learn of my family, of my land and where I was born.'

Kallimachos immediately put the dragon's body onto his shoulders and took it outside. Then he ran like an eagle to the furnace,[(640)] took fire, and burnt the hateful corpse. Returning to the lady he opened the room and brought her a remarkable, finely woven garment.

When she had put this on and sat down again, she began to speak of her ancestry and of everything in detail; her family, her upbringing, her country and all the other bitterness of unjust Fortune:

'I was the fair and noble daughter of a famous and powerful emperor and empress. I was endowed with great riches. This dragon loved me for my beauty—where is it now?[(650)]—and wanted to take me as his wife. He forced my royal parents to agree to a bitter alliance and unnatural marriage. Through fear of the monster they consented. He had completely stopped the water of the river on this mountain top from flowing down into the lands and cities of my father's kingdom. And it was through my inhuman Fortune that within the whole circumference of my parents' kingdom there was no water[(660)] except that from the river which was under the control of this raging dragon. They agreed to the compact but I was unwilling, and the wild beast . . . [*A short gap*] . . . or rather he became a dragon again as always. He immediately gulped down all the animals of my native land as though they were but a cup of water and again made his request. They did not want to give me up and began to lament. In his anger the dragon again showed his true nature,[(670)] again made his threats and demanded me in marriage. I refused to marry him, come what may. Not even in a dream did I want to live with a dragon. And then everybody, great and small, every man and woman, old and young— he immediately gobbled them all up without leaving a single person. The whole land and its people went into his stomach.[26] And then he came to the rulers—my parents, the emperor and empress. O misfortune and grief! O shame! How did I endure it? How do I live? How shall I go on living?[(680)] He ate them—gobbled them down without leaving a trace—and left me alone, completely without hope. The only favor he did them was to kill and eat them on their own, separate from the rest, both common people and nobility. O shame! How did the ugly[27] belly of that greedy dragon not then split and burst? Well! What happened after my parents' death and after these disasters? He seized me and wanted to possess me though I was unwilling. I did not obey in any way and I suffered great miseries.[(690)] But after so many tortures and woes, I conquered the dragon's pitiless heart and I have kept myself up to now, a spotless virgin.'

In reply, Kallimachos said, 'Love, whom you see seated on his shining royal throne, has himself watched over you and protected you. He is now placing you in my hands. He, the universal king, grants me forever the lovely charms which adorn your face.'

With tears she again addressed him:⁽⁷⁰⁰⁾

'The terrible wounds and injuries which you see . . .[*A short gap*[28]]. . . but, as I realize, I am afflicted by doubts. The thread of my Fortune and Destiny was made to be unhappy and again my cruel fate is spun with the bitter and unhappy thread of Aphrodite.[29] Leave me alone today to bewail my Fortune. Know, sir, that I have, to my misfortune, been struck out by Destiny's pen. Do not wish to be assigned the same fate. My wretched Fortune is rapacious and spiteful. She can change the nature of a man⁽⁷¹⁰⁾ and turn even your kindly heart into that of a dragon. Let me bewail my wounds and escape from this woe. I cannot bear to live in the land of my dragon enemy, the bitter tyrant, even though you have burnt him by fire after pitilessly killing him as he did many others. But, I beseech you, do not put me to the test. Show yourself kinder than my envious Fortune lest it involve you with me and write you down for misfortune. If you do get implicated in the unhappy decree of my spiteful Fortune, if you do become bound by it, or even if you only come to know it,⁽⁷²⁰⁾ you will be afflicted for the rest of your life. A single happy day you will never see.' The lady said this in great pain and with much sighing and weeping. But her grief, her tears and her sighs, ravished Kallimachos all the more with love. They captivated his mind and soul and made his heart Love's complete slave. Often beauty appears amidst sighs.

In his great happiness he embraced the maiden⁽⁷³⁰⁾ and when he had covered her bruises with kisses he begged her with these words, 'Give up this gloomy air! Give up your much weeping! Breathe again! You were being suffocated and overwhelmed by your sobbing. Tears do not befit a person of good birth. You may curse Fortune's decree as wicked and inhuman, but I bless that same decree because it rescued you from the dragon's mouth, made you mistress of his wealth, and in addition subjected me⁽⁷⁴⁰⁾ and all my heart to fearsome slavery.'

She sighed weakly and replied, 'In this, too, recognize my unhappy destiny. It has not in fact rescued me from my misfortunes, but it has turned your heart to iron, your soul to adamant, and your mind to stone.

You see all the wounds on my poor limbs and your soul becomes even harder. However, as I know my Fortune well with her manner of fighting and her wicked nature,*(750)* I shall not condemn you if she has turned even your royal heart to iron and made it pitiless.'

After much talking their words changed and became sweeter and gentler. What happened in between I shall not describe in detail. It would draw out my story and length brings satiety. So let us pass over the superfluous particulars. After some time, after many days, they formed the wish to unite their souls*(760)* and they joined their hearts in indissoluble links, duly binding their love with most terrible oaths.[30] Love, the king, was present at their words, received their oaths himself and wrote the contracts; contracts for which he stood between them as guarantor. The lady's natural beauty shone out now that it was completely rid of the dragon's ill-treatment. After all the many other delights which a loving heart learns from nature, they went to the pool and bathed.*(770)* Only the tongue of Aphrodite could describe the pleasure and charms of their bathing. A mortal hand and pen will not suffice to tell and describe them all; how Kallimachos caressed the maiden's wounds and from touching her bruises he received an inexpressible freshness and from her kisses a dewy sweetness. He could not take his fill of her charms. | He looked at her and as he looked he reaped the sweet fruits of pleasure.*(781)* I mean something sweeter than everything sweetest. Time alone saw the remarkable sight, the pleasure beyond words, which they enjoyed in the pool.

In the presence of the dread sovereign Love they unite their passion with terrible and frightening oaths.

The fair Chrysorroi and the young Kallimachos revel, take joy and are happy together.

The Graces gave their services and joined the lady there in her bath. All were astounded at her beauty. What person, what tongue shall describe her grace?*(790)* No-one could count so many charms. But if you had happened to be at the pool you would have then witnessed a remarkable and fair sight. In the lovely pool her body was completely beautiful. In it, her most noble body, her crystal skin, increased in grace and charm.

They climbed out of the pool. On the ground at its edge stood a couch with coverlet. The water of the pool seemed to be all gold, but what was this compared with the beauty of the golden pavement!*(800)* The couch stood there but many were its colors when its beauty was enhanced by the lady's body. Who shall tell of the delights which they enjoyed on it? Who shall describe and enumerate their joys? The rulers of the golden castle were living at the height of pleasure and happiness.

A superb description of the lady Chrysorroi. The lady was completely alluring. She inspired love. Her charms were beyond compare, her beauty beyond description, and her graces outdid those of the Graces themselves.[810] Her hair flowed down in rivers of lovely curls and shone on her head with a gleam which surpassed the golden rays of the sun. Her body, which was whiter than crystal, beguiled the sight with its beauty as it seemed to blend the charm of roses with its color. Just the sight of her face alone shook your entire soul, your entire heart. Indeed, the lady seemed to be the image of Aphrodite and of every other beauty that the mind can conceive.[820] But why prattle on? Why describe at length the beauty of her body? A few words suffice to define it. All the women that the world has produced, whether before or after her—or her contemporaries—can only be compared to her charms as one might compare a monkey to Aphrodite.

The lovers' games lasted a long time, but on a spring evening they arose from sleep and their pleasures | and, quite alone, leaned over the castle wall.[830] Close to the bank of the river

*The story tells how they leaned over the castle wall. stood a beautiful little island, a place with a strange charm as it was full of every variety of red flower and their color resembled that of a rose petal dyed from the blood of Aphrodite's lovely foot.[31] They saw and marveled at this fair spot, and all the more because the zephyr then blowing from it brought a breath of perfume. When they looked at this island once every week, they felt new life in their souls and no small joy.[840]

Yes, wicked Destiny, yes, raving Fortune, satisfy your appetite, do what you want! But what brings joy also brings sorrow, as you already know from the preface. Hear the story and you will learn that this is so. . .

There was another noble and mighty king of boundless wealth. His army could as easily be counted as sand. If you had met him and seen his build and stature,[32] his handsome face, his strong hands,[850] I do not know how you could have compared him to anyone else. But he was without a wife, unmarried, completely free. His one great passion was for hunting, deeds of valor, and the clash of battle. Also, he always loved to visit places and countries, mountains, rivers, fountains, cliffs, plains, caves, and the monuments of the Hellenes.[33] Anyone who happened to have seen countries, wars and strange events, or who had wondrous tales, came to tell him. He loved their company.

Now I do not know whether it was chance[(860)] or someone's destiny or the lapse of time or someone's mischance or whether it is simply beyond my knowledge, but something seized him and brought him from far away to this desolate place, to Dragon's Castle. It seized him and brought him to the golden fortress. The guides, the pioneers and the advance guard, who were at the head of the army, came and took up a position at a distance. They saw the splendid castle gleaming like a star or like the sun itself at its brightest. They immediately sent a message to the king.[(870)] 'If you come, Your Majesty, you will see what men call a great marvel.' The king came up running to join them, stopped and looked. He was utterly amazed at the distant sight. He gave the order for all to assemble around him. 'This place,' he said to them, 'is to be our camp. It has trees, a river, and a large meadow. There is also a thick wood to hide foreign scouts or raiders and freebooters | such as all of us who come here today.[(880)] I

Yes, wicked Destiny, shall go alone with three horsemen and
yes, raving Fortune! if I can, I shall approach this castle and
  question anyone I come upon. Do not
become alarmed if perchance I am detained for a second or third day, or even a fourth. See[34] that no-one disobeys my order or my sword will be his death. But if perchance four days pass, then ride out to search for me and do what you can to discover the best course of action.'[(890)]

With these words he immediately set out for the castle. As there was no road for him to take, he went along hidden beneath the trees. When he came close to the golden castle he found a small wood and dismounted within it. It was the end of the day. The sun set and the moon rose with the beginning of night. The king gave the horses to two of his men with the order to be on their guard, and taking the third as his companion he spent the whole night going around the castle.[(900)] He heard no voice or sound of guards whatsoever, but just when night had ended he arrived at the castle's gates and saw the dragons and the huge serpents, the guardians and gatekeepers who never slept. He was terrified and straightway turned to flight. He came to his companions and gave them a frightened account of the gates and the guards he had seen at them. The advice of his men was to wait a second day. 'Perhaps someone,' they said, 'will appear from the castle.[(910)] We think that some company of live human beings must live in this splendid fortress we see. But if perchance the castle contains only dragons and wild beasts like the ones we saw guarding the gates and is completely devoid of human life, then it is a strange place. However, let us wait.'

And so they stayed where they were. The third day came, the sun rose and climbed to midday, but towards evening, at the time when it was cool,[920] the king saw the lady leaning over the castle wall, fair in her person and fair in her manner. But not only her did he espy. Leaning over the wall with her was the castle's monarch, the slave of his queen, the gardener of the matchless lady's graces, the keeper of her beauty, the harvester of her charms.

Love for the lady immediately entered the king. He could not live or breathe if he did not win her. Such is the power of beauty over those who are sensitive to it[930] that it can enslave through the eyes alone. The king's senses, mind, reason, emotions and heart were utterly vanquished by love. It shattered his strong soul and left him a lifeless corpse, wholly extinguished. With great difficulty he finally recovered his senses. Night followed evening and the moon had come out when he took his soldiers and went back to his army. He got there, but in what a state of torpor! But still, let me confess, he got there.[939]

The bitterness of an evil Destiny arrives. When, on his arrival, he saw his army and the army saw their emperor, his troops asked those who had accompanied him for information. The latter described the castle's splendor, the strength of its towers, its precious stones and pearls and its gold. They told of the guards they had seen at its gates. But as well they told of the superb woman whom they had seen playing with Kallimachos and covering him with kisses.[949] | In conclusion they related how the sight of her had thrown the king into confusion, amazement and terror, how it had annihilated him utterly.

*Yes, wicked Destiny, yes, raving Fortune, bring your misfortune and your malice to a close.

Despite all this the king held council and summoned his lords. He asked them how they could attack the castle and capture its mistress. All considered the castle to be impregnable in battle when they saw its supernatural walls and battlements; it could not be taken; its strength and its size rendered it completely invulnerable to ruses and impossible to conquer.[960] What they heard of the serpents at the entrance acting as guards to protect the castle's gates, confirmed their opinion and they said,

'Who can fight against wild beasts? But if it is your command, Your Majesty, let us take counsel.' The king bade them do so and said, 'Give me your advice.'

One of those present, a man distinguished in ancestry and years, stood up and replied with these words:

'When we all left your castle, your kingdom and our country, we gave no thought to battle and war(970) or to bearing arms or to leading troops into battle to fight an enemy. We brought no provisions or siege engines or equipment. You simply set out, as you are accustomed to do, for diversion and relaxation, and also for some purpose wholly unknown to me. We have traveled for a long time and we have come to a strange and unexpected place. If now you wish to make war and engage in battle, everybody will be at a loss as to how to fight.(980) But, Your Majesty, with your permission let us go back to your castles and assemble an army. Let it be announced to all that you are declaring war on this castle. Seek an allied force with your neighbors, prepare siege engines, do all that is necessary, and then set out to attack it. Fall on it! Strike it! You will win! You will hear no complaint at all.(988) | This castle, you must realize, will put up a hard fight. You see the precious stones and pearls and all the gold? These must have been collected by a huge, an infinite multitude of people.'

Yes, wicked Destiny, yes, raving Fortune, finish your inhuman designs.

The king sadly returns with sad thoughts and a sad heart.

The advice pleased everybody except the king. | All were glad, all were delighted to be escaping the terror of the wild beasts and to be returning to their lands. The king alone was in great sorrow.(1000) 'Better,' he said, 'for me to become food for the wild beasts and to lose my life than to be deprived of that woman.' But the matter could not be diverted from its destined end.

However, I have drawn out the length of my story and tired my reader. When the king had gone back to his own country,[35] he stopped and said to his followers, 'Go to your homes and quickly make preparations for our return to attack the castle.' They dismounted, did obeisance to him, and departed.(1010) The king was left alone with his senate and went to his own palace. Another deluge came to overwhelm him, and with what a flood of care and grief! He spent three days alone in his room lying face down on his bed. There was uproar and confusion, disorder and turmoil throughout the length and breadth of his dominions. People were in a frenzy of activity in preparation for an attack on the castle and for battles and skirmishes.*(1020)* Men took up arms and tried horses. Everyone without exception was in a turmoil over the business. The elite and the famous of the entire aristocracy were engaged in the fuss about the war but were also grieved by the plight of the king.

So what happened? All gathered, went to the king and addressed him with respectful mien and sweet words:

'It would have been better before all else, Your Majesty, for your heart not to have fallen into the cares of love.*(1030)* But since this has happened and there is no escape, if it is your wish, let us take counsel together as to how we can get possession of the castle and the lady. The castle is strong and is guarded by serpents. Let us take care! A group of dragons or a company of demons lives there. If we were fighting against a castle inhabited by men, our army could without any doubt put up a fight and be victorious. But no man can wage war against dragons or do battle with demons.'*(1040)*

When all had spoken, they fell to silence with the thought in their minds that perhaps the king would hesitate. When, however, he kept to his purpose and preferred to die before his time rather than be completely deprived of the lady's love, they changed their minds. The king gathered his allies, counted his soldiers, enlisted his armies, and began to leave for battle. And to help him in this great and noble undertaking he used the vast wealth of his treasury which served his power and his activities.*(1050)* But faced with Dragon's Castle, serpents for adversaries, and walls of boundless height which were not of stone, all shrunk from battle in despair and ignored advice even before the time of battle. So the king, dying from his passion and wholly overwhelmed with despair, was ready to give up his kingdom in the event of failure.

But to further my long story*(1060)* and give my readers an accurate picture I shall tell the whole incident in detail . . .

Yes, wicked Destiny, yes, raving Fortune, do what you want. Do it! Finish it off completely![36]

The beginning of the story of the old witch.

There was a certain sly old woman, a demonic creature who controlled spirits by magic and was versed in astrology. When she heard about the king, she took her walking stick and went to the palace where she found a page standing in front of the doors.*(1070)* She stopped and, being alone with him, said, 'If you take my message to the king and arrange for me to meet him. you will be rewarded, not by me who am lowly, but by the king. For, my child, I, more than anybody else, can give him a cure for his lovesickness!'

'Ah! What are you saying, mother?' he replied. 'You can really provide a cure for the great and unbearable passion of his love? You say that you can succeed where no wise man has had the least effect?*(1080)* Mother, I see you are poor and wretched, an unfortunate and very miserable old woman. Be careful that you do not do me a disservice rather than a favor.'

She said to him, 'Don't worry about that, my child. Even if I appear to be an ugly and wretched old woman, miserable and unfortunate, as you say, nevertheless I have great skill in medicine. Time, my child, and old age and rags put no obstacle in the way of healing.'*(1090)*

The page listened and said, 'Mother, sit down and give me your blessing so that by chance I suffer neither torture nor ill treatment nor insult. What profit would you have in getting me killed?'

The page went off, leaving the old woman alone. He ran quickly and, on coming to the king's room (his bedroom), he hastily went inside. He did not act discourteously but he stood back a little and touched the head of the bed, shaking it gently—once, twice, three times.*(1100)* The king, who was mentally turning over his troubles and had his mind weighed down by anxiety, took some time to realize that his bed was being shaken. However, after the third shaking he got up, opened his eyes and asked what was wrong and why his bed was being shaken. The page, who was standing there, replied, 'An old woman claims she can treat you. She promises to relieve your pain and cure your suffering.'

The king said, 'Where is she? Fetch her! Why stand there? Why wait?*(1110)* Why delay? Answer me! Move! Be quick!' The page left and ran to the old woman whom he took by the hand and led to the bedroom.

The light was now drawing to a close. The old woman entered, did obeisance to the king, smiled and said,

The prologue of the old beldam, or rather of balm. [37]

I 'The mighty lord, who is unconquered in battle, strong in war, the terror of many—is an amorous look enough to slay and destroy him?[38] Your Majesty, why do you suffer? Why do you sigh?*(1120)* Why resign the government of your empire and seek the comfort of death if you do not win the fair lady as your queen and fulfil the longings of your desire? I shall put myself at the disposal of the imperial office. I shall serve your plans and your desire and I shall bring the lady for your feast of love. In the very fire which comes from the flame of Love's furnace you will find love's cooling dew.'

The king revived on simply hearing this.*(1130)* Even a light remark spoken at random can often assuage Love's pangs. So he said, 'When can this be, my good woman?'

The old woman said in reply to the king, 'If you simply tell me in detail everything that happened, without any evasion, I myself shall give you relief within a short time.'

So the king began to tell the old woman how he had originally started, why he went to Dragon's Castle; how he saw*(1140)* the shining gold, the gleaming precious stones, the silver and pearls, the castle wall and its extent and size, the height of the towers, and then how he ordered his army to wait while he went with only three companions; how he approached Dragon's Castle but heard no sound and saw no watch, just fearsome and ever-wakeful guards such as no-one had ever placed as sentinels at his gate; then how they were seized by fear and ran quickly back like cowards*(1150)* to their companions; how they changed their minds and stayed for all the second day, and the third as well, to get information and to see if anything would happen; and how in the evening they saw the noble lady walking for relaxation along the wall.

The king again falls into a deadly faint.

Yes, wicked Destiny, yes, raving Fortune, bring your will and your misfortune to a close!

When the king came to this point in his story he immediately fell back as though dead.*(1160)* His limbs shook and his heart beat so fast that even the old woman thought he was dying. Nevertheless, she approached, looked at him and, taking his head, muttered something to herself. Then after turning around and making a magic sign she spat as though in anger and stamped her foot in order, I think, to frighten the demons. The king lifted himself up and sat on the bed. He grabbed the old woman and implored her:

'My good woman, do something to make me gain what I desire,[1170] and you will be called my mother and I your son. A golden statue of you will be set up in the palace. You will receive great favors and gain enormous wealth. But I shall draw the thread of my story to a close. I saw that fair, amorous lady playing with a man and kissing him passionately. And, mother, how was I able to see her? That I cannot say. I lost my feeling, my mind, my powers of reason and judgement. Mother, I became a stone, I stood motionless. In my distress I had difficulty in making my way back, lamenting all the while.[1180] I related the story, I told them everything. I put the matter before them and gave my advice that we should subdue the castle and that I should capture the lady. But all were against this on the grounds that no-one has ever waged war against serpents. What, then, did they advise? To return home, summon allies, pay wages, make machines for the siege, and then start our war on the castle. This, mother, is the rest of my tale.[1190] Now we are about to leave for battle. So I beseech you once again, mother, do something so that I do not court danger in vain.'

'Be quiet, Your Majesty,' she said to him. 'Worry no more! I shall attend to the future. Do not grieve. You are going to get the lady as surely as if you had her now.'

'And when will that be, my good woman?' the king said.

Yes wicked Destiny, yes, raving Fortune, carry out all your whole plan, you worker of mischief!

She replied, 'Three clear days[1200] after our arrival at Dragon's Castle.'

The king was impatient of delay. A soul in the grips of love and passion . . . [*A short gap*] But whether he liked it or not there was nothing else he could do. So what happened to bring the matter to a close? Using letters of evil magic, and incantations, the old woman placed the charm she desired on a beautifully made apple of pure gold. On it she wrote a double spell:

'If anyone puts this apple into his bosom[1210] he will straightway fall dead; his breath will fail immediately. But if this golden apple is held to the nose of the dead person, he will come to life, go, walk, and traverse the world with the living.'

The old woman prepares the magic apple and gives the king the following advice.

The old woman completed all her preparations and said, 'I do not want you to bring a large army. Take only a hundred men with you. It is not the time to fight but to await[1220] the results of what my old hands have created.'

The king set out and went with the old woman and the hundred soldiers that she required. They took three months to journey to the castle, to get to the land of the dragon's fortress. But, to be brief, they arrived there and assembled[39] everything in the place where they had previously pitched their camp. The old woman did not neglect her arts at all. She kept demons with her, she talked to them,[1230] she conversed with them, she ate with them, she journeyed with them, she became one of them until she completed the trickery and sorcery to be used for her scheme to make Kallimachos a corpse and to enable the king to take the lady from Dragon's Castle. All of this I shall soon reveal. . . .

Yes, wicked Destiny, yes, raving Fortune, bring your oracular decree to a close!

Once every week the lovers were accustomed to look down from the castle at a spot a little further away.[1240] Here was the fair island with the strange beauty of its shores, with its charms, its perfumes and smells, full of delights and roses, plants and cool waters. The old woman discovered it by a trick because once every week Kallimachos and the lady leaned over the castle walls together and enjoyed the view. Consequently she decided to hide there until she had done her intended mischief.[1250]

Observe and marvel at the old woman's evil trick!

What then did she tell the king to do? 'You see that fair and charming place— the little island with its strange beauty? I am going there to hide and to complete my machinations. My express order is that no-one should make the least movement. Listen carefully for my whistle. When you hear it, all run and come to me.' With these words she set off straightway at midnight and concealed herself as she desired.[1260]

*[A large gap which is preceded by the rubric: **The treacherous ambush carried out by the old woman's magic**. It seems likely that a leaf is missing from the manuscript, in which case about forty-six*

lines have been lost. The text resumes with Kallimachos talking to Chrysorroi.]

'<I heard> the voice of a person crying. I do not know what has happened. Perhaps another dragon was in the vicinity and was treating people with brutal cruelty. But where is there the least trace of a human being here? Who would have had the strength to climb to Dragon's Castle? Who would have been able and willing to penetrate a mountainous country like this with its wilderness bereft of humans?'

They were silent for a moment. Again Kallimachos heard the voice.*(1270)* It was clearer and louder than before. He heard it and straightway trembled. Time did not allow him to escape what was fated. They were troubled, they wept and the lady said with a sigh, 'Kallimachos, my darling, the dragon has a relative. Perhaps this relative has come and is hiding to attack us. Stay close to me. Hold me. Do not go outside.' But Kallimachos ran to his room, took his sword, and raced off. He ordered the gates to open and they opened immediately.*(1280)*

Yes, wicked Destiny, yes, raving Fortune, do what you want quickly. Do not drag it out.

He was bounding towards the voice when he heard a whistle. A fearsome dragon, the creation of the old woman's magic arts, emerged from the wood holding her in his mouth and apparently eating her. The dragon eyed Kallimachos suspiciously as he angrily advanced brandishing his naked sword. The dragon dropped the old woman and charged straight at him. For his part, Kallimachos made for the dragon, smote him with his sword,*(1290)* and straightway cut off his head. But the monster was simply a trick of magic, a creature of illusion. When the old woman saw this she ran towards him shouting loudly, 'My hero! My savior!' and pretended to kiss his footprints.

Chrysorroi, on seeing Kallimachos fight and cut off the dragon's head, took a golden urn and went to the pool in order to get water to wash his hands. She also wanted to welcome the abominable demon of an evil old woman.*(1301)*

Yes, wicked Destiny, yes, raving Fortune, do what you want quickly! Finish it off completely!

Before the lady arrived, the evil witch— who was the demons' tool, the lightning's companion, the thunder's mother, the devil's nursling, the grandmother of the Nereids;[40] indeed an accessory to every wickedness—threw the golden apple at Kallimachos with the words, 'Here's an apple for your trouble.' He took it, looked at it and admired its beauty.*(1310)* He put it into his shirt and straightway fell down dead.

After the lady came from the castle with the urn she found Kallimachos stretched out dead on the ground while the witch was shouting and whistling loudly. When the king (who was in a constant state of worry and alarm) heard the whistling, he jumped on his horse and advanced with his hundred men. He found Kallimachos lying dead, the lady completely unconscious and dazed, and the old woman frolicking like a child and dancing erotically.*(1320)* The horsemen did not lose a moment. In no time at all they snatched up the lady and the old woman with her, and the king went quickly back to his own country.

Once again I am spinning out my tale and extending its length, but a little patience! Wait just a moment and you will learn the whole story in detail. . .

The apple alone is responsible for Kallimachos's death and return to life.

While Kallimachos was lying there dead on the ground, without breath, without consciousness and without speech,*(1330)* his Fortune was busy and went to the trouble of visiting his brothers to inform them of what had happened and of his plight. In their sleep the brothers saw a woman clad in black I who was hitting herself, tearing her hair, scratching her cheeks, beating her breasts, and shouting to the brothers, 'Quick! Come to Kallimachos. He is in terrible danger!'*(1340)*

*Yes, wicked Destiny, redress your evil, soften it and make it milder.

The brothers saw her and were terrified by her cries. The eldest woke and aroused the other: 'Brother, did you dream about Kallimachos?'

'I saw a woman in black,' he replied. 'She shouted at me as she hit and scratched herself. She cried out, "Quick! Come to Kallimachos's aid. He is in terrible danger." '

Troubled and distressed by the dream they saw about Kallimachos they hasten to his aid.

The brothers said, 'Kallimachos has come up against a trial. Today he is in peril; at great risk.*(1350)* He is in peril; in a terrible storm of danger. Let us go quickly and show the love of brothers.

As brothers let us seek our brother and let us face this trial with him. Let us sacrifice our lives, our entire bodies for the love of our brother, our Kallimachos. Let us be quick. Our departure brooks no delay. Away to Dragon's Castle!'

They left and set out on the road they had previously taken, and on the way they shrieked in loud voices,*(1360)* 'Kallimachos! Our brother Kallimachos! What is the terrible danger you face? What caused your trials? What caused your peril? Who has dared oppose you? If you are still alive wait a little for your brothers. We are coming today and we shall free you or we shall die with you like true brothers. Dear Kallimachos, how is it that you are alone in danger, deprived of your brothers? Death is in the midst of your dangers, Kallimachos, but you do not see your brothers*(1370)* to give you courage, to give you hope at least in your fight. Perhaps he has been defeated—but that is inconceivable!—and vanquished. Perhaps Kallimachos lies there dead in battle despite his acts of valor, despite his many victories, and we who live, labor under a cruel sentence: we shall not die with Kallimachos.'

With such thoughts and with such words they went along the road. Only after much trouble did they come to its end, and with bitter and distressed hearts they found golden Dragon's Castle and its city.*(1380)* In great fear, with much weeping and grief they ran around the walls and came to the little island near the castle. There they found their brother dead.

Yes, wicked Destiny, redress your evil, soften it. That's enough for the present.

They sat beside him and began their lamentation. Nikokles, the eldest, addressed his brother in a loud voice: 'Kallimachos, who fought with you? If you were hit by a sword, then where is your wound?*(1390)* You lie dead but there is no sign of blood. So how were you killed? Did you die from sickness? But why were you not buried?'

Xanthippos, the second brother, said, 'So you are dead, Kallimachos, but your brothers live. They now sit beside you in tears and lamentation. They cover your body with kisses, but you are insensible. If you could hear your brothers here weeping,[41] you would share their tears and share their pain.'

After their mourning and grief,*(1400)* their laments and cries, they embraced the corpse and were silent as death because they had lost their voices with weeping. Then with difficulty they looked at their brother again and searched for injuries. They undressed him but instead of wounds they found the fatal apple. Around it ran the words: 'If a lifeless corpse smells this apple, it will immediately gain consciousness and return to life.' They put the apple to the nose of the dead Kallimachos and he immediately revived,[(1410)] came back to life and sat up. He saw his brothers and was astonished. On reviving he looked for the lady. He went with his brothers into the city[42] and, amid sighs, again searched for her. The other two thought their brother was raving and said, 'What do you mean? What lady are you calling for?' But he kept running and looking for the lady and when he did not find her he started shrieking and shouting. They held him back and again questioned him,[(1420)] imagining that he had lost his wits. Kallimachos then related the whole story to his brothers: how he entered Dragon's Castle on his own, how he had found its luxurious splendors and the lady hanging in the dragon's room. He told them of the inhuman tortures that the wondrous lady suffered, then of the slaying of the dragon, of the lady's graces and charms, her beauty, her elegance, her voluptuousness and indescribable allure, and finally her dress;[(1430)] and how a wily woman, a demon of a witch, by misleading him with her weeping and tears and her deceitful words, had brought him down from the wall. 'After that I was dead. What happened later I cannot tell.' And again he sighed and started to search for the lady.

After telling his story to his brothers Kallimachos, in tears, again searches for the lady.

'Where have you gone,' he said, 'O fairest among women? Where have you hidden yourself? You were certainly killed. But how? Why do I not see your dead body? Certainly it will be bitter to look[(1440)] on my beloved, lifeless and smitten by death, but still I shall sit beside you, I shall lament you, I shall weep for you, I shall hold you, I shall embrace you, I shall sing your dirge, I shall cover your dead body with kisses. But how can I speak these words and not die instantly from the pain? How can I both live and pronounce this complaint? I shall start a great dirge, I shall tear out my heart and shed a mighty torrent and rivers of tears. I shall bathe again but in a pool of bitter water. With you I took a bath of joy[(1450)] but now we shall share a bath of tears. Love was our attendant when we bathed. Now I shall embrace you in death. To say this makes me swoon. But why do I waste time sitting idly here? Why do I not go quickly and make a search for my lady? Why do I live, exist, and look upon the day without her who is my breath, my life, and day itself?'

To his brothers he said, 'This fair castle with its splendor, its gold, its precious stones and its pearls, is a fountain of riches and a river of all wealth.[(1460)] If you need a residence, then dwell here. If not, take a goodly

part of the money, the precious stones and the pearls back to our country.
I am leaving you again and going in search of my lady.'

He immediately said farewell and set out. He cried as he made his way,
and he made his way as he grieved. With sighs and tears he passed through
the country. He did not wish to see either the sun or its light and he said,
'I have lost my illumination; my light has been taken from me.*(1470)* A
dark and dismal path it is that I shall tread in my mind's distress and my
heart's gloom.'

In his search for the lady he journeyed through many countries. His voice
was sad, his words lifeless. With sorrow, with terrible and deep laments
which are beyond the power of number to count, he went over plains,
mountains, defiles, rivers and rocky places. He did not know what country
to enter or what road to take in order to find what he wanted. But as he
was, at random and without guide,*(1480)* he wandered about, he hastened,
he searched in the hope of discovering someone whom he could ask.

Behold! Destiny cuts And at the fourth hour on a certain day
short Kallimachos's he came upon a man ploughing his
journey from one evil to land with his yoke of oxen. He wore
another and then to black and his head was shaven.
something worse. Kallimachos went up and greeted him,
thinking that this man too seemed to
have grief and sorrow. The sight of the black mourning garment*(1490)* and
the shaven head brought Kallimachos instant comfort as he thought he
had found an unhappy and afflicted man with whom he could share his
grief and talk. If a person in distress sits with another troubled by anguish
and misery, and shares his woes, he finds some comfort and relief.

'Sir, I see that your appearance is one of grief,' he said after greeting him.
After a moment he continued, 'I expect that you have your troubles or that
you are afflicted by grief.'*(1500)*

The ploughman replied, 'My mournful appearance and my shaven head are
not caused by my own bad fortune or trouble but by the crazed will of an
accursed girl. I am not alone in being dressed for mourning nor am I alone
in having my head shaven. Everybody these days, entire cities and castles,
a multitude of people beyond number, is dressed in mourning because of
the king's command. I Since the woman will not wear anything else[43] on

Kallimachos gets a little information about golden Chrysorroi from the ploughman. her body[1512] we go hungry, we die through abstaining from meat. This woman, this dragoness, this offspring of a dragon, lived, they say, in Dragon's Castle but the king, through a cunning scheme and trick, abducted her and keeps her in his palace. The story goes that she demanded that everybody dress in this black clothing and adopt this gloomy and mournful appearance.[1520] So a general order went out from the king and even little children are running about in the dress you see and with their heads shaven. The queen controls the palace and has imposed this sentence even on the poor.' From these words Kallimachos recognized the lady and her story.

Yes, wicked Destiny, yes, raving Fortune, carry out your ill-starred wishes! He immediately took leave of the ploughman.[1530] He ran the whole distance with all haste and at great speed. His head was swimming as if he were suffering agonies from dizziness. Along the way he met men in mourning with shaven heads and all dressed in black. These too he asked about their appearance and he received the same answer as before. 'The king took the dragoness from Dragon's Castle and keeps her as queen in the palace. On her command we are all dressed in black.[1540] O Heaven, why do you endure this? Why do you not break and fall upon her? O Earth, why do you not open up and swallow just her who has brought this misfortune on us?'

Kallimachos found some solace in learning this again and his spirits rose as he ran to the palace. But he railed against Time because he could not get there in an instant. He began to curse human nature for not having given him[44] wings for greater speed. While he was dead he had lost, as it happened, the fair and wondrous ring[1550] which made the human body winged.[45] He had, in fact, encountered three supernatural objects: the golden ring which had the virtue of allowing the person who wore it on his hand to fly; the shining gown covered with pearls which was inside the dragon's abode and which had the virtue of curing its wearer of even supernatural cuts, of supernatural bruises and wounds, everything that one would think beyond the power <of medicine>;[1561] and the third was the witch's evil apple which had the power to kill and to bring back to life. If we have diverted a little from our story and its action we shall now take up its thread again. . .

After much running and effort, Kallimachos came within sight of the palace where he saw the mourning citizens dressed in black and with their hair shaven. Kallimachos, with his wretched appearance, approached it in the guise of a wretched traveler*(1570)* and sat down in a sorry plight. He found a woman in black sitting there and fell into conversation with her. After some talk she began to tell the lady's story: first, how she had been deceitfully kidnapped and with what[46] terrible trick and magic device; then, how she had not recovered from this mistreatment but was always crying and lamenting; how the king had left on a journey, how long he had been away, and what a mighty battle he was fighting.*(1580)* The lady had been left completely on her own and had time to cry and lament. She was always fainting, every minute she sighed. In her tears she shouted a name and immediately dropped as if dead. 'And the name she shrieks out is, I think, "Kallimachos! Kallimachos!" Perhaps the dragon is called Kallimachos because the queen, they say, is a dragoness, though it does not appear in her sweet appearance. Her tears and laments never cease. If, sir, you saw how lamentation and trouble have blighted her loveliness*(1590)* before its time, like a rose which wilts in summer, except that even though she has wilted and faded her charm blooms anew. After she faints and drops from her trouble and tears, she only recovers when water is brought, and those guarding and comforting her have a device to supply it. Just to see the lady's tears and laments would frighten you. She has completely faded and has finally been consumed by grief.'*(1600)*

Kallimachos sighed and said, 'I feel sorry for the lady.' He held out a moment and then fainted and fell lifeless, a corpse without breath.

The woman revived him and asked, 'What happened to you?'

'Sister,' he said, 'what you have told me would move even lifeless stones to tears.'

She replied, 'Has my simple tale distressed your heart and stirred your soul? If perchance you were to go and see the lady, it would certainly astound you and drive you to madness.'*(1610)*

But as Kallimachos had the power neither to remain there nor to endure separation from his beloved lady, he immediately left and went to the garden.

When Kallimachos learns everything he goes to the garden.

Yes wicked Destiny, yes, raving Fortune, turn your spite. Mollify it, soften it and bring it to an end.

There he found the gardener doing his watering and he sat down for some time by the gate.[(1620)] While he was sitting there he recognized from the amount of water used, the flame of the lady's passion, the furnace and the fire which engulfed her. He wanted to speak but was silent and collected his thoughts. He heard[47] an order shouted at the gardener and it instantly tore at his heart.

'Quick, gardener! Put water into the basin. Fill the pipe for the water to flow as they said, so that at any time it can be poured on the queen.'

Kallimachos's heart began to bleed and he said, 'It is not good to sit expectantly[48] here[(1630)] and wait for an opportunity or for the right time. I must go and greet this gardener.' He immediately got up, went into the garden and greeted the gardener with, | 'Greetings, good sir! You have indeed much to do. I marvel that an old man like you is able to manage on his own in such a large garden.'

*Observe Fortune's course and Time's thread. Never, never judge a man happy before his end.

'My child,' he replied, 'I can do[49] the work[(1640)] but I cannot manage the supply of water. A curse on the time, a curse on the hour when the witch's spells carried off this queen and brought her to the palace! The witch tortured her. We are vexed and everybody is condemned to wear black.'

Again Kallimachos spoke to the gardener: 'I see that you have a large garden which needs much upkeep. But I am a gardener too, though a poor wretch. If you wish, employ me for my bread alone.'[(1650)]

The gardener was overworked and wanted a hired laborer. He was looking for an assistant to help with the water. When he found this young and unhappy stranger who could cope with such a task . . .[*A gap of a few lines in which Kallimachos is formally engaged*]. . . and the old man who had charge of the garden was pleased with the arrangement for the large amount of work, but Kallimachos himself, the hired laborer, found it wonderful and very pleasing. To him it seemed bliss and he said to himself, 'I shall again serve the wondrous body of the matchless lady.[1660] I who once cleaned[50] her wounds, her bruises, her injuries, I who once inspected and treated them, today I shall again render her fair service by bringing her water when she requires it[51] and by giving her comfort. . . If you recognized the one who toils to refresh you, the flame in your heart would be completely revived. But the time for this is close. I thank Fortune that she has again had my destiny enrolled with yours.'

He sighed as he poured the water onto the garden and he began a dirge in these words:[1670]

Read the dirge of the unhappy Kallimachos, the hired man, the gardener and carrier of water!
'Cease now, Fortune of mine, this long wandering. Cease the wrongs and tortures you have inflicted on me. Cease your rage and your malice. Sufficient the sorrow you have caused me, sufficient my misfortunes. Fortune, how did I offend you? What did I do to you? What madness did I conceive against you to make you persecute and abuse me so much? Now I carry water as a hired servant[1680]—in this you have had your fill in testing me. O Moon with your fair light, you see what I endure. In the evening, I beseech you, send down a tiny beam, let it enter the palace without being observed and let it tell Chrysorroi the good news: "The one you love has been found, the one you know has revived and today tends the garden as a hired laborer. He now fills your basin with water to quench the flame of your soul. But his body, his lips, are charged with the dew which quells the flame of Love's furnace."[1690] Perform this trick for me, O Moon. Do me this service.'

He repeated this dirge many times. His eyes were running like a river. Little by little his watering took him to the palace. He went up the steps and made himself known. Everyone there met the gardener's hired laborer who carried the water. Everyone came to know him and take notice of him.

On one occasion Kallimachos recognized the lady's weeping. He fainted on hearing her voice and remained as if dead.[1700] But soon after, the lady's voice revived him when she sadly called out his name with a voice of passion and of grief that tore at the roots of his heart. He fainted at the sound. At other times[52] he sat close to the lady and hoped that she would soon recognize him. He could not endure her cries for the whole day. Her sufferings made him lose his breath, her agonies tortured him. But he endured them as he was trying to devise a way[1710] of making himself known to the lady and putting an end to her weeping without the knowledge of the rest. He was afraid that he might be recognized and so reveal the reason for the lady's silence.[53] Consequently he considered how he might talk with her without people knowing. He thought, he struggled, he racked his brains. Finally, after long and ceaseless reflection, he came upon a way of being recognized by the lady. When they had bathed together in the pool, that wondrous pool laden with all charms and pleasures at the golden castle,[1720] he had taken a small ring from the lady which her mother, the queen, had given her. This was the only token she had from her parents. 'When she sees this ring she will know it immediately and realize who sent it and how it came into the garden today. In this way and with this plan we shall meet again, if it pleases Fortune, since it is Fortune who guides the wheel of mortal affairs.[1730] I shall know her immediately, I shall hold her in my arms, and she in turn will recognize her Kallimachos. When we have met we shall embrace. I fear that in some indescribable way our hearts will straightway stop beating at that terrible moment. But I shall hold the charms of the peerless lady and revive our dead and battered souls. I must consider every aspect of this plan.'

He carefully began his stratagem and plan to see the lady and speak to her.[1740] He sought out a tree in the garden where the lady often went in her weeping. There in her grief she would sit like a corpse, and from this tree she would look at a bitter orange tree like a person without feeling or reason. With much care and attention he tied the little ring to it.

Necessity often suggests a cunning ruse like the one[54] Kallimachos was now forced to carry out. In the course of time, the lady came to the tree with her accustomed lament[1750] and sat under it. She looked up, stretched her head and saw the bitter orange. 'Kallimachos,' she cried, 'now I have certainly failed all my vows. You are dead in Hades but I live, I exist, I walk and I have sight. But though I am alive my senses are wholly dead. Though I live I am only a copy of living things. Though I have sight I see only you, despite the fact that you are not with me.'

With these words she stretched out her hand to the tree, held its leaves and saw the ring.[1760] She took it, put it on her finger and experienced a great shock. The fruit of the bitter orange gave her an indescribable joy. From the tree she took a blend of happiness and pain. Overcome with fear and tears of grief she fainted and fell onto her couch. She was tortured by worries and shaken by anxious thoughts. She thought she saw

Kallimachos's finger and this revived and comforted her. Again, holding the ring made her anxious and faint. She felt giddy and agitated.[1770] She pondered in her heart and reflected, 'This is certainly the ring which I wore from the beginning of my royal destiny. It was in the pool that Kallimachos playfully took it from me, in the warm pool. When I remember the place, the time and that pool I die yet again. He took it and put it <on his finger> with much love . . .[*A short gap*]. . . and my envious Fortune <has snatched away> all those pleasures and bitter-sweet delights. When I now do no more than remember them shall I not straightway die?[1780] But perhaps someone saw Kallimachos lying dead and took the ring from his finger. However, no-one was allowed to go near, either to approach or touch his corpse in any way. But if someone did not take the ring from the golden fingers of my golden Kallimachos how then is it here? Perhaps it happened that Kallimachos did not die then but the cunning old witch overpowered him with some mighty spell. Because they quickly snatched me off like wolves[1790] I had no time to touch or look at him. I stood there speechless and devastated by the disaster. But I did then catch a glimpse of Kallimachos stretched out, a lifeless corpse, in the middle of the island. Well, my Fortune is today preparing something. She wishes to give me yet another bitter drink. What does it mean? Are you alive, Kallimachos, though you have not appeared? I think there is certainly a trap involved. And how could his corpse have now come back to life? My Fortune has assuredly resumed her rage against me[1800] and wants another disaster with which to plague me. But perhaps my envious Fortune has reached some surfeit with my troubles and unhappy laments. Perhaps she will show a little kindness and I shall be united in joy with him. Without a doubt she is not so wholly insatiable that she can never be appeased or have her fill. If Fortune relents her trials somewhat and Kallimachos returns to life!—but that is impossible. Nature does not allow the dead to return. If perhaps he is alive and he did not die, then who will look at his living body?[1810] Who will clasp him, embrace him, and swoon sweetly from pleasure? Let us see whether he comes to look for me if he really lives.'

The lady went through every explanation in her mind as she sat by the foot of the tree where she had found the ring token. With these thoughts she spent the night. At dawn she went out with her tears and accustomed lament as though to walk around the garden. With a pensive air she approached the tree[1820] and looked at it once again. She examined its leaves to see how the ring had come to be there. Kallimachos was about,

On seeing the lady the unfortunate Kallimachos suffers a terrible shock of legendary proportions.

The lady addresses and questions the gardener and he in turn makes a suitable reply.

but at a distance. He saw the lady and recognized her perfectly. I Only a sensitive heart can portray the effect she had on him at that moment. Neither speech nor written word can describe it. By chance the queen called out to the gardener,[1830] 'Old gardener, come to me. I Are you the only person who brings water to refresh me? Do you alone care for the plants of all this enclosure? I am surprised that on your own you can manage such a large garden and the numerous varieties of vegetables which I see. How can a single person cope with such an area?'

'Up till the present,' the gardener replied, 'I looked after the whole garden on my own and had no assistant.[1840] But since we have needed water to refresh you, the work has been too much for me and I have taken on a hired laborer, a poor stranger from abroad. I do not know his origins or how he comes to be here, but he seems sensible and he has suffered much. He does not seem equal to carrying water and he may return home shortly as he cannot stand the effort.'

A moment of sweetness shines for Kallimachos and he enjoys a little of Fortune's compassion.

Chrysorroi said, 'Summon him. I want to learn of the country[1850] of this hired gardener.' The gardener shouted out for his assistant who immediately came running. The lady fainted and fell to the ground. The assistant fainted on the spot. The lady's comforters sprinkled her with water.[55]

The gardener called his assistant and said, 'My boy, are you mad? Have you lost your reason?'

He replied, 'I almost did, but I suffered a much worse shock when I saw the queen faint as though she were dead.[1860] Who could look upon the queen and such beauty and not die immediately?'

The lady recovers from her faint.

The lady, distressed at heart, spoke to those present: 'Leave me a moment. Retire for a little while and leave me so that I do not now go completely mad. I am tired of your talk. The crowd here is killing me and I am suffocating in this place and its palace. I want you to build a beautiful pavilion in this garden with equipment to make water flow around it.[1870] Surround it with a curtain and give me a few servants, or rather no servants, just one maid. I have been exasperated beyond human endurance. Some unbearable evil is awaiting me.'

When they heard the queen's words the attendants carried out her orders to the letter. A pavilion with running water rose immediately. A splendid and wondrous screen, beautifully embroidered with gold thread, formed the curtain surrounding it, and on its floor stood a bed of great charm.[1880] There was just one maid there to help. The queen, with a distressed and wild air, got up and ran to where the pavilion with its bed stood. She asked for food to be brought and placed on the pavilion's floor. To the maid she said, 'You alone will wait on me and serve this food. No butler or cook or waiter, or any servant at all, no-one is to approach. Let me live in solitude, let me recover on my own.[1890] I was suffocating and I cannot bear it. If my worries and troubles begin again let me face them on my own. I do not want witnesses.'

The table, the food and the meal of the lady Chrysorroi.

She sat down. She started to eat her solitary meal from the floor. I She was alone in the pavilion and alone in the garden. Immediately she felt faint and said to the maid, 'Tell the gardener to give roses to the hired laborer. Let him bring them to cheer me up.'

'Gardener,' the maid said, 'give your hired laborer[1900] a large quantity of roses and send him to us with them now.'

The hired laborer had the roses in a trice. His senses, wits, hearing and discretion, were all ready for this request. To the fair Chrysorroi's great relief, the roses were with her while she was still speaking. She then dispatched the maid—I do not know how; it escapes me; I forget what she did—and with an artful smile she said I

The sweet and happy words of the lady to the hired man.

'And how did you, a miserable foreigner and hired laborer, dare to approach the royal table,[1911] to bow before me, bring me these roses, without a word to anyone?'

He leaned down, he kissed the queen passionately; he seized her and stole a delightful kiss. As he held the roses, he planted a kiss on her lips which were fairer than a rose, and another kiss he took in payment for them.

The queen haughtily gave an order to her maid (she had returned after dutifully carrying out her mistress's command):[1920] 'Take the roses from the hands of the hired laborer.' She took the roses and gave them to the queen. With them she brought the laborer's breath. Again haughtily, and in the manner of a queen, the lady issued an order that the gardener should be honored with gifts but that the laborer should receive a mouthful of bread, just a morsel. This she threw to him, and with the gesture she breathed on him all the charms of the cupids. She was gamboling with the cupids and Aphrodite. Straightway she was released from the countless worries, the tears, the lamentations beyond number.[1930] In this way she spent the day in joy. Night came and with it the charm of love. Darkness brought love's light, a light which equals that of the day. Night made her pleasures tangible with the charms of the body.

The lady enters upon a scheme to be rid of the crowd and to be left alone. The maid immediately drew the curtain. The queen went out by herself, bowed,[56] and said to the others, 'This place has afforded me some relief.[1940] But I have no desire to be suffocated. I do not want to see a crowd. My unhealthy appearance, my bewildered mind and the terrible confusion of my heart I blame on crowds.' With this she dismissed them and they withdrew. Night came and she immediately said to her maid, 'Let me lie down to sleep. But to you I give this order: Retire beyond the pavilion and curtain. I cannot bear to hear the breathing of another person.'

The mistress's order was carried out. And after the first or second hour of night[1950] the hired laborer ran up and crossed the garden. He approached the pavilion, went up to the curtain, and there spied the queen, who also saw him. She rose trembling with desire. He came to her as though on wings. Words, no matter how fair, cannot tell of the passion, the joy, the love with which they embraced. It can only be described by a tender heart. The ineffable sweetness of their kiss[1960] watered their fair but dead hearts like a river. Just as a river waters dry trees, so a kiss revives a dead heart. If you had been there and seen the kisses of that night . . . [*A short gap*] . . . they could never be separated. And when they had spent the greater part of the night kissing, he joyfully took Chrysorroi to bed and their bodies were united. She in turn embraced Kallimachos and they then experienced a delicious rapture beneath the trees, a rare and wondrous pleasure.[1970] Their dead hearts began to beat again in unison. Then it was that they returned to the living. Their souls, which had completely suffocated under so much passion, revived and came back to life. Streams of a fountain[57] of joyful tears poured down. They derived much pleasure from this flood that rose from a spring of happy weeping.

The night ran its course and came to an end; the night which had abounded in delight and flowered with joy; the night which had refreshed and shone on their pleasures.*(1980)* The lovely dawn began to appear but for Kallimachos its loveliness resembled darkness. Amidst weeping, sighs and lamentation, and through fear of the crowd, their bodies parted. The hired laborer, a laborer again, went out into the garden as if to tend the plants and put in trees. The queen, a queen again, he left on her bed. During the day she adorned the royal couch and the splendid pavilion with every grace. The lord[58] of the cupids performed her toilet.*(1990)* In their joy the lovers were free from care. The queen, her heart happy and relaxed, rested in her fair bower. Some distance away the laborer in his capacity as hired gardener was stretched out on the lawn under a tree.

The crowd of the lady's followers and comforters approached and sat down. When they saw the maid and questioned her they were told that the queen was resting. 'She did not speak during the night,' the maid told them, 'and, as you see, she is still sleeping.'*(2000)* When they learnt of the queen's recovery and sleep they were exceedingly pleased and continued to wait.

At midday the queen woke and said to her maid, 'Bring in those who wish to do obeisance to me, but let them leave immediately. The quiet and the solitude here are indeed giving me relief.' The maid called in the trusty followers who were waiting outside and they all entered humbly and did obeisance.*(2009)* | They saw that the lady

*The lords do humble obeisance to their queen, the golden Chrysorroi.

was somewhat rested and were delighted at her excellent recovery. She said to them, 'Once again I tell you: today also I am finding comfort in the solitude of this beautiful little spot. But today and this evening as well I shall again remain by myself and rest until late. So please withdraw and let me once more retire alone. I am now condemned to this seclusion.'*(2020)*

The nobles reply to the beautiful lady—I too call her beautiful just as you say.[59]

They replied, 'We were with you in your distress and your many woes. We shared your daily swoons, your constant tears and the agonies which wasted your noble body. Now, if you have revived a little and if you have recovered sufficiently to spend one hour without lamentation or weeping, we welcome this as a great blessing and favor.*(2030)* We shall retire. It is enough for you to relax. The king shall learn of your recovery. Even if he is suffering the hardships of war, the news that you have found relief will revive him, and we shall the sooner rid ourselves of our clothes of mourning.'

All left at her command. The queen, with the appearance of amusing herself, went for a walk on her own in the garden and strolled among the plants. | She came upon the gardener who was tending his beds.[2040] The hired laborer was with him, picking roses and singing a wonderful song:

The lady's delightful walk in the garden.

Learn of the song of the unhappy Kallimachos.

'The man who two days ago was afflicted, who yesterday was grieved, is today full of joy. The whole garden, which wept at his laments, now sees him and rejoices with a great joy. The man who with many tears told the sun to share his pain and come to his aid, now tells him to be happy, to be bright, to shine[2050] and run a straight course along his road. The man who with many tears asked Fortune to show a little pity for all his woes, today thanks her, glorifies her and sings her praises.'

Hear what the lady said to the gardener.

The lady said to the gardener, 'When I want roses I shall only accept them and reward you if you obey my order quickly. This hired laborer of yours has brought luck. He has relieved you of the labor of carrying water[2060] and, to provide you with a little entertainment, he can sing.'

She looked at the laborer there and he looked at her. From the scene Love made a fair sketch of yet another pleasure. After a short time the gardener moved off to attend to the garden and care for his plants. The laborer was left alone with the queen. At one time her words were sweet and her tongue full of love, at another time her manner seemed serious and grave, but her gravity was part of Love's game,[2070] a lesson of Aphrodite and a picture worthy of the Graces.

The queen's charming words in feigned anger to the poor hired laborer, Fortune's victim.

The lady said, 'Fortune makes me a queen. I shall in no way transgress my royal destiny as universal empress, queen of the garden, ruler of all its plants, and sovereign of its hired laborer. As queen and sovereign I go to my bed. How would a laborer dare to approach it? If he does dare he will suffer until he learns better.'[2080]

Kallimachos's excellent reply.

He replied, 'Fortune that makes you queen has decreed that I pluck roses. You are the ruler of the plants and I am the protector of the garden. When you go to bed as queen you will have your laborer to protect and defend you. He will also pick your roses and tend your plants.'

In this way, surrounded by the plants and roses, they assumed playful airs and talked much as love suggested and desire devised.[(2090)] Chrysorroi then left and went to the pavilion's fair retreat while Kallimachos remained in the garden. Later, the sham laborer came again to the curtain and when he found the queen there he entered as a king, fell down with her and embraced her. They lay together and sported the whole night. After their embraces and words of love, as night was drawing to its close, their words were:[(2099)]

Kallimachos takes counsel with Chrysorroi.

'How long can we steal the pleasure of our love? How long can we reap its joys in secret? How long can the laborer stay with the queen now that after the tears, the sighs, the laments; after the great trials and the long delays, Fortune has had her fill and after abandoning her cruelty, seems to have by chance taken on a kinder aspect? Let us see how we can flee this land and return to our golden city to reap these pleasures but not as thieves.[(2110)] There we can spend the rest of our lives as sovereign rulers in freedom and without care.'

After speaking they embraced and again kissed. They watched the dawn appear even though they found the darkness bright by comparison. With much reluctance they separated, but separation had little sadness. The laborer went back to his garden. The queen lay there in splendor on her bed and slept like a queen until evening.[(2120)] When the king's notables who were guarding her, saw her completely relaxed sleep and how she had ceased her lamentation and her tears, they wrote of the good news to the king and in great haste sent the following letter:

The letter of the nobles to the king.

'We, your faithful servants, write to congratulate Your Majesty. The lamentation, the suffering, the agony, the bewilderment, the restless petulance and the terrible anxiety which you saw in our queen and mistress[(2130)] are at an end. They have settled, receded and passed away. Now come days of joy and happiness. Tears have stopped, grief is banished, and in their place come ease and freedom. When you have finally overcome your enemies you will certainly find what you desire on your return. Your servants take the liberty to inform you of this.'

The queen awoke, and the maid again called the group of comforters. They approached the queen as servants,[2140] did humble obeisance and once more asked if she had enjoyed another restful sleep.

She replied, 'From the solitude of this retreat . . . [*A short gap*] . . . and I have somewhat recovered from my terrible grief. As you see, my poor unfortunate body had been exhausted with lamentation and weeping. I hate all words of consolation because they bring me tears and make me lament. What I love is solitude. I hate crowds[2150] and I shall continue to remain by myself in this solitude. I do not want to see anyone. This is what gives me relief.'

They withdrew and went away, again leaving the lady as she desired, alone with her one maid. . . . [*A short gap*[60] *in which Chrysorroi goes out into the garden*] There she found the laborer and she played with him. He alone had won the queen's love and they embraced with frequent kisses. The garden became the bridal chamber of Aphrodite, the mirror of the Graces and the dwelling place of Love. They spent the day in much happiness.[2160] The night returned with all its sweetness. On its arrival winged Love again took the laborer and with every joy of desire brought him to the queen.

Misfortunes and sadness return once more. The hired laborer approaches Chrysorroi for the third time.[61]   Love was with them and remained as a servant in the royal employ. Love, the lord and king, gave his service to a true passion and pure affection. But, not to draw out my story, I shall not describe[62] at length all the nights and days,[2170] the pleasure of the day and the joy of the night. I only say this and this alone: they lived happily in this fashion with their minds intent on planning their escape.

Misfortunes and woes return once more.   When the lady's many comforters and guards saw their queen's strict solitude, her sudden change from grief to joy, and that she slept without break for the entire day,[2180] they were curious and started to wonder. They reflected on the reason for the great change and said to the maid, 'Stay close to her and learn if she is still spending the

night in tears. Is she using her solitude as a pretext for grief? Stay awake
and alert. Take note of what she is up to. Is she still torturing herself all
night and lamenting bitterly without her comforters? In a word, whatever
happens, do not close your eyes.'

The sly maid's nasty   The space of the entire day passed.[2193]
trick reveals the artifice   The sun's flaming light disappeared
and the love of poor   bringing darkness and death to the
Kallimachos and the   lovers' good fortune. The moon's
lady Chrysorroi.   golden rays shed their sweet light.
Bright disk, why did you not hide your
light in cloud rather than see mortal woes and death? But alas! The trick of
the evil eunuchs and the deceit of the wicked maid[2200] were so well
hidden as to be unsuspected. So what occurred? The queen, unaware of the
plot, reclined in royal state on her lovely bed. The maid lay down to sleep
for the night but was on the watch and discovered everything that
happened. She went up close to the queen's bed but on the other side of
the curtain. She there saw how the laborer embraced the queen on her
golden couch.

When day shone again the company returned. The maid called the eunuchs
aside[2210] and when they were alone said to them, 'I have seen her
deceitful little game. The gardener's laborer, the one who does the
digging—she is embracing him, she is sleeping with him! I watched all
this last night and I saw her playing with him, kissing him, sleeping
with him. O what a wicked and unnatural deed! But if you want to see the
horror yourselves, spend this coming night in the garden.[63] We shall sit
together and wait.[2220] You will learn the tricks of this little whore.'

All this she said to them in secret.[64] They went and made their usual
obeisance—the maid returned by another path—after arranging to watch
together that evening. They entered, did obeisance and immediately left
according to their custom and rank. But why speak at length? The day
passed, night came on, its darkness spread, and three of the trusty
eunuchs[2230] sat in hiding with the maid to keep watch on the lady. As
usual, at the accustomed hour she went to bed again with the laborer, in
complete happiness, as she knew nothing of the trick nor of the
treacherous eunuchs sitting outside. The lovers' secret was revealed. The
evil fortune which was the lady's foster sister[65] came again to her
chamber. The lady did not perceive the treacherous plot. She was unaware
of the plan and she imagined that she was escaping notice.[2240] Those
faithful guards, the three eunuchs, after discovering the full secret, fled
from the lady's harlotry as though from fire and said, 'A curse on her tears,

a curse on all her laments, on her many sighs and her sad air!' They wrote to the king of the lady's harlotry; of her dishonest solitude and how this concealed her union with the laborer; and of the garden's secrets.

They write to the king about the whole affair. These are the words of the scoundrels' letter.

'We previously wrote of joyous news[2251] and the message which we dispatched to Your Glorious Majesty was full of happiness, but the present one is painful and bitter. Do not imagine, sire, that her tears, her confusion, her misery and affliction have returned. Everything was a wicked deceit. Two days ago we sent you the most wonderful and joyous news[2260] that the empress whom you set over us had ceased her weeping. Well, while she was carrying on with her tears and mournful sighs, she was concocting a way of furthering her own ends by saying that in solitude and isolation from crowds she found comfort, as well as a distraction that gave her relief and a cure for her sorrow. But it was a clever trick and deceitful fabrication. On her orders we put up a pavilion in the garden. She used to rest there by herself, as she explained it. Consequently, not knowing her purpose, we withdrew. But she set up a deceitful trick and showed herself a harlot! (O fearsome news!)[2270]—Not with some noble or important man—but with a laborer; the gardener's boy! This is no lie. Do not suspect our motives. Do not believe otherwise. For this reason we send our report to Your Majesty. Order[66] your servants as you wish.'

When the king received the eunuchs' letter, his anger was aroused and he flew into a violent rage. He was grieved and embittered. He cursed what had happened. He marveled how she had abandoned all the violence of her tears[2280] and lamentation to give her love to a laborer.

'Perhaps people are indignant? Perhaps they are tired of having their heads shaven, of wearing black, of fasting from meat, and of mourning? Or is it rather this scheming and envious race of eunuchs, who are two-sexed, or rather have no sex at all—have they fabricated[67] this to incense me, to put me in a rage and frenzy against her so that they will be freed of the nuisance of dressing in black?[2290] But, on the other hand, how have they dared to resort to such a lie and write such an implausible fabrication? Has this golden lady now become a whore? These filthy eunuchs are lying! But, on the other hand, what made them do it? However, I cannot stop at the moment because we are approaching the critical point of the war. So I shall sit down and write out my orders to these eunuchs in my own hand, not through my secretary.' So he sat down and wrote to the eunuchs as follows:[2299]

82   *Three Medieval Greek Romances*

He sits down and writes
his orders with his own
hand. Hear what he said.

'We have received a letter from your hands announcing a strange and terrible circumstance (which has almost killed and destroyed us), how this came about, and its cause. Nevertheless, we now write to order you to apprehend the laborer, put him securely in irons and lock him up. But the lady, whom you claim to be an adulteress, you are to continue to regard as your queen. Our command is that you apply yourselves to showing her all possible goodwill and attention.*(2311)* . . . [*A short gap followed by a line (2313) which is unintelligible without the previous words and is here omitted*] We expect to rout our enemies shortly and, after so doing, we shall return quickly to you. On arrival we shall examine the matter, make a judgment, and pronounce a sentence. Do not concern yourselves with this matter in any way. Farewell, our three eunuchs.'

When they received the letter and read its contents*(2320)* they considered it difficult and inappropriate to approach the queen and to seize the laborer openly because, if she discovered the trick, she might, through fear or, more likely, through anger, make some fatal attempt on her own life. Their hesitation was in accord with their master's orders. Consequently, after luring him far away by cunning, they carefully apprehended the laborer, put him into irons and threw him into prison. They did not allow him to suffer any ill treatment,*(2330)* either in respect of his cell, his bed, or his comfort, so that they would hand him over alive to their ruler.[68] As for the fair lady, their queen, those sons of vipers treacherously showed boundless humility and much submission.

But why speak at length and draw out my story? The ruse deceived the fair lady for just three days. She started to look into what had happened and asked the gardener, 'Tell me, old gardener, where is your laborer?'*(2340)* At first the old man, through fear of the eunuchs, completely denied having seen him. 'Perhaps he left because he had to carry too much water and he was tired from digging,' he said.

The queen makes
enquiries about
Kallimachos.

The queen replied to him, 'Old man, the task of carrying water was heavy at first. But now that this place, this tree and this pavilion*(2350)* have given a little relief to my grief and freed me from my woes and sufferings, the need to carry water has come to an end. Why then has the sweet laborer left exactly when those days have passed?'

The gardener was upset at what had happened to the laborer because the burden of the garden had fallen to him and he took the opportunity of telling the queen everything. | Her weeping and her lamentation started again but they were worse than before, double what they had been previously.

Misfortune and grief begin again.

Amidst her tears and sorrow she sang a mournful dirge[(2360)] and bitterly inveighed against her Fortune:

'Deceitful, raging Fortune of mine, accursed, evil, bitter, empoisoned, again you have come and overtaken me. I imagined that I had escaped your foul decrees, your misfortune and your cruelty. For the space of an hour, a minute, or even just an instant, I seemed to have found some relief from your woes, but now I see that you have caught up with[69] me again. O Fortune, if only the whole disaster had fallen on me[(2370)] and not on Kallimachos, the light of my eyes, my benefactor, my savior from troubles. Better, I think, better for you to have left me to the dragon's punishments than to have sent me an avenger and now to hand him over to tortures and condemn him to irons and prison.' Such were the laments of the queen.

But the golden, the ill-starred Kallimachos, royal by birth but made a laborer by Fortune,[(2380)] the man who had killed the dragon but whom she, Fortune, had made a corpse, he who was graced by every virtue but was now in chains—in his bitterness, his grief and his tears he cried out, 'Again, my Chrysorroi, again, my love, you, the beauty of the world and the flower of the Graces, again you have slipped through the arms of your Kallimachos. I used to say that if Death were to come to take you I would engage him with my sword and do battle. But now Fortune's malice has taken you from me without the help of Charon or of Death.[(2390)] Alas for our misfortunes! Alas for our bitter woes!'

I have drawn out my story. My readers may think that my tale is dragging, but soon afterwards the king returned from his expedition. On his arrival all his subjects did obeisance to him. What happened next? The king took aside the eunuchs and privately asked them about the queen. They showed no hesitation in freely telling him everything in detail.[(2399)]

The three eunuchs, workers of evil and misfortune, tell the monarch about the queen.

'After you ordered us to guard the lady, the queen, and to give her solace, she showed no inclination whatsoever to be silent. Her grief doubled, her weeping knew no limit, she did not want to hear the least word of comfort. Faced with such a problem we were all at a loss. A certain time later she went into the garden and ordered us to make her a pavilion with curtain and to put a bed on its floor.*(2410)* After we had carried out everything according to her instructions she said, "I hate to see a crowd. Leave me alone by myself, just me and my maid. She will suffice to attend to my table, my bed, and all my leisure."

'Her distress grew less, her weeping ceased. We too enjoyed some relief. She was alone with her one maid, as it seemed. Who would have guessed at*(2420)* her cunning trick, her thoughts, or what she would do? However, when we saw how much she was sleeping—you could say she was in bed the whole day—we chanced to say to the maid, "Stay close to her and see if she weeps and laments during the night but wishes to hide it." So the maid took a position in the garden—what tongue could go on? Who could describe the horror of the dreadful business? She saw the laborer, the man who looks after the garden*(2430)* the one whom the old gardener had hired to carry water and do the heavy work in the garden—she saw him together with the lady! She called us and told us everything in detail. But we, master, were sceptical of the matter and stayed up all night to watch together. And we saw everything as we have told you.'

The king becomes angry and gets into a rage.

The king ordered that the queen be brought into his presence, and the laborer with her, so that he could exact retribution*(2440)* by inflicting the terrible misfortune of a merciless punishment. I They brought the lady. She stood there with her hands bound. They also brought the laborer who had his legs in irons. The three eunuchs were there with the evil, cunning maid, ready to give their evidence. The executioners were preparing themselves to carry out the sentence on the king's command, the accused to endure their punishment. Then the lady, with a firm and noble air, addressed the king as follows:*(2450)*

*Behold! The end of the troubles draws near.

Chrysorroi's words to the king.

'O judge, lord of many subjects, eminent for truth and justice, I wish to speak to Your Majesty. Restrain your temper. Check your anger. Afterwards, deliver your sentence as you see fit. A man plants a vine with his own hands, hoes it, prunes it, puts a fence around it, weeds it carefully, tends it, spends the whole day with a sling[2460] frightening away birds who wish to destroy it, walks around by night to guard it. He suffers hardship and agony. At harvest time another man comes and seizes possession of it for himself. He harvests it and eats its fruit. As for the previous owner who planted the vine and labored over it, the second man wants to kill him. Do you consider this just, or do you consider that the first owner should enjoy the fruits of his labor?'

The audience was silent and the king spoke:

'I judge that the previous owner should enjoy the fruit of his toil[2470] and that the evil robber and thief should be beheaded to frighten others who might wish to do wrong or steal.'

The audience roared in applause at the king and praised the beauty of justice.

'My thanks, Your Majesty.' The lady continued: 'And indeed what wrong did the first owner do to make others want to harvest his labor? This is the king whom the witch rendered a corpse with her spells.[2480] This is the king who rescued me from my woes, who killed the dragon, who is my true lord. Whom did he wrong in enjoying the fruits of his labor?'

When the king heard this, he was silent for some time. He shuddered in amazement. 'But how did he return to life?' he asked the lady.

She replied, 'About this, inquire of Kallimachos. I was in your castle, in this palace, lamenting my bitter woes and unable to bear this preposterous circumstance.[2490] I thought my life bitter, my existence a poison, and so, because I did not wish to be silent, I brought trouble on everyone.'

The king softened a little. He was silent for a short time and then said, 'Well, Kallimachos, tell me of your family and your country. Tell me how you took possession of Dragon's Castle and the lady, how you killed the dragon, how you escaped death and, after your wanderings, came here.'

'Your Majesty, you double my grief, my lamentation and my agony*(2500)* when you ask me to tell of my country and my parents. However, at your command I reply:

Kallimachos tells the	'My father was a powerful king who
king in detail about his	ruled a large and fair country, excellent
family, his country and	beyond all others. He had three sons,
upbringing.	including myself, handsome in every
	way. He issued an order and declared his

wish. "I do not want to make any one of you king unless he shows himself superior to the rest in his behaviour."*(2510)* So we made up an army, took tents, provisions and many accouterments necessary for travel. We went over much land, past many countries and castles, and finally we came to the mountain whose thick forests made it difficult and frightening. We thought, "It would be pointless, contrary to good tactics, and against all reason to lead such an army with our tents and baggage up a mountain so sheer and hard to climb. So let us send back the host, and alone, with our own arms, let us go on."*(2520)* We took no road for there was none to take. After mastering the difficulties of the terrain by taking detours we arrived at the top, at the castle of the dragon. The country we saw was strange and beautiful. When we got to the castle we saw the serpents guarding the gates. We considered turning back in retreat and I was left there alone because I did not want to abandon the beauties of the castle.*(2530)* My brothers left.

'I planted my javelin in the ground, jumped over the castle wall and enjoyed the various beauties of the castle. After traversing many quarters, among other wonders, I found this lady hanging by the hair. After slaying the dragon when the opportunity arose, I freed the lady from her torture. Then we bound ourselves with terrible and unbreakable oaths to guard our love, until the treacherous malignity of Fortune changed again for the worse.*(2540)* The witch's scheme, the trick of the apple, how the lady was kidnapped and whisked away, my own demise through a spell—this you know well, better than I do. But out of fraternal affection and prompted by dreams,[70] my brothers came along the road to Dragon's Castle in their search for me. They arrived after difficulties and found me dead. Weeping bitterly, they looked for the cause of my death but found neither cut nor any wound at all.*(2550)* However, they did discover the witch's magic apple and saw the letters which read: "If anyone puts this apple into his bosom he will immediately become a lifeless corpse. But if anyone puts it to the nose of the dead person he will return to life." When they took the apple and applied it I quickly revived and straightway saw my brothers. I was stunned. They were amazed. I sought to find the lady and asked if they had seen her.*(2560)* I left my brothers and again went off alone to look for her.

I was as one dead. In my agony I kept on my journey, for how long I do not know. Finally I came to Your Majesty's kingdom and this castle. I learnt about the queen. I looked for some way, some scheme by which I could see her.[71] Well, I found her and became a laborer, the gardener's hand, just so that I could see her. This, Sire, is the end of my story,[(2570)] the end of my many sufferings and woes. Now everything depends on the pleasure and the goodwill of Your Sublime Majesty.'

In his grief, the king gave a terrible sigh, but his humanity prevailed. He summoned the witch. She was brought before him and in the presence of all, he addressed her:

'You foul, black baggage, you accursed, evil mother of devils, tell me the reason[(2580)] why you gave the apple its double power of death and life? Did someone compel you? Did someone apply force and make you act against your will? Was it because of this that you did what you did, you devil incarnate? You are the evil devil in human form, the baneful spirit that today I am going to wipe from the memory of the human race.

'Light up a great blazing fire! Burn her body even if you cannot destroy her soul! She is a devil and will quickly escape from the flames.'[(2590)] Before a moment had passed the order was carried out.

The king then freed Kallimachos from his chains and gave him to Chrysorroi. The king, I think, felt pity because of Fortune's cruelty and, bestowing on them a not undeserved favor, he ordered a detachment of the army to escort them wherever they wished.

So Kallimachos and Chrysorroi took the road to Dragon's Castle. Happy and free, they made their way with much pleasure and joy.[(2600)] They came to the castle and, now by themselves, they tasted indescribable bliss and pleasure. And, by the grace of God, our Savior, freed from their woe and bitter grief, they regained their previous happiness.

The present book is now at its end through the will of Christ, our God and Redeemer.

Amen

Notes

1   For the text see Knös.
2   Our poem also uses the later form of the word (δράκος) at *l.*492.
3   See R.M. Dawkins *Modern Greek Folktales*, Oxford 1953, p.23.
     Dawkins's characterization of the δράκοι of Greek folktales (*very big,
     very strong, and very stupid, generally living in companies of forty;
     often in caves*) certainly does not fit what we are told of the δράκων
     of *Kallimachos*.
4   See the dictionaries of Liddle-Scott-Jones and Lampe for antiquity.
     Kriaras gives the meaning of *snake* but simply terms the creature in
     Kallimachos a legendary monster, which avoids the issue.
5   Digenis Akritis Gr VI 69f.
6   Following the text of Hatziyiakoumis (p.205) in *l.*54.
7   Emending the last two words of *l.*56 to τῆς αὐτοκρατίας (cf.
     *l.*66).
8   Following the text of Hatziyiakoumis (p.179) in *l.*98.
9   Text uncertain.
10   Following the text of Hatziyiakoumis (p.180) in *l.*129.
11   The ferryman of ancient mythology became the personification of
     death in medieval (and modern) Greece.
12   Reading ὡσάν for ὅσα in *l.*245 with Kriaras.
13   This rubric should come before the previous two sentences. Other
     rubrics are similarly misplaced in the manuscript.
14   Reading ὑπέρ for ἀπό in *l.*284 with Kriaras.
15   The pool is inside its own building and presumably takes up most of
     the floor space. There are windows in the building's walls and when
     the shutters in the windows are opened the plants in the garden outside
     lean through and hang over the sides of the pool.
16   Following the text (καρπόν) of Hatziyiakoumis (p.181) in *l.*314.
17   Reading πύλης for πόλης in *l.*367 with Kriaras.
18   Following the text of Hatziyiakoumis (p.206) in *ll.*383-385.
19   Following the text of Hatziyiakoumis (p.206) in *l.*402.
20   Following the text of Hatziyiakoumis (p.182) in *l.*437.
21   Following the text of Hatziyiakoumis (p.206) in *l.*459.
22   Following the text of Hatziyiakoumis (p.182) in *l.*480.
23   Following the text of Hatziyiakoumis (p.206) in *l.*502.
24   Following the text of Hatziyiakoumis (p.183) in *l.*598.
25   Following the text of Hatziyiakoumis (p.206) in *l.*634.
26   Adopting Lambros's emendation in *l.*676 which, though not wholly
     satisfactory, is better than the other suggestions that have been made.

27 Following the text of Hatziyiakoumis (p.183) in *l.*687.
28 Adopting the lacuna after *l.*701 suggested by Lambros.
29 Adopting Lambros's emendation in *l.*705.
30 Following the text of Hatziyiakoumis (pp.183f.) in *l.*762 (with καλῶς).
31 An allusion to one version of the story of Aphrodite and Adonis in which the goddess, when coming to the aid of her fatally wounded lover, pricked her foot on a rose thorn. Her blood permanently stained the rose, which had previously been white.
32 Following the text of Hatziyiakoumis (pp.184f.) in *l.*849.
33 i.e. the ancient Greeks, whom the Byzantines called "Ελληνες (Hellenes). Themselves they called 'Ρωμαῖοι (Romaioi).
34 Following the text of Hatziyiakoumis (p.185) in *l.*886.
35 Following the text of Hatziyiakoumis (p.206) in *l.*1006.
36 Following the text of Hatziyiakoumis (pp.186f.) in *l.*1064 (the same correction in *l.*1303).
37 The play on words is in the original.
38 Following the punctuation of Hatziyiakoumis (p.187) in *l.*1119.
39 Following the text of Hatziyiakoumis (p.188) in *l.*1227.
40 Christianity had at an early stage downgraded the pagan divinities into instruments of evil and servants of the Devil. The daughters of Nereus, who had been minor sea divinities, were transformed into water demons (see Oxford Dictionary of Byzantium *s.v.* Nereids).
41 Following the text of Hatziyiakoumis (pp.188f.) in *l.*1397.
42 In the Middle Ages the distinction between a large castle and a small city was often small. The word used here for *city* (πόλις) has already occurred in connection with Dragon's Castle (*l.*1380).
43 Following the text of Hatziyiakoumis (pp.189f.) in *l.*1512.
44 Emending ταύτην to αὐτόν in *l.*1549.
45 The ring which Kallimachos had received from the eldest brother at their first separation (*ll.*261ff.).
46 Following the text of Hatziyiakoumis (p.207) in *l.*1576.
47 Reading γνωρίζει in *l.*1624 and ἔλεγαν in *l.*1627 with Hatziyiakoumis (pp.190f.).
48 Following the text of Hatziyiakoumis (p.191) in *l.*1630.
49 Following the text of Hatziyiakoumis (pp.191f.) in *l.*1640.
50 Following the text of Hatziyiakoumis (p.192) in *l.*1662.
51 Reading στὸν καιρόν (Gouillard) in *l.*1664.
52 Following the text of Hatziyiakoumis (pp.193ff.) in *l.*1706.
53 This clause would have a satisfactory meaning if we could suppose that the phrase *the lady's silence* is an obscure way of describing her refusal to conform to the king's wishes, but this seems unlikely.
54 Emending εἰς ὅ to ὡς ὁ in *l.*1749.

55 Following the interpretation of Hatziyiakoumis (pp.195f.) in this passage.
56 Following the text of Hatziyiakoumis (pp.196f.) in *l.*1939.
57 Following the text of Hatziyiakoumis (pp.197f.) in *l.*1975.
58 Following the text of Hatziyiakoumis (p.207) in *l.*1990.
59 Following the text of Hatziyiakoumis (p.198) in *l.*2022. The author of the rubric here addresses the author of the romance. Elsewhere he addresses the reader.
60 Postulating a lacuna after *l.*2154 (Hatziyiakoumis p.207).
61 Following the text of Hatziyiakoumis (pp.198f.) in *l.*2166.
62 Following the text of Hatziyiakoumis (pp.199f.) in *l.*2172.
63 Emending παρέξωθεν to παρέσωθεν in *l.*2219 (there is no question of the counselors staying ouside the garden).
64 Following the text of Hatziyiakoumis (pp.200f.) in *l.*2222.
65 In modern Greek folklore Fate attaches herself to each person a few days after birth and subsequently never leaves (Pichard).
66 Following the text of Hatziyiakoumis (p.207) in *l.*2276.
67 Reading σκευάσασι in *l.*2288 with Kriaras.
68 Following the text of Hatziyiakoumis (p.203) in *l.*2332.
69 Following the text of Hatziyiakoumis (p.204) in *l.*2369.
70 Following the text of Hatziyiakoumis (pp.204f.) in *l.*2545.
71 Following the text of Hatziyiakoumis (p.205) in *l.*2567.

Introduction
to
Livistros and Rodamni

In *Livistros and Rodamni* we have two stories combined and narrated in a rather complicated way. The whole poem is told in the first person by Klitovon. Within Klitovon's narrative, after he and Livistros have met, we start with Livistros telling his newly found friend more than half his own story; and then Klitovon does the same for Livistros. After this exchange of histories Klitovon joins Livistros in his quest. Only here, after the mid-point of the poem, does Klitovon begin to present the story directly to his audience as he himself has seen and experienced it. But even in this latter part we get recapitulations of the kidnapping scene, first from the witch and then from Rodamni herself; each recapitulation adds further information which supplements the first account, as well as furthering our acquaintance with Rodamni and Verderichos, not to mention the witch herself. The element of suspense and the interplay of characters which this technique allows give *Livistros* a sophistication and depth that we do not find in *Velthandros* and *Kallimachos*.

Livistros is a frame or boxed story. The original author seems to have been influenced in this by the twelfth century novel of Makrembolites (see p.xix) which has a similar structure (and which also contains a description of the Twelve Months and other motifs which occur in *Livistros*). Whether *Livistros* owes anything to the collections of boxed stories of the sort which were popular in the Arabic medieval world is doubtful. Two works of this nature, originating in India, had circulated in different middle eastern languages and were translated into Greek in the eleventh century with the titles *Barlaam and Ioasaph* and *Stephanites and Ichnelates*. Both became very popular. But boxed stories of this sort (the *Thousand and One Nights* is the most famous example) are different from *Livistros* in one important respect: their stories, which need not be related to each other, do not make up a coherent narrative. In *Livistros* the boxing is used to provide an added dimension to the plot, which we see from the perspectives of all the main characters except Verderichos. *Velthandros* and *Kallimachos*, on the other hand, are narrated almost wholly from the point of view of the hero.

Text

There are five surviving manuscripts of *Livistros*. These have been designated by scholars with the letters E (late 15th century), N, P, S,[1] and V (all early 16th century). Of them only E and V are complete (or nearly so). V gives a shorter version (3811 lines against E's 4405) where brevity is achieved by condensing (but not abridging) the story as it appears in the other manuscripts. It is the version presented by the other four manuscripts that is presented here in translation. The verbal differences between even these, however, are sometimes great. Scribal carelessness has only contributed to this to a certain degree. As suggested in the General Introduction (p.xxx), it seems that scribes were under no constraint to preserve the exact words of a poem which they were copying.

As an extreme example of this type of variation we may take a line from the text when Klitovon realizes that Livistros wants to hear his story (p. 149). In the manuscript followed at this point in the translation he expresses his feelings towards Livistros: *The foundations of my heart hold you within them* (S1470). But in ms. E the words that Klitovon says are: *You are rooted inside my limbs* (E2614). Not all differences between these manuscripts are as striking, but the lines do show that even E, N, P, and S can present separate versions. While they do not differ from each other as much as any one of them does from V, they nevertheless do not allow us to reconstruct the original author's words as can normally be done, or at least attempted, with most surviving Latin and Classical Greek texts.

Mainly because of this complex situation no satisfactory text of Livistros has been produced up to now.[2] Ideally, each manuscript would be edited separately, and we would be able to catch the flavor of each version. Among the differences to surface more clearly would be that of language because there is a difference in the Greek employed in each. But this, unfortunately, would not give us four versions of *Livistros* in its entirety because there are considerable gaps in N, P, and S while E, though virtually complete, has sections so corrupt as to be unintelligible. This means that we are forced to take the manuscript which presents the best text (S) and supplement its gaps (and sometimes correct its mistakes) from the others. If it is objected that the result is a version that never existed in the original Greek the reply can only be that we have no other choice.

This method has been followed in establishing a text for the present translation. The first quarter of the poem, which is missing in S, has been supplied from N; in this case (and elsewhere) the reader will be able to discover the provenance of a passage by the manuscript letter prefixed to the line numbers. But even in the combination of S and N there are further gaps, ranging from one to sixty lines. These have been filled from P, and very occasionally from E and V.[3] The translation of passages which supplement gaps in N (up to *l.*979) and S has been put into italics; in all cases the provenance is given, either in the actual translation or in an endnote. Occasionally italics indicate that a half line or more in N or S has been replaced with what stands in another manuscript.

A transcript of manuscripts S, E, and N (up to *l.*979) has been published by Lambert[4] and the line numbers in her book have been followed. For P and N (after *l.*979) I have used the numeration in a transcript of these mss. For P the misplaced folios 84-91 have been restored to their proper position and numbered accordingly; to have attempted to reconstruct the numeration of Hatziyiakoumis, who follows the present order of folios in the manuscript, would have inevitably led to errors. To make the shorter supplements taken from N (after *l.*979) and P easier to identify I have, in the endnotes, added the first words of the line or passage in question to all line references. The manuscript N also suffers from misplaced folios but as these are all within the section published by Lambert (they occur between *l.*280 and *l.*487) I have not attempted to renumber them.

Rubrics occur in *Livistros* which are similar to those in *Kallimachos*. These have been supplied in the translation where they occur in the manuscript used at any given point. None occur in the latter part of the translation because of their absence in S after *l.*1438.

Nearly all the corrections made to the text of N and S by Lambert in the critical apparatus of her edition of these manuscripts have been adopted without comment. Other changes are indicated in the endnotes.

Livistros and Rodamni

The very romantic verses of the story of Livistros as told by his friend Klitovon to Myrtani

All sensitive people schooled in love,[5] who have been reared and instructed by the noble Graces; who have been subjected to love's torments; and all you of low degree; every soul of goodwill who is versed in love, every heart of noble grace which is devoted to virtue—come now and hear with me of love's passion in the fair story which I shall tell. And you, lady Myrtani, who are the queen of the Graces,[(N10)] a spring flowing with love and esteem, the living embodiment of the Graces, mistress of Aphrodite, join with all the glorious land of the Litavians and your noble kinsfolk down to those of low degree; men, noble women, old, young, let all come and gather round me. Today, my lady, I am going to tell a wonderful tale of love and of the terrible sufferings endured by a man of many trials and woes whom Love persecuted.[(N20)] From my story of passion's fury everyone will learn of the bitterness of Love and will marvel at how a man innocent of the world suffered so much from the time he began to feel desire.[6]

And now I shall begin my story of the love of the unfortunate Livistros and the lady Rodamni.

His friend Klitovon begins the story. On a narrow path beside a flowing river a sorrowful young man was crossing a sloping meadow. The meadow must have been a place where strangers camped and the fair river a source of refreshment for the afflicted;[(N30)] the meadow charmed them with its trees, its flowers and springs, and the river gave them comfort with its clear and sweet water. The man crossing it was very troubled. He was a noble Latin[7] from abroad, a capable and good-looking young man, of very handsome build and features; blond, tall, beardless, with his hair close-cropped on either side. He was mounted on a horse, in his hand was a hawk and behind him a dog followed on a leash.[(N40)] He was girt about with arms and as he went along the road he drenched himself with his tears. His sighs were frequent and they scorched the path.

I too had left my country, hounded by passion, afflicted by love, and burnt by desire. In my grief I had gone and was roaming the world to find relief and ease from my many woes. And, I know not how, I too had taken the same path *as that handsome Latin*.[8] I had been traveling for one day and on the next I caught up with him.[(N50)] I was behind and he in front, bathed with tears and frequently sighing. When I saw that he was in pain and so troubled, I was distressed and wanted to ask him who he was, from where he came, and the cause of his sighs. Finally, in my great distress I could hold out no longer. I drew up to his side and boldly greeted him. I said, 'Fellow traveller, from where do you come?'

But his mind was torn by grief and instead of turning and greeting me[(N60)] he kept on the path's narrow track. In his sorrow he went on, with his eyes on the river. Again I spoke to him and greeted him many times: 'Bear up, sir, do not grieve, do not distress yourself so much. You are wandering in a wild region. If in your troubles some new woe befalls you, you will be without consolation here in a foreign land.'

At one point he sighed and turning to me in a very piteous and sombre fashion he replied, | 'Sir, what is it you ask me? Are you pressing me so much[(N70)] to learn the reason for my

Livistros replies to his friend Klitovon.

grief and frequent sighs? I am a man and I suffer. Do you seek the cause of my suffering? *Fellow traveller, fellow stranger, when you learn it*,[9] even if you are made of rock you will, I think, burst with grief. I swear by the woes I suffer for my love that even a stone, if it came to learn what I have endured, would break into a hundred pieces and crumble like a clod of earth.'

When I realized that love was the cause of his suffering I conjured him by terrible oaths to tell me of his sorrows. I said, 'Stranger, learn what the proverb says: "On a journey a brother is better than a mother."[(N80)] If you do not tell of your woes and hide them within yourself *they will suddenly flare up and some day you will have trouble; you will become more stricken and desperate*.[10] A person who conceals his troubles does so at his own peril.'

Livistros again replies to Klitovon.

At one point he suddenly turned and looked at me. Tears were streaming down from his eyes like a river. | *'Friend and fellow traveller, hear the woes I suffer for love and give me your sympathy.*[11] Learn how here in the world my Fortune has changed me. Instead of father, mother, brothers and friends, today, here in foreign parts, I have only you and I want to tell you what I have suffered in the world. If you have in truth learned to feel for the unhappy*(N90)* you will swear an oath with me that we shall not part.'

Without delay, he eagerly got off his horse to swear an oath with me and to ratify it. When I saw him do this, I dismounted, and we both swore that whatever danger might occur, we would not part. And immediately after the oath he said to me from his heart:[12]

Know—I swear it by the troubles I bear in my soul—that I have spent a whole year wandering and searching the world. I live from my falcon, I am nourished by my dog, my horse is my life, my weapons are my soul. I have come to this madness, my friend, because my sword has been like Charos[13] to me, my breastplate has been as death, and my weapons as the grave. Now learn also why it is I lament.*(N100)* | Friend, in my country I was a mighty man, a ruler, wealthy,

*Livistros tells Klitovon of his ancestry.

feared, of great courage. This, I think, time will show you. Joy was my companion, serenity my friend. Never was there any happiness or pleasure which I lacked. And amid so much joy, amid so many pleasures, amid all my wealth and prosperity, amid the many luxuries and delights which I possessed and had at my command and in which I took pleasure, no concern[14] for love ever came to me.*(N110)* My mind was completely free of passion. The thought of love did not enter my mind. I lived unsubdued, in freedom, without Love's tortures, and beyond desire. But further, my friend, if ever any of my family or my friends became involved in thoughts of passion or notions of love, I taunted them much and berated them a thousand times.

One day I decided to go hunting with my kinsmen and my friends.*(N120)* I went to mountain slopes, to a wooded hill and searched to find a partridge. I wanted to release my falcon and see if it would give chase. I spent the whole day on the plains, on the slopes and in the mountain valleys without ever being able to set loose my falcon. It was only late in the afternoon at the close of the day that I found two doves sitting together on the branch of a tree and covering each other with kisses. I tied down my falcon and took out my bow.*(N130)* I mounted an arrow on it and shot one of the two. Then I witnessed a strange and frightening thing. As soon as the bird that had been killed fell to the ground, the other flew up and rose to the clouds. Then, at that great height, it relaxed its wings and fell down dead on its mate. I saw it and was astonished. I was gripped by anxiety. I felt sorry for the bird and I asked a kinsman of my group why it had killed itself. When he learnt what had happened, he started a constant search for*(N140)* some way to tell me of love's pangs and to instruct me in the bitter-sweet of passion. When I asked, he replied in a few words: 'Attend, Livistros, ruler of my land and country. If I sit down and instruct you about the bird you see, care will enslave your now care-free mind and you will glorify the power of love mightily.'

Straightway I drew my kinsman to my side and questioned him about the bird, the amorous dove, and about the nature of Love's fearsome power.*(N150)* He attempted to instruct me in Love's mysteries and the bonds of passion.

'You see this bird, the dove?' he said. 'It always makes for the mountains as it flies through the air. But if its mate is killed and quits the world, it never perches on a tree which has green leaves, it never drinks fresh water from a spring. It sits forever on a rock and laments inconsolably. It chokes itself with the tale of its loss. But what do you expect of a bird which has feeling and sight?*(N160)* Consider the palm tree and marvel. If a female palm has no male, it drops no fruit to the ground but stands in constant grief. Next, marvel at the lodestone. Because of its passion, it attracts iron. Take also the moray eel. Its passion makes it rise up from the sea floor and unite in love with a serpent. Wonder too at how the river called Alpheios*(N170)* runs through so much of the sea to get to the harbor in Sicily.[15]

'Yet why, Livistros, ruler of my land and country, should I go into details to teach you the mysteries which Love reveals in lovers? I am sure that even if you are more insensitive than a stone, you have come a little way towards understanding desire and you fear the power of the lords of love.'

And after this long account which my kinsman had given to instruct me in passion, I went to my quarters, got off my horse*(N180)* and, as I wanted to recover from my weariness, I entered by myself. I considered what my kinsman had told me of love, and without the wish to do so I began to brood. My heart resolved not to get entangled in love's woes.

The evening called in the day, the sun set and night came on. I was drowsy with the care in my soul and went to bed to sleep. Hear what I saw:

An account of Livistros's dream of woe. I dreamed that I was alone and that I was going through a meadow,[N190] a most beautiful meadow with countless flowers. Fresh, cool water gushed forth among thousands of trees. If you had seen it you would have said that the place with all its beauties and colors had been created by the hands of an artist. I looked at the sloping meadow, I examined the trees, I was delighted by the plants, I admired the springs. My mind was entranced by the flowers. The place intoxicated me. As I went on by myself I said, 'Happy the man who lives in such a meadow and spends his days amid such beauty![N200] If he yearns after Paradise he is no true knight.'[16]

I was passing through the fair meadow on my delightful journey and as I was examining it I glanced up and at a distance saw armed men. All had wings and they were coming towards me. They were racing over the meadow in great anger. When I saw their number my heart sank. I dismounted from my horse and went to draw my sword, but before I had it out they fell upon me. They surrounded me and shouted in angry voices,[N210] 'Throw down your weapons or you will suffer harm.' When I saw that they were many, that all had weapons and wings, and that all breathed fire, I faced them almost as a novice since I was now at death's door. I resigned my life. I threw away my sword, I threw away my bow and, crossing my hands on my chest, said to them, 'I am your servant, let me live.' One of them, extremely handsome and of pleasing build and appearance, with wings on his shoulders and armed,[N220] came up peacefully and took hold of my hand. He tied me by the neck and said, 'Follow me. And give up your terrible arrogance. It will not help you at all.'

We began to cross the meadow. On one side and on the other, in front and behind, I had Love's executioners who punish crime.[17] How can I describe to you, my friend, how can I relate to you the threats and menaces each made? But I shall tell you of the admonitions of the one who had bound my neck and was leading me:[N230]

'Livistros, Love is warning you. Passion is commanding you. Sir, do you want me to be silent? Interpret this as you wish. If you were not fashioned from earth, if you were not of this world, if you were born of iron or were a lump of rock, I would not find it strange at all if you felt[18] the boundless power of lords of love. There is no way that anything, whether with or without life, rock, tree, iron, or stone can exist without receiving Love. And you, a mighty man, a handsome youth,[(N240)] do you despise Love? Do you not care about Passion? Now, if you heed me, you will take up Love's cares. Give up your arrogance, bend your neck to the yoke of Love's servitude, enter into the bond of Passion, bind yourself to Desire, give yourself to Longing, look towards Care. They will now speak to Love and beseech him, and he will give up the terrible rage which he feels towards you, he will change and pardon you. And, to speak to you, human that you are, do you wish to endure no passion, do you wish Love to forget you and pass you by?[(N250)] Why do you suppose that you are outside loving desire? Desire becomes you; see this for yourself. Observe what befits you. I swear by the two-edged sword of Love's madness that I am telling you nothing by way of flattery. Even though you are handsome in build and appearance, if you do not put on Passion's yoke you will suffer. You will suffer Love's tortures and, as is right, you will realize that you are nothing. Learn this from me. And hear what I now command you. When you now go and do obeisance to Love,[(N260)] approach him with bent neck and lowly face. Assume an abject look to show your fear. Cross your hands tightly on your chest and fall to the ground in front of him. Speak from your heart and beseech him. But when you are entering his dwelling and you see the ivory sign on the lintel above the door, read what the writing there says.'

After these many warnings we came to Love's camp and entered the courtyard of his domain.[(N270)] | At its gates I saw a stern man who was naked with drawn sword. His face was very wild and his appearance terrifying. One hand he stretched out and in it he had a sign covered with writing. Hear what it said: 'Every man who is not a servant to Love's power, who has not been driven by passion to feel desire, let him remain outside the courtyard of Love's domain. But if he wishes to enter and examine it, let him subscribe himself as a servant and give himself to Love.[(N280)] *Then he will see the charms which the lord of passion has. But if he refuses to enter and enrol as a servant let him know that my sword is his death. I shall act as a harsh tyrant and brutally[(P250)] cut off his head. He will disappear from the world!' Further on, the sign had: 'The keeper of Love's courtyard and of Desire's gate.'* [19] *And <the cupid> who was looking at the gate said, 'Read this.' I saw the letters and was greatly distressed. I read, 'I am now enslaved to Love's bow.'*

Livistros describes in detail the beauties he saw in his sleep. He speaks in sorrow.

We then entered the courtyard together; myself, the cupid who was executioner, and my torturers. And, my friend, how shall I tell you? How shall I describe to you the arrangement of the courtyard, the statues it contained,(P260) the cool waters, the trees around the fish pond, the picture on its wall, the walking statues? If I tell you of everything in detail I shall need the space of an entire year. Leaving all that aside, I shall tell you of one thing which I saw and marveled at in Love's dwelling.

I first entered a portico. Its floor was wholly of chrysolite and was covered with representations of Love. There you saw various beautiful trees, and in the branches of each(P270) were birds, some sitting, some about to take off, and others flying low from one branch to another. And Love was depicted in the middle of the mosaic in green marble, and Love's birth was shown with wondrous art. It showed how Aphrodite gave birth to him as an archer, and how he in turn fired an arrow at her. On the portico's roof was depicted the judgment[20] of Paris, whom he passed over and to whom he gave the apple.(P280) In the portico's corners stood cupids skilfully made of fine plaster and sitting on the lips of each[21] I saw a strange reed. Whether it happened through the wind's breath or through a stream of water or by some other means I do not know, but the cupids were shouting in turn. The first said, 'Leave the place where you are treading, you who resist passion!' The next said, 'Let the servant of disloyalty be killed!' And the next, 'Has the fire no effect? Does it not inflame him?' And the fourth shouted, ' Give yourself up and stop!' (P290)

I looked at the portico and marveled at everything. I was amazed at the beautifully worked marble. I admired the representation on the roof. My mind was in agony over the words of the four cupids and was afraid. I was directing my attention to this and that, and I simply did not know what to praise first. I spent some time standing there and examining Love's fair abode together with those who had ordered me to stop and look.(P300) I stood there lost. My mind marveled at countless beauties which I was seeing in my dream.

After an endless time the one who was leading me by the neck went out. He again held the rope in one hand and put the other around me as a warning.[22] He now said, 'Take care, mortal, to remember what I said to you as we were coming so that he will pardon you.'

In his sleep Livistros meets Passion.

When I left the portico I was met by Passion, an extremely handsome man, fair, with blond hair. On his head he had a chaplet of daphne and in his hands he had a sprig of the same. When he met me he began to speak words of rebuke and warning:

'I marvel now at Love's patience.$^{(N440)}$ Why is he so tolerant of a mortal? Why are you not his servant? Why are you insolent? He has drawn his bow but has not shot you. I shudder at the burning fire which you hold in your hands. How has it not yet consumed your entire heart?'

Then he asked, 'You know me?'

I replied, 'No.'

'I am Passion,' he said.

I said to him, 'I do obeisance to you. I tremble at your power. I shudder at your might. I submit to Love and become his liege.'

'If you were minded to become his servant,' he replied,$^{(N450)}$ 'and to conform to the charter of Love's domain, you would have a sweet time and carefree days. You would begin upon a very wonderful life.'

While I was talking to Passion and had my eyes on him a beautiful and enchanting woman appeared. She was fair and tall, with her head uncovered. Her hair was the color of milk and was made up into two plaits hanging low with curls in places. On her head she had a chaplet of myrtle which was in fruit and had clusters of flowers.$^{(N460)}$ She wore a dress in the Latin style[23] which was gold and white below, with no girdle. Above, it had fur. The lady was holding roses in one hand and in the other a sheet of paper, but what was written on it I do not know.

The one who was leading me said, 'This is Desire. Become her servant now and *do obeisance to her. She has said that she will intercede on your behalf*[24] and, together with Passion, will make peace for you with Love. They will speak on your behalf and he will pardon you.'

Desire approached and stood with Passion.$^{(N400)}$ To the cupid and to Passion she said, 'Is this the man with whom the lord of love was angry two days ago? Is this the one who caused so much violence and uproar?'

'Yes,' I replied. And as I said this I did obeisance to her. Falling at her feet I went on, 'Desire, servant of Love and his true kin, and you, Passion, also his servant and true kin, I have not known Love and have not been able to enter his service. Do something for me, sweet Desire and Passion.

Find Love and make this appeal to him:*(N410)* "I was a peasant and I did not know who you were. For this reason I did not enter Your Majesty's service." Make yourselves sureties for me. Speak fair words and I shall swear by Love's bow and flame to be his servant from this day and to obey his will.'

My words and the appeal I made to them, my friend, would have moved a robber to pity. And when I had beseeched them with many tears, Desire bent over, raised me up from the ground and said, 'Passion, we shall speak to the lord of love*(N420)* and win a pardon for this man.'

Passion said to me, 'Calm yourself! Have no worry! Since you are now in Love's service and you swear not to be unfaithful, you will have the love of a virtuous and noble lady as well as Love's pardon and goodwill.'

And the cupid who was guarding me said to the other, 'Let him now go inside with you to where Love is judging.[25] Let him gain Love's pardon, swear by his arrow and take up the bond of desire for the lady.'

Desire and Passion moved away from me.*(N430)* They were holding each other by the hand and kissing secretly.[26] And they went off to Love's court.

The unfortunate Livistros describes in detail the wonders of the pool which he saw in his dream. There was a low terrace built of marble[27] and round it stood slender, hewn columns. On the front of each were fair sculptures of cupids which seemed to be alive. Little creatures were sitting about on their chests and all drinking water from the cupids' mouths. Beside the terrace was a pool which was filled with the freshest water, cold as ice. In it stood a column and on its top was a marble basin.*(N370)* Inside the basin I saw a man—he seemed to be alive and to move. In front of his chest his hands held a sign with verses that said: 'Let him who sees me grieve. Let him who looks at me suffer. Let him whose eyes turn to me feel sorrow. The sentence which I expiate with my sufferings was imposed upon me by Love, who condemned me because I neither knew nor feared him.'

I quickly read the words*(N380)* and I shook my head in fear lest the mighty and dread lord of love might so condemn me too. I looked at the man who was holding the message and saw that the tears dripping from his eyes were seething like boiling water and bubbling like a cauldron. On his head a snake was lying curled round his temples. Its mouth was fastened to the man's forehead. When I was looking at him he seemed[28] to shout to me, 'Take care lest you suffer what I have suffered and lest you endure countless tortures.'[(N390)] When I heard his voice I seemed to freeze.[29] I began to pity the youth, to lament his sentence and to suffer for him. The cupid whom I had with me said, 'He is being tortured for the error he committed.'

After a little while I saw that the gates where Desire had gone inside with Passion were open. A cupid came out and said to my guard, 'Bring him in!'

The latter asked, 'What do they say about him?'

To prevent me hearing, the other furtively replied, 'Desire is interceding for him and Passion is standing as surety. Love pardons him. He will not suffer.' And to me he said, 'Proceed. From now on do not be distressed.'

I went inside with them[30] and found a large crowd. There were tens of thousands of people and their cases involved desire, love, and discretion in passion.[(N290)] And, my friend, learn what was in their midst that amazed me. My eyes saw and my mind was astounded.

Love was sitting on his throne and had three faces. His first face was that of a small child; soft, delicate[31] and of a blond complexion. If you had seen it you would have certainly pronounced it a work from the hands of a master painter. It was beyond censure. The second was of a man in his prime, with round beard and skin like snow. The next face you saw was of an old man[(N300)] with form, shape, build and appearance to match. The first face had hands, feet and the rest of the body complete. The next was only from the shoulders up. I noticed that the faces were placed in order of rank. I looked at this triple form and said, 'Who fashioned this? What is this strange creature I see? What is it? Who can tell me what it is I see? Who can explain it? What kind person will instruct me?'

And, at one point, while my mind was troubled with this problem,[(N310)] my own case came up. A cupid shouted, 'Let the rebel come forward!' The order rang out on either side of me and my guard said, 'Go forward and do obeisance.'

In his dream Livistros falls before Love, falls before him and beseeches him with many tears.

I went up to Love and fell to the ground before him. My tears began to flow and I said, | 'Love, my master and king, sovereign of the whole earth, ruler of things lifeless, lord of creatures with life,[32] inspector of every heart, true judge of Passion, partner of Desire and friend of Esteem;[(N320)] if I was insensitive towards you and showed you scorn, mighty lord of love, take no note of my offense, do not be angry. Realize that I was a peasant and pardon me. You have terrified me—that is enough! Now show pity. I shall swear to be your servant, a menial at your orders, a liege at your will and your command.'

When I had finished my appeal, Love said, 'Rise! Because Passion has interceded for you and I have Desire's guarantee[(N330)] I shall now have pity on you. I shall be merciful and forgive you. What you did I shall disregard and forget. And now, receive desire into your heart, and passion for a virtuous lady of supreme beauty; passion for Rodamni, the daughter of King Chrysos.'

I raised myself from the ground and did obeisance to him.[(P470)33] I noticed, my friend, a frightening and remarkable thing about him. When this face was speaking you would have said that it was that one; the three mouths shared the one voice and you heard the resonance of the sound from all three.[34] You simply did not know which started and which finished as Love did not utter his words from where you would have thought.

On either side of Love's three faces stood two women, beautiful in appearance. One was wearing a chaplet, made only of pearls, which was as white as fair untrodden snow.[(P480)] The other also had a chaplet on her head—red rubies which stung like fire. The garment of each[35] was as shining as her chaplet. The two had their right hands[36] on one of the knees of the lord of love as a fair sign of his oath to Good Repute.

Hear how <the cupid> explained to me the significance of the two women: 'You see the fair woman all in red who is standing on the right side of Love? She is called Truth. She swears that Love[(P490)] will not be false to what he has promised in the world concerning passion.[37] The one who stands on the left is called Justice. She swears that Love will defend what is just and never make false judgments through partiality. The one is all in red and the other all in white. Think of the latter as ice from the clouds and the former as fire from the earth because of her honesty.

Wonder, mortal, at the forms of the two women. When you leave from here and proceed further you will come to Love's weapons and take a vow on them.(P500) *And then for your instruction you will also see the prophet who will tell you of what you are going to suffer and when you are going to win your love.'*

When he had talked to me he left me and went. Again I looked at Love and again he spoke: 'Livistros, why are you standing and looking? Come, swear! Desire, take him! Passion, secure him! Make the guarantee for him. He will swear by his life.[38] *Let him be hit by a cupid with an arrow of passion for Rodamni.'*

*A beautiful description of Love's oath. We find this written on one of the room's double doors. Hear what it said. Hear also what was depicted on the doors.

Immediately I did obeisance and left.(P510) *Passion was on one side and Desire on the other. We went to the room of oath-taking. | Above, Love was represented naked with a whetted sword in one hand and a lighted torch, all red, in the other. Hear the inscription underneath:*(P520)

'Inexhaustible Love who goes to the sky and the depths.' Passion said to me, 'There is no-one in the world who has avoided Love. Be informed that there is no-one who has escaped from Love's archery.'

Passion and Desire left and we [Livistros and his guards] went inside into the fair room for taking Love's oath. On top of a gold and red cabinet I found the arrow of Love and his strung bow. Between them was a sign with these words: | 'I am Love's law. This is my arrow(P531) *and this is my bow. All of you, swear to be its*

*The terrible oath of the cupids. He swears not to transgress it.

lieges[39] *and servants, and not to transgress it. I am at a loss as to why you wander and why it is you transgress. Where can you escape him?*

I shudder that you flee him. If you fly into the heaven he has an arrow and will reach you. If you go down into the depths you do not escape him. If perchance you wander the earth observe his bow. His aim is very accurate,[40] *and there is no way you escape Love's archery.*(P540) *So I bid you who are of the world: become Love's servants. Let him who swears to Love not transgress his oath since what Love says is certain.'*

And below this sign was written: "The room of Passion and place of Love's oath.' I read this, I saw the picture and I leant over the arrow and the bow. I said, 'I swear by this arrow and well-aimed bow that I assign myself to Love, enter myself as Passion's liege and that from now on I shall be faithful to Love and Desire. *(P550)*

I took the oath. When I had sworn the prophet came and after <my guard> had explained to him that he had seen me swear the prophet told me with great assurance:[41]

The prophet tells Livistros what he will suffer. 'Livistros, ruler of a Latin land, mighty governor, man of great wealth, prince[42] over many people, you are destined to go into exile from your native land because of your passion for the fair Rodamni. It is ordained that you become master of Silver Castle[43] and succeed Chrysos, the illustrious father of the lady Rodamni, in his land and that you rule the world. After a space of two years you will lose Rodamni through a cunning woman, an evil witch, and you will go out in search of her.*(N340)* You will wander for two years before you find her. And when you do find her through the help of your true friend, a further period of a year will pass and you will again become master of Silver Castle. You will die with the wondrous lady.' So spoke the excellent prophet in his account of the future and I awoke immediately.

Livistros wakes from his dream; he awakes all in a dither and with countless anxieties. My mind was in confusion and there was fear in my soul. Desire was causing my heart anguish and distress. In my anxiety I lay down for a long time to see*(N350)* when my wits would come back—if they were not really lost. After a while I recovered and my senses returned. My mind rose from the depths of the dream. I immediately cast sleep from my eyes. I sat down and my mind was shaken by fear. I looked to see if my back was still tied and if I was the same as when they were dragging me in bonds. My mind was fixed on Love and his three forms. I marveled at the terrace and the fair pool. I seemed to be still able to see with my eyes the scene of Love's oath. I was here, there, and in the world beyond. I wanted to consider this but reflect on that,*(N470)* to think about something else but not to let another thing escape me. Believe me, my mind was breaking into a hundred pieces. After some time I informed my kinsman who had been telling me of Love's power.

Livistros tells his relative of the dream. 'Hear what happened to me yesterday. Love sent a dream which, it seems,[44] I still see. Love fashioned a fearsome vision to make care for my mind and worry for my soul. I still see it perceptibly as it passes before my eyes.'*(N480)*

He said to me, 'Livistros, master, ruler of the land, lord of my country, speak! Tell me your story.'

And I began, my friend, to tell my kinsman the dream of love. When I came to the name of the lady Rodamni he said, 'Stop, Livistros, I have information about the lady you mention. Listen. The time is now passed *but it was, I think, two years ago that I went abroad to a certain country. The land I am speaking of was plunged into misery on account of its ruling prince who had gone to the lady you mention.*[45] And calm yourself, do not lament, have no worry since the man who is prophet and seer has foretold your future. It is true that you will bring sadness, grief, worry, distress and death to your country and all your people*(N490)* if you leave on a search for the lady Rodamni. But win the lady whom Love promised you and you will in turn comfort those whom you have grieved.'

For my comfort and relief my kinsman began to tell stories of love and to turn me towards other things. He spoke fair words to console me. The whole day passed. The night came, it grew dark and the moon appeared.*(N500)* My kinsman, who had been with me, left. I dined with my friends and engaged in talk. *I then went to bed. Hear again, my friend, of the dream*[46] which Love fashioned for me in the loom of night:

I seemed to enter a lovely garden planted with countless trees. Everything was in flower. It was decorated by Love the king, adorned by Passion[47] and beautified by Desire with her wondrous gifts. I wandered around, examining the garden, running up to this tree, leaning on that one. I lay down by this tree and that, I ran up to another.*(N510)* I plucked fruit from this one and a flower from that. The beauties of the garden knew no limit. Love's garden, I thought, was large and I ran to look at this part and to examine that.

I met Love but it was the small child who was sitting there with his two <other> faces. On his shoulders he had wings. In one hand he held a silver bow and in the other he held the lady, the beauteous lady Rodamni.

He held the lady—endure, my much-suffering heart,*(N520)* lest you now suffer, burst[48] and die of the pain!
He held the lady—endure, my soul, do not swoon!
He held the lady—take care, my soul, do not faint!

He held the lady—reason, do not leave me!
He held the lady—she is the repose of my heart!
He held the lady—my friend, she is the light of my eyes!
He held the lady—what shall I say? Endure, my soul, do not depart!

I met Love, the old man, the child, the beautiful child in the prime of life. *(I have just forgotten to tell you one thing, my friend. Remind me later when I finish my dream and I shall tell you what I saw.)*[49] I met Love, Love and the lady,[(N530)] the lady and Love holding hands. He came up to me. He looked at me, he first looked at me for a time and then shouted, 'Livistros, approach!'

I looked, I recognized who he was, I approached and did obeisance.

'Stop! Have no fear!' he said. 'Return to your senses.'

I stopped, looked at Love and gazed at the lady. I looked carefully at Love, then admired the lady and said to myself, 'This too is Love. But he has transformed himself and become a woman. *And he does not have his arrow —where is he hiding it? If it is a woman her face certainly surpasses that of Love in harmony. It is a woman—it must be Love's mother; her appearance is similar to that of Love. It seems that Love's mother, who is called Aphrodite, is alive and goes with him. However, what I see is strange; before my eyes there is, it seems, a maiden who is beyond doubt unmarried.'*

After the many thoughts with which I was fighting,[50] Love said to me, 'Livistros, this lady whom you are looking at[(N540)] with amazement and much admiration is Rodamni, the daughter of King Chrysos. I promised her to you. I said I would give her to you. Well, here she is. Take her! I make you a present of her. Stretch out your hand and take the lady now. Spend your years with her and die with her. Bend your neck, as yet unbent, to love for her.'

I heard Love's words and stretched out my hand. Love gave me her hand with assurance. I covered Love with kisses and moved towards the lady.[(N550)] But the excess of joy woke me. I woke with death and great pain as my companions. I woke to sighs and countless pangs. I woke to find myself ablaze and tortured by my woes. I searched for the garden, for Love, for the lady, for the trees and the beauties which I had seen in the garden. I was in torture. I longed for the night. My mind yearned to see the dream. I forswore the light and hated the day. Night was my queen but the dawn I did not wish to see.[51]

Again I spoke to my dear kinsman.[N561] Again I told him what had
happened in my dream. Then I talked with him about my plans for going
in search of Silver Castle, for meeting Chrysos, its king, and for setting
my eyes upon the lady Rodamni.

To begin, my kinsman said, 'First, send men out to search. Let them
announce who you are and from where. The whole world is full of your
fame and rings with your bravery.[N570] Everyone knows of it. Through an
agreement you will achieve your desire.'

Livistros sits and takes
counsel with his relative
as to what he should do
and how he should look
for the lady.
But when he saw that my mind could
not be moved in the matter he sadly
gave me this advice: | 'Livistros, ruler
of my country, prince[52] of the land of
Livandros and its comfort and
adornment, since you are aflame with
love and wounded by desire, since your heart suffers the blow of
passion[N580] and you go out a willing servant of Love,[53] I advise you, I
beg you, I beseech you: first of all, consider the good of your native land.
Until you find what you desire, until you meet with what you seek,
appoint a man to rule the land in your place. Take from your country all
the men you wish and go out on your quest for the lady Rodamni.'

I accepted this counsel and advice and said to my dear kinsman, 'You are
the leading man and my first kinsman.[N590] It is you that I leave here in
my place until I find what I desire, obtain the joy I long for, and boldly
return to my country. I am leaving my land and my home to go and roam
the world in my quest for Silver Castle and the fair Rodamni. If any friend
or kinsman wishes to come with me and *share my suffering, I thank him.*
Let him come[54] and let him be assured that he will be a great comfort in
my afflictions.'

And the nobles, the rulers of my land, heard the news.[N600] Men vied[55] to
be the first to give their sons to comfort and serve me. So I departed from
my country and left my home. I had with me, my friend, a hundred men
in all, who, I swear by my heart's countless woes, could have conquered a
thousand with their javelins alone.

Livistros sets out from
his home in search of
his love, the lady
Rodamni.
So I departed from my country and left
my home. How shall I tell you, my
friend, of the great desire,[N610] the great
anxiety I felt as I went along the road
with those hundred companions before

we found Rodamni's castle? I shall not describe to you, my friend, what happened in the intervening time, the good and the bad we suffered together before we came upon her castle. When we were close to it we came out of difficult ground and entered a meadow. At first we lay down[56] to rest ourselves after the past years.[(N620)] It was evening when we came to the meadow, my friend, and we immediately encamped and slept.

The unfortunate Livistros finds Rodamni's castle after much misfortune and much longing.
In the morning the sun rose and the castle appeared. The sun's rays shone out and struck the castle, and other rays from the castle hit the sun. You would love to see it, my friend, and if we live you shall. The castle vied with the sun in splendor. If by chance you had wished to gaze at the sun,[(N630)] it was there, striking the battlements, and you saw it clearly and beyond question as it rose at dawn from within the castle. But if by chance you had wished to gaze at silver you would have seen the castle's stones shining like pure sterling, refined to the utmost. You would have seen the contest between the sun and the castle. The sun was in its glory and the stone was turned to silver.

At dawn the sun rose and woke us all. I went out of my tent and when I saw the castle facing us[(N640)] I shouted in joy to my countrymen, 'Look! Silver Castle! We're there!'

The hundred also saw Silver Castle and we were seized by joy. Our sorrow left us. *In their delight all shouted ecstatically,*[57] 'Livistros, from now on live! You have found what you desire.'

I unfolded my tent and raised my standard. After assembling my men and companions I announced my decision that we should remain there in the meadow. They all released their horses. The place was thrown into confusion and the meadow thundered with the neighing of the hundred chargers.[(N650)] Without a care, we spent the whole day at rest. Towards the hour of evening, the hour of repose, we all caught our horses, saddled them, and, to relieve our many woes, I rode together over the lovely meadow. We began to sport and joust.

*Livistros mounts his horse and sports with his javelin in the company of his hundred fellow countrymen.

They heard the noise inside the castle and saw the large gathering and our camp.[(N660)] A messenger came from Silver Castle to discover what the commotion made by the large crowd was and to whom the camp and tents belonged. One of my hundred told him:

'It is the chief of the land of Livandros, the splendid Livistros and his men. For two years now he has roamed and searched much of the world. Countless are the misfortunes he has seen and the hardships he has suffered. He has come to this place and has found great relief. After the many labors he has endured[N670] he wishes, good sir, a little time to refresh himself. And what, good sir, is the name of this splendid castle we see? And the name of its king?'

'This is Silver Castle and its king is Chrysos. His daughter is the virtuous lady Rodamni.'

When the messenger learnt who was making the noise and whose camp it was, he went and gave King Chrysos a clear account of it and of my men. When the whole day had passed[N680] and with the approach of evening the night drew near, I dined and took counsel with my hundred young men.

I said to them, 'As soon as we see the dawn breaking we shall strike camp, approach the castle and pitch camp within an arrow-shot of it.'

All approved of my plan. My men bade me good night and left me alone with my squires inside my quarters. Now hear again, my friend, what the night wove[N690] and what the lord of love and passion again showed to me. I After I lay down upon my bed I immediately fell asleep. Again I saw Love in a dream. He flew up and brazenly entered my quarters. When he came in he grazed my head with his arrow and said, 'You are sleeping, Livistros?' He immediately woke me. 'From now have no worry. Do not grieve,' he said. 'You have reached your goal. You can already see Rodamni's castle.[N700] Know that I now leave you and go to pierce the fair one[58] with desire for you. And now farewell, Livistros. Have no worry.'

The woebegone Livistros's third dream about Love.

He went out of my tent and disappeared. When I woke from my dream I again looked, in much confusion, to find Love. The night ran its course and departed. Again I saw the dawn begin to break and I rose joyously from my tent. *I went out to my young men and walked around to them all, explaining the web of my dream.*[59] All said to me, 'From now on rejoice, my lord.'[N710]

And I said to my friend, 'Let me
interrupt you a moment. Tell me
something that escapes me. I bring this
to your attention again for an
explanation.'

*Klitovon asks Livistros
about the previously
<mentioned> three faces
of Love.*

**Livistros instructs his
excellent friend
Klitovon in the even-
handedness of Passion.*

And he said to me: About the three
faces of Love which the prophet
described and explained to me? | The
prophet told me, 'Livistros,[60] hear and
learn about the three faces of Love
which you see.*(N720)* I shall teach you what this means. When he arouses
desire, Love does not distinguish between faces. One person is old and
uninterested in passion, another is of the right age and *should be
concerned with it, and another is an utter child and not yet ripe for love.
But whether it is an old man or a child or a man in his prime, desire and
passion are the same and there is no distinction between them when it
comes to loving. And because of this you see that the expression people
use* respite <from desire> *is without meaning, no matter who uses it.
Every nature, whether of old or young, or of one in the prime of life or in
first infancy*[61]—know that the passion which you have seen in yourself
goes to them all. Be assured that the lords of love have no preference for
anything. This I swear by the sword of Passion.' This, my friend, is the
explanation given to me by the prophet about Love's three faces. Now
listen again and attend to my story*(N730)* of how we left the camp and of
the kingdom we found at Silver Castle.

But, my friend, evening has now overtaken us and we have come to a
town. Let us find an inn. When we start again and take to the road I shall
resume my story of how we found the castle and entered the realm of the
lady Rodamni. Now is the time for sleep, my friend. Let us go to bed.

We spent the night together and the next day*(N741)* we again mounted our
horses and took to the road. Again the love-afflicted man began his tale.

'You remember, my friend, where I stopped the story of my love which I
told you yesterday?'

And I replied, 'Yes, it was with the three faces of Love and *how you were
about to approach the castle,*[62] and how you fell in love with the lady.'

The second part of the story of the love of Livistros and Rodamni.[63]

He went on: Yes, and I related the dream I had. This I told to my men and they said to me,[(N750)] 'Why do you waste time, Livistros, lord of our land? Why do you let slip the occasion for your venture? Why are you waiting for another two years to pass? Why, tell us, do you still wish to suffer woes?*[64] Why are you dithering? We are angry with you. Why are you gripped by anxiety? Why are you tortured by fear? Why does danger disturb you and make you wait? Here is the castle. You have found it. Why wait? Tell us!'

*Livistros addresses his hundred men.

When I heard the anxieties of my men I said to them:[65] 'Dear friends who have borne my troubles, you who dwell in my land and share my castle,[(N760)] for two years now you have suffered with me, you have borne my many woes, you have shared my many afflictions, you have endured my many misfortunes, you have joined in my unbearable sorrows. After the many miseries we bore together we have now found what we always sought and have come to a sweet place of freedom. But take care that we are not over-hasty and that after so many toils the fruit of our great labor is not wasted.[(N770)] Rather, let us wait. Let us examine the castle and discover where the lady's bedroom lies. Let us set up camp near there and stay a month, taking care to establish friendly relations with the castle. And we must be always gathering information and examining the area. With a subterfuge of Passion we shall, little by little, come to see what we desire. Love does not deceive us. We shall live years with her and find happiness and joy. Passion has confirmed that he will not change his goal. Love is making his poison turn to sweetness.'[(N780)]

My friend, all my men were pleased with my plan. We started at dawn and came to the castle. We saw its beauty and its construction. As far as I can describe it, your soul will be amazed.

Description of Rodamni's Silver Castle.

Rodamni's castle, my friend, had three sides and on each there were twelve towers. On all the battlements stood men of brass and stone. The artist had represented them in arms.[(N790)] If you had seen them, my friend, I think you would certainly have said that they were alive and were standing in line for battle. The artist had fashioned others as well. *One was playing a mousiki,*[66] another a lyre. A third was playing a flute skilfully and with feeling and you heard every note of each reed sound with the breath[67] of the wind as it came from the artist's invention.

You would have supposed that whole castle was from one block as there were no separate stones with joints.[(N800)] Carved on the left side near the gate I saw the Twelve Virtues. *Each held a sign in her hand; all contained writing and one was displayed in front of each female figure.*[68]

Description of the   The first was Wisdom holding a sign.
Twelve Virtues.   She was represented as standing pensive
                          and noble and, with one hand bent up
to her forehead, she indicated with a finger the honesty of her thought and the purity of her mind. With her other hand she held her sign.[(N810)] Hear, my friend, what the letters said: 'Intelligence knows to look to the conclusion towards which matters tend and then attempts the beginning with a view to the end.'[69]

I saw Bravery standing beside her with bold appearance and *in one hand she held a sign and in the other a spear.*[70] The words on her sign said: 'I judge him a coward who looks to the conclusion towards which matters tend. I judge him without boldness and bereft of courage.'[71]

Next I saw Truth standing intrepidly with a red rose in one hand.[(N820)] In her other was a sign and its words said: 'Honest intelligence achieves boldness; it does not fail. It accomplishes what it desires and never shrinks.'

Beside her was Faith[72] and she was represented as pensive and serious, with a contemplative mien. In one hand she held a cross and in the other a sign. The letters written there said: 'Know that, when you lack faith, even if you tell the truth you are erring in respect of the truth. Be assured of this by me.'

Hear how I saw Justice beside Faith.[(N830)] She had a joyous appearance and a pleasant glance. One hand held a balance for weighing and the other, my friend, a sign with the letters: 'Without deeds you are futile;[73] learn this from me ... [*Three unintelligible words*]. Believe what I tell you.'

Beside her was Prudence bending slightly to the ground. One hand held a myrtle sprig and the other bore a sign with the letters: 'You may be truthful, just and of correct faith, but all merits are part of prudence.'[(N840)]

After her I saw Humility standing there. She had a gentle demeanor and very pleasant appearance. Her face was kind and one hand she kept to her breast. In the other she had a sign with the letters: 'Every humble person possesses faith and truth. Without doubt, he certainly knows what is just.'

After her was Affection.[74] *She had a trace of shyness.*[75] She was leaning over and looking at the ground and her appearance was serious. The words on the sign she held said:[N850] 'You may be humble but if you do not observe affection your feelings are not to be relied upon. Be informed of this.'

Next I saw Prayer, a woman in appearance, weary and sober. She kept her eyes on the ground, and the words on the sign she held said: 'Do not pray, O mortal, only for those you love. Pray also for those who hate you.'

Next I saw fair Patience, pensive and sober. You seemed to be looking at an angry person who was standing there tongue-tied in rage.[N860] One hand was on her cheek and the other held a sign with the writing: 'Anger and vexation are blamed by all, but everyone admires patience.'

Standing beside her I found Hope. She was gazing up at the heavens and pointing there with her hand that was next to Patience. In her other hand was a sign whose words said: 'Mortal, be bold! I bid you never to despair. Put your hope in Heaven for assistance.'[N870]

Then I saw fair Charity standing with one hand laden with money which she was giving to the poor. In the other was a sign, my friend, whose words said: 'You who are fortunate, look to those in distress. Pity those who weep[76] lest you be condemned to die.'

I read the messages of the Twelve Virtues which I found on one side of Silver Castle. And carved on the other side of the gate stood the Twelve Months.[N880] These too all had signs with writing.

Livistros also describes   March appeared as an armed soldier,
the Twelve Months.[77]   covered with steel from top to toe. He
                                 was girt about with weapons and with
one hand *he brandished a lance and in the other he held a shield. On his shield was*[78] a sign with the words: 'I am the year's leader, a soldier ready for war. At this time do not stay seated, move against your enemies!'

Next was April, who appeared as a shepherd, hatless, with dishevelled hair and unkempt appearance.[N890] There were sheep in front of him which he, as their shepherd, was grazing. One hand held a shepherd's pipe and the other a sign with the words: 'As a shepherd I tend and pasture many sheep. Frolicking lambs are my joy.'

Next I found May, a man of handsome appearance, fair in build, and also in appearance. My friend, on his head he had a chaplet of flowers, and in one hand he held red roses, in the other a sign with these words:[N900] 'Men of complaisance, savor the world's beauty. Do not pass by its blessings. Enjoy and relish them.'

Then I saw June, a stout man. His shoulders were broad, his head large and his waist thick-set. His arms were naked up to the elbow and he lay stretched out in a blooming meadow. In his hands he held flowers of various colors and among them a sign on which these words were written: 'I rejoice in the beauty of the sweet season. I delight in the scents of its many flowers.'[N910]

Next I saw July, who was also stout. His arms were bare and his dress all gathered up. On his head was a chaplet made from ears of corn. One hand held a scythe for harvesting while the other labored at collecting the corn. Behind him was a sign on which these words were written: 'I harvest the earth's produce which I have labored to sow. I shall increase my crop tenfold at the harvest.'

I next saw August, also a stout man, my friend. He was standing by a pool, *washed and groomed.*[79] He was thirsty from the heat. In one hand[N921] *he held a cup with wine and he was drinking because of the heat. In the other he held a sign with writing. Hear and learn, my friend, what it said:*[80] 'Let those whom the heat of the pool burns and inflames to thirst drink cold water *and not put aside wine.*'[81]

I found September gathering from the vine . . . [*An unintelligible line*] . . . and in his other hand was a sign with these words: 'I gather what my eyes have guarded for three years. I eat the harvest and drink its sweetness.'

Next I saw October in human form.[N930] He was a hunter, but of small birds. *In one hand he held a cage with birds and he kept his gaze on the sky. In his other hand he had a sign*[82] on which these words were written: 'I watch, I track, I hunt and catch birds with my skill. This is my delight and my amusement.'

After him I saw November too, my friend, a farmer in build and in appearance. In his sack he had wheat for sowing and in his hand a sign covered with writing which said: 'I sow the earth and next year I harvest the seed. For all I give to the earth it repays me threefold.'[(N940)]

Then I found December standing there, also a farmer. In one hand *he had a sack with seed, a stick and a goad. The other hand held a sign with writing. And hear, my friend, what it said: 'At this time all farmers have rightly stopped their sowing. The weather is wet and does not mature the seed.'* [83]

January was next and he too was standing, a complete hunter, totally bold in appearance. A dog followed him and he held a falcon. In his hand he had a sign on which these words were written:[(N950)] 'No hunter *should be idle lest he let the time go.*[84] The season cries to him to go hunting.'

I saw February in the form of *a very old man, to judge from his hair and his appearance.*[85] He wore a fur coat in front of a fire that he was lighting to warm himself against the season's cold. In front of him lay a sign on which the words said: 'Because of the season's bitter chill I am warming myself. Do not abuse me because you see me old.'

Such were the messages of the Twelve Months which the wondrous stone-carver had made.[(N960)] And on the back wall, which was on the other side and where the lady's chamber was placed, the Twelve Cupids were standing with signs, all inscribed. I shall tell you of each, my friend.

The first was Longing and she had this message: 'Romantic longing *has skilful words and needs a persistent soul if it is not to be neglected.*' [86]

Next was Respect and she had written: 'Desire born of respect tells no lies in the world[(N970)] but its sweet charm wins praise in lovers.'

The words in Affection's hand read: 'Affection binds even amid shame, and all the world's envy, even if united, cannot break its bond.'

Beside her stood Friendship and on the sign she held were these words: '*There is no fairer thing in the world than friendship, especially if it comes*[87] from the heart of a young woman in love.'

Then I saw Fondness and she had this message:[88] 'Show fondness in your longing so that you never part. Expectation is a fair thing and gives full recompense.'

After her I saw Remembrance with the message: 'Remember with passion, I command you, whenever you are separated. Always keep love's yearnings in your mind.'

I also saw Recollection and on her sign was written: 'In your passion keep the recollection of love. Never for one moment dismiss the thought of its aptness from your heart.'

Standing by her I saw Good Repute, and in her hands she held a sign with the message:[S10] 'He whose desires are in accordance with good repute wins much fame because good repute is great in the world.'

Next to her I saw Probity standing and she held in her hand a sign which said: 'A person who shows probity in love never fails. He will attain all he desires.'

Standing by her I also spied Courtesy with her sign. Hear what it said: 'If a person is courteous and loves from his heart, his courtesy will not fail to gain him his wish.'[S20]

After her I saw fair Patience standing with a message which cried out: 'In the art of love the patient man and he who waits for a year have an advantage over the impatient.'

Next I saw Expectation and she too had a message: 'Wait, do not give up if what you desire delays for years. Yearning plants patience in the soul.'

These were the fair representations that I saw on the other side <of the castle>. I was affected at the sight and my mind was in suspense. As I went around examining the signs[S30] and looking at the figures around the castle which held them I saw where the lady's bedchamber stood. I then told my men to set up my tent opposite. From here I could see the Virtues, from there the Months, and from another point the Cupids and the figures above them. My mind was breaking into a hundred pieces as it contemplated how to begin courting the lady and what stratagem to use. I spent one day. Two days passed,[S40] three, four, and then one of my men gave me some advice.

But, my friend, after the passage of many days I noticed that men and women, old and young together, were bending over the castle's walls to see our camp and tents. And at the point where lady Rodamni's bedchamber stood I saw fair young women leaning over the wall with an extremely handsome eunuch who was the lady's confidant[S50] in her talk, her secrets and her hidden counsels. Hear then the advice which one of my hundred youths gave me.[89]

He gives Livistros   He said, 'Livistros, many days have
advice on his love.   passed and we have now become known
                                to the castle. Do you see the eunuch
there who is leaning over the wall? I am now prepared to strike up a
friendship with him as he will be of service in courting the lady. But my
advice is this—follow it without delay:[(S60)] write a message on an arrow.
When you notice one of the lady's fair women leaning out from her
splendid bedchamber to look at us, *pretend that you see a bird on the
chamber*[90] and gently shoot the arrow, taking care that it falls inside.
Then you will create an opportunity for love to begin and you will
discover how you can succeed in your venture.'

I was heartened by his counsel and his words pleased me. 'First,' I said,
'try the way of friendship[(S70)] so that, with you as an ally inside, I shall
learn what the situation is. Likewise, I too shall be ready for the venture.'

*Livistros's first   He went out of my tent, leaving me
attempt at declaring his   there. I He dressed as a merchant,
passion to the lady.   entered the castle and somehow or other
                                 won their friendship. That was all I
knew. Days passed and I noticed him lean out of the castle from the place
of the lady's bedchamber, make a sign of greeting to me,[(S80)] then
withdraw inside quickly so that no-one perceived him. After I had seen
him I sat down and wrote a letter onto an arrow, my friend. Hear what it
said:

He writes a letter on an   'Arrow, if you can hit a bird as you
arrow and fires it to her.   have hit me, your archer must have a
                                 rare hand. But if your success is only in
a human heart, hit the lady in the castle as well as me, that fairest lady of
all,[91] and let her suffer as I have suffered.'

I finished the letter and went out of my tent.[(S90)] After loading my bow
and taking note of the bedchamber I pretended to aim at a bird and drew
back the arrow. Around the lady's chamber there ran a balcony and it was
onto this balcony that the arrow fell. Again I went inside my tent. Again
I searched for the right moment to show my love of the fair one and
pondered on how to start:

The unfortunate Livistros's painful reflections.

'At any rate I have now already wasted two years. I have gone through many places and endured suffering.*(S100)* After many miseries I have found what I desired and my mind has attained what it passionately longed for. How am I now to begin upon my love? In what friend can I confide what I desire? Shall I first send a messenger? But to whom shall I send him? Shall I then write a letter? But who will read it? Suppose I find a friend and tell him what I am suffering. How will he venture to inform the lady? Imagine that by some trick he tells her. If she is haughty will she be angry with this?*(S110)* Neither is she acquainted with me nor does she know who I am. Perhaps the young woman will take action against me. But I cannot think that lies come from Love's mouth and I know that he has promised to hit her with his bow. He told me that he would grant me her love. Suppose he lied. What made him do it? Suppose she agrees and, in accepting my love, falls in love herself. How shall I know this? Will she write to me? But this is not proper. So I think I should write to her first.*(S120)* If she accepts my letter this will be a great success. But if she does not accept it I shall try again. I shall write three, four, five letters or even more. From so many she will accept one.'

With these ideas I searched and deliberated. Deep in thought, I rose, went out of my tent, and stood there troubled, holding one of the tent-ropes. My mind was in confusion from such a difficult situation. While I was standing there with my endless troubles and looking, I noticed the lady's room*(S130)*—I directed my attention to her bedchamber and saw the fair women around the balcony fighting as to who should have the arrow. One took it and ran, then another grabbed it. All were in confusion as to who should have it. At one point there was silence. The young women stood still. One held the arrow while the others stood and read what was on it. And when all had read they ran together and entered the lady's room. Whether the lady had seen the writing on the arrow or whether she had not read it (as I afterwards learnt),*(S140)* when she saw the girls quarreling she asked them the reason for their argument and what they were fighting about.

They gave her the arrow with its writing which they had found. She snatched it, read it, looked at it, examined it, and when she understood what was written on it she asked where they had found it and from whom the message came. They told her where they had discovered it and the young woman calmly said, 'And who could have written on it? Take care to find out.'

The lady took the arrow but did not give it back. She held it in her hands and gazed at what it said.*(S150)* She kept giving orders to find out who had written the message. A short time after, Rodamni left. She played with the arrow, to which she had taken a fancy.

The noble lady walked around the castle's battlements with a single maid, her fancy still taken with the arrow. She stared at me, and talked to the eunuch. I recognized who she was from her appearance. She realized to whom the arrow belonged. My mind was anxious to write a letter.*(S160)* Hear, my friend, what I wrote to her in it:

The beginning of the | 'If your soul had learnt of me, if you
letter which Livistros | knew who I am and for whom I suffer,
wrote to the lady. | if there were anywhere a person to tell
you how much time I have spent for

you, how many dangers I have run and woes I have endured, what manner of things have happened to me because of you—I think that if you had feelings of stone and a heart of iron you would take pity on me when you learnt what I suffer.*(S170)* I have no-one who could tell you of me. I have only Love and I have confidence in him. I hope that he puts concern for me into your heart. He is slow to act.[92] He is sluggish in what he promised me. I have no-one to whom I can tell my sufferings.[93] Believe me, my heart is being torn by my troubles. Here now is my letter, read what I suffer. Know whose message it is. Have mercy on him. Pity him. For two years now he has been wandering because of desire for you.'

I wrote this message, my friend, and sealed it up with a ribbon.*(S180)* Again, at the hour of twilight, when evening was beginning, I fastened it to an arrow, I shot it at the lady's quarters and again I landed it onto her balcony.

But at about midnight that evening my man who had gone to seek friendship with the eunuch came to me. He entered my quarters, approached me and said, 'Are you sleeping, Livistros? Arise from your slumbers!'

I got up and when I saw him I embraced and kissed him. He said to me, 'You can now rejoice. Have no worry.*(S190)* I have now made the eunuch my friend. He has spoken to me in private and told me his secrets. We have sworn a terrible oath that we would conceal what we say to each other and that no-one would hear it. After I had won him over and he had gained confidence in me he said, "I shall tell you something now that the occasion has passed. The lady had a dream in her chamber. A winged boy came to her. He flew through the sky at an eager pace and after entering her chamber said to her,*(S200)*| 'Livistros, prince[94] of the land of Livandros, the country of the Latins, has been

Love talks to the lady in her dream.

wandering for two years from desire for you. He has seen terrible dangers and endured woes. From now receive desire for him into your heart. Take up love of him. Enslave yourself to him. Bend your neck, as yet unbent, to love of him. Throw away your haughtiness. Give up your pride. He has suffered much for you. Do not resist.'

' "When he had addressed her and was leaving*(S210)* he shot the untamed girl right in the heart. In her fear she woke, shouted for me and said, 'Vetanos, go! Catch the murderous archer who has wounded my heart and cut me in two!' I arose, saw her, and took her by the hand. 'Stop, don't be afraid,' I said. 'Surely you had a dream.' She replied, 'There was a young[95] boy here with wings and when he had addressed me and was leaving he shot an arrow at my heart and disappeared.' Everyone was in confusion and afraid for the lady.*(S220)* King Chrysos came, stood by her, and asked if she had been dreaming during the evening,[96] and what was it that she had dreamed. The lady did not admit it was a dream but said, 'A robber holding a bow entered, rushed over[97] and shot me. I was panic-stricken and my fear woke me up.'

' "The confusion and turmoil came to an end. All dispersed and we were left alone. King Chrysos went to his chamber. The lady remained and talked with me.*(S230)* She talked about Livistros, the prince of Livandros, and told me endlessly about her dream. From then on care entered her mind so that she scarcely ever rested night or day. Her mind was forever troubled by her dream and the boy she saw in it. When Livistros came and set up camp the lady saw him and realized that the arrow was from him, but she was afraid of the bad opinions that people might have. She said to me, her eunuch, 'Go, take him greetings from me,*(S240)* and say to him, "Write, do not hesitate. The lady desires your letters. There is no way she can be swayed by a single message from you. The lady is fair and she bears her beauty as befits her and is proud of it." ' Attend to this now and I trust you will win the lady's love with your letters." This, Livistros, is what the eunuch told me when I had won him over and gained him as a friend.'

And after he had spoken I asked him, 'How did you approach the eunuch and win him as a friend?' [98]

He replied, 'Do not ask me now. It is night and I am anxious to enter the castle immediately because I have orders*(S250)* that the morning star should not find me outside. But know that the lady is keeping the letter you wrote. She looks at it, reads it, and recites its contents. I know from her manner that she is yearning for you. Farewell, Lord Livistros, ruler of my land.'

He went off in great haste leaving me reeling in the depths of longing. When day came I arose from sleep, went out of my tent and saw my men. I told them to come to me and they began to address me, and to converse*(S260)* on various topics. A short time after they bade me farewell, leaving me in my tent with my squires. I stood watching the lady's chamber and my eyes roamed over the balcony. After a time the fair lady, preceded by her eunuch and followed by her maids, came from her chamber. In her hands she was holding the letter I had written—the eunuch had the first arrow. The lady came out and cast a glance from the tower.*(S270)* She went up and down and had the appearance of being in love. She read the letter, looked at the eunuch, seemed to smile, looked at the wall again and then went inside her chamber.

When I saw that the young woman was again holding the letter I wrote another. Hear it, my friend:

Another letter which Livistros wrote to the lady. 'When are you to walk in the castle of my soul? When are you to enter the tower of my heart and plant imperious steps upon me?*(S280)* When are your hands to lock its gates so that they never open again? When will you sit in my loving heart and rule as its sovereign so that its trust[99] is in you? Instead of this, I am enslaved by desire for you; instead, the castle of my heart is betrayed, fair one, by tyrannical love for you. I would not find my bondage strange if it were by your choice and your will, and if it were not[100] in spite of you that I am drowned.*(S290)* So much am I being tormented by love for you and it is without your knowledge or your wish. But I have faith in Love, I trust his honest nature. He said that he was telling no lie and that he would bring this to completion. You alone will subdue the castle of my heart. You will imperiously enter the tower of my soul. Envy's plot will vanish from our midst and, after being a slave, I shall win my freedom. I shall enjoy the fruits of my woes. Envy will not be victorious.'

I wrote this letter, my friend, I tied it*(S300)* onto an arrow and again fired it up to the lady's noble chamber. It must have been the hour of breakfast.

The eunuch came out, looked and recognized the letter. He knew from whom it came. He stooped, picked it up from the ground and immediately went into the fair lady's chamber. What he said to her about the arrow I learnt from my man.

'Madam Rodamni, queen of the graces, look! I have found a message which was lying on the balcony.*(S310)* What it contains I do not know. Take it and read it. Tell me what it says and for whom it is meant.'

She stretched out her hand, took it and untied the ribbon. She unrolled it, looked and read its message. When she had finished she threw the letter down and seemed to sigh. She said to the eunuch:

'Vetanos, I do not know whose the letter is nor for whom it is meant, but my command is this: if I find any of my maids or my ladies receiving a message or sending a reply*(S320)* let her know that I shall immediately put her to death.'

When he heard the lady's angry reply he stood his ground and replied with these words: | 'Give up your anger, my lady, it does not become you.

Give up your great rage against
The eunuch boldly   passion. Give up your wrath against
replies to the lady.   those suffering from love. Fear lest by
                                 chance you be caught in desire's bond.
See that you do not step into affection's depths. Beware lest the furnace of passion burns you.*(S330)* Take good care that you do not drown in a sea of longing. Beware lest a wave of yearning lashes your heart and you drown through your own violence. If this happens, you will suffer what others have suffered through desire, you will pity those whom the flame of affection burns, you will swoon with those whom yearning torments, your eyes will see those whom the hands of cupids have shot with their arrows, and your soul will suffer.'

When he told her this, the eunuch went out and left her to brood on his words.*(S340)*

I went out again and stood by my tent. My inner being was wrapped in passion's distress. Because of my desire for the lady I resolved not to fail. Shortly after, my friend, I chanced to see both the eunuch and my own man. The two were leaning over the wall and indicating to me, 'Write!' I left where I was, entered my tent, and, my friend, I wrote another letter. Hear what it said:

*Another woebegone
letter of the woebegone
Livistros.*

'Love, you are aware of[101] the ill treatment I have suffered in the world,[(S350)] I know. It has not escaped you. Love, I remember all the promises that you made me in the dream you sent. Nothing has escaped me. Now, because of your promise, I alone have renounced my place, my country and land, my home, my native city, and the world. Because of you and your promise I have entered into captivity. Because of the dream I threw myself into troubles[102] and, for two years, suffered countless woes. I came to this land of sweetness. I found what the dream had mentioned.[(S360)] But after my misfortunes, of which I have often told you, I found the haughty lady and I have spent six months here. My hands have written letters every day but she does not accept a single one. Now, dear Love, I beseech this of you. Consider what I tell you. If you have fired your arrow at her too, let me know this. Let her receive my letter. Let her read what I have written. Let her learn of my desire and write a reply. But if you have made my heart grieve alone and your arrow has not touched her, know that you are wronging me[(S370)] and that I shall fill the world with your injustice.'

I wrote the letter. It too I sealed, and, once more, shot it onto the lady's balcony. The eunuch came out immediately, looked, recognized it and said again:

'I have found a letter, princess.'

She replied, 'Let me see it, Vetanos.'

He gave it to the young woman. She untied its ribbon with her hands, stood and read it, and said to the eunuch:

'Give me the other letter as well which you found some days ago.'

He produced it and gave it to her. She put the two together,[(S380)] tied them into one bundle, as I afterwards discovered, and gave them to her maid, to whom she said, | 'Alas for this man! Who he is, I do not know. Many

*The lady's distressed
words of acquiescence.*

are the woes he has suffered in the world for his desire, great is the bitterness his soul has endured for love, and fearsome are the troubles and hardships he has withstood. He is afraid to confess for whom he suffers this. I would, in the name of truth, like to know who he is and for whom he endures this. I could then feel sorry for him.'*(S390)*

'The eunuch seized the opportunity to address the lady and again taking a bold stand said to her, | 'Pity those smitten by desire, feel sorry for those

The eunuch warns the
lady about love.

burnt by passion, grieve for those whom Love in his anger has afflicted. Consider the letters and learn for whom they are intended. They are not for your maid, madam, they are for you. Think of the dream, my lady, which you had. Consider for whom it said you were destined.'

The lady listened to the eunuch and sighed.*(S400)* Tears sprang to her eyes, and she said sadly, 'Happy the man whom Love's bow has not hit! Happy the person whom Desire's bolt has not struck! He has lived a happy life and days without pain. But alas for the man whom Love's bow has hit and Desire's bolt has consumed! The years he has lived have been filled with anguish.'

After she had spoken to him, the lady left and in her distress went to her bedchamber. She was drowning in the depths of her desire for Livistros.*(S410)* When the eunuch saw her affliction he sadly went to his bedroom and said to my man, 'I congratulate you. The fair one is smitten with desire for Livistros. Go and take care to tell him that letters should not stop coming from his hands.'

That day came to an end. I saw the sun set and the evening draw near. I noticed that the moon was shining. The night passed and day appeared.*(S420)* After some time the young woman came out, preceded by the eunuch and followed by two maids. They sang me a charming song. Hear what it said, my friend:

The lady's song of
passion to the young
man.

'A young man left his country, the captive of his desire for a fair lady, and suffered countless tortures. This knight wishes that the lady too should learn what he suffers. But he cannot speak of it, and his woe consumes him. He complains loudly and is choked by his grief.*(S430)* In his great affliction he tells his story to Love.'

Further painful reflections of the distressed Livistros.

When after a time the young women had finished their song, they returned inside the bedchamber. I But I watched the tower where the lady was. Finally, I went away, entered my tent and fell on my bed, seized by Love's desire. Of its own accord my mind began to reflect and ponder:

'When shall I enter the castle and climb its tower?
When shall I receive the lady's joyful message?[(S440)]
When shall I hold her letter in my hands?
When shall the fair one's mouth say, "Livistros"?
When shall I see her chamber and hear her talk?
When shall I tread joyfully in her room?
When shall I hold her hand, kiss her lips and have her fill my mouth with sweetness?
When shall I fulfil my yearning and embrace the crystal skin of the fair one's neck with endless kisses?
And when shall I stretch my hands over her entire body and make her dance with desire as I feel her every limb?[(S450)]
When shall I enjoy what I crave and gain my wish? Will it happen?
When shall I find happiness? When shall I leave behind the troubles which I suffer daily?'

When I had done with such great longing my man arrived from the castle, came into my bedchamber and said to me: 'You are sleeping?'

I replied, 'No.' I took him and again covered him with kisses. From his bosom he took a letter which the eunuch had written and gave it to me. Hear, my friend, what the eunuch's letter said:[(S460)]

'Though to you I am an unknown stranger, I am your servant. You have as yet neither met nor spoken to me. I am sending you this letter, Livistros, lord of the land, so that you may know from what I write that I am at your service. Because I am not known to you,[103] take note of the help I have rendered you. Know that the lady sighs with desire for you. She has fallen in love with you and suffers for your woes. But young women give themselves a haughty air. If she has not yet yielded to you, do not think that she does not desire you.[(S470)] This is through the haughtiness of the lady who was born of the sun. But write, write, Livistros, write. Do not be indolent. She has your earlier letters. She keeps them and reads them. She examines them word by word and her soul reflects on your misery of two years.'

I read the message and was somewhat comforted. Again I asked my man to tell me how he had won the eunuch's friendship. He replied:

'Do not worry now. I am anxious to leave. I shall tell you later—do not make me explain at this moment.*(S480)* But you should write a reply to the eunuch immediately.'

So I sat down and wrote myself to the eunuch. Hear what I said to him in my letter:[104]

I send another letter in   'Friend whom I have not met, servant
reply to the eunuch.   whom I do not know, I thank you for
                                   your service. I marvel much at how
you have served me and have shown a liking for the unknown man with
whom you have never sat. In this I see the probity of your upbringing,
your courtesy towards me, and your nobility. Although you do not know
me, you desire my affection*(S490)* and wish to be bound to me by service. I
hope that you will come to know my friendship and you will become
inseparable from me for all the days of your life.'

My friend, I gave the message to my man and let him go. When alone, I
again fell to thought, and my mind exhausted itself on what I should write
to her who was born of the sun. Hear, my friend, my letter to Rodamni:

Another reply of   'Comfort of my soul, sweet love of my
Livistros to the lady.   heart, passion which I embrace, and
                                desire in which I find joy,*(S500)* hear my
sufferings, learn of my griefs, pity me for my distress, give me comfort,
cast aside your disdain, give up your pride, see what is killing me and
have pity. I am drowning in the depths of desire for you. Separation's
dread wave is beating down upon me, it throws me down into the abyss of
despair. Sit and reflect on how I have been tortured, the many griefs I have
endured and the dangers I have faced. If you are the offspring of Love and
have been instructed by the Graces,*(S510)* if you have been reared by Desire
and are possessed by Sensibility, share my woes, pity what I suffer. Take
my letter in your hands, read it with your soul and write me a reply. Let
me receive a letter from you and see your writing. Let me revive a little
from what is choking me. Believe me, my heart has suffered much for
you. It groans under the load of misfortune's burdens. It is laden with a
huge mountain of grief. If you do not give up your pride*(S520)* I shall now
kill myself and go down to Hades.'

You have heard this letter, my friend. Now learn of the next:

*Another painful letter of
Livistros to the lady.*

'They say that if[105] a drop falls constantly on a rock, whatever the nature of the drop and the nature of the stone, *the steady beating bores through the stone*[106] because the water's dripping cannot be averted. I used to find this extraordinary. I was always amazed how a drop can pierce stone. But when I examine the matter I do not believe what men say. I do not think that a drop can bore through stone.[*(S530)*] My passion, as it beat on the rock of your heart, should have worn it away. For drops my passion has these many letters, my fair messages, my words of love. I think that if my letters' words had fallen on stone, even though it were rooted in Hades, the stone would have been wrenched up and would have come to understand[107] my letter; however lifeless it was, it would have been transformed into intelligence.

'So a drop is powerless against stone. It does not have the quality they say and their words are lies.[*(S540)*] A virtuous woman's heart surpasses a rock in hardness. The dew of my soul is now powerless and the spring of my heart cannot drip. It remains for me to beseech you, for me to confide my heart's woes in you. *It has submitted to the judgment*[108] of your love, my lady, and the courtesy of your mind.'

You have learnt the contents of this letter which I sent with my heart in turmoil. Hear what the lady wrote to me[*(S550)*] and how she received my message.

I again drew my bow and again shot the letter onto the lady's balcony. I then waited to see who would take it. After some time the lady came out, looked about, recognized the letter, picked it up furtively, then undid the ribbon and immediately unrolled it. After she had stood reading it she looked it up and down, called for the eunuch and said to him:[*(S559)*]

*The lady surrenders to
love for Livistros and
talks sadly to her
eunuch.*

'Well, you see how your urgency has affected me and into what depths your words on desire have plunged me! Your warnings have thrown me onto a precipice! You have dragged me into a sea of tenderness! Know that I have found yet another letter. It contains reproaches and I pity him. Hear this letter too, Vetanos.'

She read out the letter and the eunuch said:

'Yield now, abandon your pride.*(S570)* Write a reply yourself, give him comfort, feel grief for the woes he has suffered on your account and for the misery of his two years of searching. Pause, noble lady, and bring him sweetness.'

The lady's distressed words to herself about Livistros.

She listened to the eunuch, stood and sighed. She talked in a solitary fashion to herself: I 'Yield, my unbending soul, my proud neck. Submit to the bond of desire. Already you are afflicted.' Then, with her own hand, she wrote a letter*(S580)* which the eunuch dispatched to me. Hear it:

The first fully joyous letter of the lady to Livistros.

'I cried out to the heavens and I spoke to the clouds. I called on the earth as witness and I declared it to the sky: I would never bend my neck to the bond of desire. I imagined that I had bidden it farewell and I was proud. But now I see that the obstinacy I maintained has been bent. I have thrown aside my great pride. I have put my mind's freedom in your service and I have retrieved what I had dispatched.*(S590)* The oath that I swore by the heavens and ratified by the clouds, I now forswear. I repudiate it, I deny it. And tell me, sir, why do you claim that my soul is more unfeeling than stone because it did not come immediately to your love? My assertion and boast were that I was untouched by Love and outside his power. And how is it that I, who was without cares, am now plunged into them?'

This is what the fair one's letter contained, my friend. Hear what I wrote in reply:*(S600)*

Livistros's reply of love to the lady.

'You spoke to the heavens, fair lady, and you cried out to the clouds. You called the earth to witness that you would not enter upon desire. You swore a fearsome oath that you would not go back on your word. In this I do not disbelieve you. I believe what you say because you yourself were an offspring of the heavens. The clouds gave birth to you and if you had still been with them there is no doubt that you would have kept the oath you had sworn. Now, since you have fallen down to earth from the clouds and though born in the heavens,[109] you spend your time in this world with everyone else,*(S610)* it is not remarkable that you go against what you have sworn. In this you do no wrong at all, be assured by me. But if you see the man who has suffered for you, you will much regret the oaths you have sworn in your heart.[110] If you had made a hundred vows you would renounce them all. I

beseech you now: if I receive a token from you with your next letter I
shall regard it as I would you.'

I wrote the letter, my friend, and sealed it with a ribbon. Once more I
dispatched it as I was accustomed to do.*(S620)* Again the lady came out and
found the letter. She untied it, read it and sighed once more. Late in the
evening, when the moon had risen and was shining, the lady's maids came
out onto the balcony and began, my friend, to sing a ditty:

A love song on   'A youth who was captive to passion
Livistros's passion.   left his home for a fair meadow and
                             there set up camp. The dawn gave him
no sleep, the night could not overcome him. He was harassed by care and
tortured by anxiety.*(S630)* When would he see, when would he win the one
he longed for? He implored the sun, he made a vow to the moon that if he
gained his wish he would erect them a memorial. Fearsome were the pains
and hardships he endured. Finally he found what he desired but he is still
in agony.'

The fair ladies sang their ditty of love—I think they would have surpassed
even the songs of the Sirens—and after a short time went inside.*(S640)*
When I had heard the beautiful song, my hands moved once more to a
letter. This, my friend, is what I wrote to her:

Another letter of joy   'Dear Moon, you know the wrongs I
from the woebegone   have suffered. How much I have been
Livistros.   tormented by desire has not escaped
                             you. When at dawn its pangs gave me
no sleep, I rose early, stood up and noticed how you were dressed in
clouds. *Do not set now. I implore you to delay a little longer*[111] so that I
can tell you what I am suffering. After that, set if you will.*(S651)*
Tomorrow night, you can tell this to the woman who was born of the
sun. And now, dear Moon, I beseech you ten thousand times to pity my
woes, to go to the lady and assure her of what I endure, of what I suffer on
her behalf. Make fearsome vows to her. Beg her to send me another letter
with a token of herself so that I may see it and gain some relief in what
my soul desires, and this will not lead to my death.—This is what I told
the moon on your account:*(S660)* it should go to find you and tell you why
I am troubled.'

You have heard, my friend, the letter which I sent. The lady sent me
another. Listen while I tell you what she said:

The lady's distressed and
angry letter to
Livistros.
'It is enough that you have the letter which I wrote and that you have now bent an inflexible mind to desire. As for your eagerness to obtain a token as well from me and receive in your hands a pledge of my love, I am amazed that you feel no shame when you say so.*(S670)* In writing this to me the violence of your passion has led you too far. You will not see another letter from me. As long as you try to make me give you a token, you will die waiting as far as a letter goes. You will certainly not see one.'

And again they dispatched the letter to me. I reached down and took it. At first I was filled with joy but when I read it I seemed to be frozen to the spot. I did not know who I was. I became a corpse. After a time, my senses returned with a jolt and I went to write her a letter. Listen to it:*(S680)*

Livistros's reply of
sorrow and pain to the
lady.
'From the letter which your loving hand wrote, I saw death incarnate leap out and imperiously strike down my entire heart. I saw a letter of love become a man's grave and words of affection my soul's death. I thought, dear heart, that the letter was yours, that it was some message of comfort for my love. I cannot describe how I held it, how I embraced it and with what joy!*(S690)* But I did not know that it held death for me, that it convicted me to a time of despair. It gave me joy but on reading it my heart was lost, my mind was slain. I did not know who I was. I sought death. The letter itself, fair lady, felt pity for the one it had killed—your message of love had laid him low.[112] Revive him with another letter. Do not stop your letter from approaching me.*(S700)* Believe me, you are killing my heart. If it is true that you are a Christian, what I suffer through you . . . [*A short gap*] . . . do this. Give up your resolve not to send me a letter.'

I wrote this letter and again I dispatched it. Again the lady found and read it. She was distressed, she sighed over its message, she felt sorry for what it said, and again wrote me a reply:

The lady sends Livistros
a reply.
'A person could be worse than a robber, he could have the nature of an assassin, he could bear the soul of an executioner or have the temperament of a wild beast*(S710)* but still feel sorry for what your letter says. *How much more a human being who receives it,*[113] a

letter which tells of the death of an honorable man? How could that person's heart not be troubled by what it says? How could it not suffer through the contents of your sad letter? Know that I felt sorry for it. I was distressed by what you wrote and I shared your pain. Even though I said in my letter that I would not send you a message, my soul again grieved for you and I am writing a letter, a letter in my own hand. Read it and recognize from what I write that your suffering troubles me.*(S720)* I faint at your woes. Do not disbelieve me in this.'

Again they dispatched the letter to me. I snatched it, held it, kissed it, opened it, unrolled it. I read what it contained. I abandoned my grief and was comforted. I wrote a reply. Hear it:

Another letter of joy 'I faced death, disaster, and misfortune
from Livistros to the because of what you wrote in a letter.
lady. But because of what you now write
death has departed and the grave has
released me.*(S730)* Again I take joy in the world and I live because of your message. I have recognized the probity of your caution. I have learnt the compassion of your love for me. I also realize from what you say[114] that you are not insensitive. I write to you, my queen, to beseech you ten thousand times that you send me a token which I may have in your stead. After your letters you must at least do this. Show some pity. Send me a token so that I may have hope of support. I trust I shall not fail. But if you again do not send me your token,*(S740)* you again make me persevere. I hope for it in the future and you put me on the rack of my passion for you. I suffer countless pains for your love.'

I wrote my letter. Again I dispatched it and again I held the tent rope. I was impatient for them to find my message and read it. My letter
contained a ring. Hear what it was like.
*A superb description of I For a stone, my friend, it had a pure
the ring. ruby.*(S750)* On the inside was iron and
on the outside, lodestone. Between, to bind the iron and lodestone, was pure gold, refined to the utmost. Regarding the ring, I wrote in my letter: 'I send this enchanting ring which my love dedicates to you. Take it, wear it, and look upon it as you would me.'

The lady found the message and the ring. She stood admiring it, she held it, she put it on her finger and looked at it. She eagerly read the letter, she danced at what it said. She called for the eunuch and showed it to him*(S760)* together with the ring which she was wearing as my gift.

'You see this lovely ring?' she said. 'It is made of gold, iron, ruby and lodestone, the four elements of attraction which bond love.'

He replied, 'Yes, it is a noble ring. It testifies to his affection for you, fair lady. Now return his love. Show him comfort and write him a letter to make him more certain of your love.'

She sat down and wrote me a letter, my friend. Hear it:*(5769)*

The lady's superb letter   'Hear, O knight, what happened with
about the ring.   the ring you sent with your letter of
                                 love. Just as lodestone, from its nature,
attracts iron, so it drew out my heart with desire for you. It has left me
without a heart but in its place I have your ring to remind me of you.
When I see its ruby, when I look at its iron and refined gold I marvel how
the craftsman brought them together and fashioned them to serve the cares
of sweet love.*(5780)* And be informed by this letter, O knight, that I name
you as my heart; I register you as my soul. You I call my lord and you I
declare my light. In turn, dear heart, I show my love for you with a ring.'

The lady who was born of the sun wrote her letter and on it, to serve as a
tie, was her ring. They dispatched the message to me. I took it, I kissed
it. Rodamni's ring, my friend, was one hand of iron and another of
lodestone, clasping each other so tightly as to be never wrenched
apart,*(5790)* and in her letter were these words: 'You see that the bond of
this ring cannot be broken. Conclude from it that my love is also such.'

I read the ring's message. Hear the reply which I wrote:

Another charming letter   'Unbreakable, fair lady, is the bond of
from Livistros to the   the ring which you sent me with your
lady.[115]   letter of love. Know that my own mind
                               is the same.*(5800)* The bond of love for
you cannot be broken. I have read your message. I have seen the ring. I
look at it—hear what it tells me, "Put me on your finger. I am the bond
of desire, I am a thing of love. Keep me because I was sent by the
longing of a young woman. Cast a glance at me and think of the fair lady
who sent me for you to look at in place of her. Love me too, remember
her, look at me and think of her. Hold me in her place. I bear a command
from her that you put me on your hand, that you look at me and that I
hold your finger tightly*(5810)* so that the memory of her love never leaves
you." This is what the ring tells me about you. It constantly calls on me
to remember you. This is the root of what is fair, the spring of affection,

the bond of esteem, the gallantry of desire. I beseech you now to let me see you and talk with you so that I can be assured of the probity of your love.'

I wrote my message, my friend, and again I dispatched it to the lady's balcony as I had the others. Late that evening, under the clear heavens, I summoned my men.*(S820)* They all came and I opened my tent on all sides. I had two squires with fair voices. Hear the beautiful ditty they sang:

Livistros's love song to the lady.   'A knight loves a maiden who was born of the sun. He is encamped on a lovely meadow. He compares her to the moon but the lady is more beautiful. Her loveliness has exiled him from his native land and he has suffered many woes to find the fair one. Now he has found her but the gallant knight still suffers.*(S830)* He sees the beautiful lady, he sighs to think of his tortures, and he grieves in his pain. He looks to the sun and tells of his sufferings. When the moon is shining, in tears he bids it to speak to the fair one so that his tortures should not be in vain.'

This was their ditty. While we were singing, the lovely women listened and were engrossed with the song. When we had finished they left and my men bade me good night.*(S840)* The lady found my message, looked at it and read it. She grew angry at its words and fumed with rage. Again she wrote me a letter. Hear it, my friend:

The lady's angry reply.   'It did not befit my heart, it did not become my mind for me to write a reply to this last letter of yours. My hands should have cut it up and banished it from the world. You would have learnt from this that, even if you do love, you should not be so brazen in showing it.*(S850)* You should have counted the time, you should have watched the days and attended to what was happening. This alone should have sufficed. You must now realize that your letter made my heart angry with you, fearsomely angry, that your soul was impatient to receive another message or token of my love.'

Again they dispatched the lady's letter to me from the castle. I took it and read. Imagine, my friend, what terrible grief entered my heart, what great confusion took hold of my reason,*(S860)* to what a cliff of misery my soul fell. What with the terrible violence of my passion and the despair that the letter caused me, it was with difficulty that I wrote another message. Hear it:

Livistros's very sad and woebegone letter.	'Ah, your letter, fair lady, it is worse than an executioner! Ah, your message, it is worse than a robber! Ah, your

note, it wields a sharpened sword, a two-edged knife of anger that desire has forged, and it tortures bodies and lacerates feelings!*(S870)* Instead of words, your letter was full of woes to slay sensitive hearts. Pity me, madam, now that your hands have written me this. Your mind showed me no whit of pity in the face of my death, but, because of a word, you raged so terribly that you have killed the man who is dying for you. Your soul conceived such madness that you wished to see a man unjustly put to death. Your hands wrote a letter of rage, a letter which has brought about my complete destruction,*(S880)* a letter whose words were able to tear out my entire heart. Ah, the misfortune that I now go to my death. Today makes up two years that I have had no other prospect.'

This is the message I wrote, my friend. I composed the letter as my soul was seething in its terrible pangs of desire and I sent it like the others. They found it but I saw no reply. One day passed, then another went; three days came to an end and I wrote again.*(S890)* Listen, my friend, and I shall repeat it to you:

'Receive a doleful letter of emotion from a soul now without emotions, a living message from a heart completely dead which your own words, madam, prematurely killed and banished from the world. Look at it, read it, see what it says. Receive its message, feel pity for what it says. See the mistake it has made regarding you. *If it was just for you to be so angry with me*[116] leave me without sympathy and with my soul in agony. But if I did you no wrong to justify my torture,*(S900)* or that I should descend into such a gulf of your anger, that I should endure the terrible furnace of your hostility and enter the woeful sea of your repulsion in whose depths I drown and have no resistance—ah, alas, I swore to her to join her in death! She sees[117] that I drown because of her but she is without pity. Ah, the spectacle! I who have suffered two years for her am now being slain by her harshness. She sees that I drown but she does not repent.—You know that I am in torture, you see that I am dying.'*(S910)*

I wrote this message, my friend, and it too I sent. She read it but I saw no reply. Imagine what I suffered, the agony I was in, the woe I endured in the expectation of a letter from her! About four days passed and then I wrote to her again. My friend, hear it:

'Shout in a wild place where nobody goes, cry out in a deserted land, and then take note how you hear a voice replying to your own. I, fair lady, am shouting to your feelings,*(S920)* I am crying out to your heart. I am speaking to your reason. I am beseeching your soul. Pity me. Show compassion. It seems that you have no feelings, that you are turning to stone, that you pretend to be deaf to my sufferings and that you do not turn towards me. Know that if you persist in this you will cast me down into Hades, soul and all, and that you will acquire the name of thief—alas! surely you will want to be called my murderer.' Again I shot this message like the others. She read it. Hear her reply:*(S930)*

Another love letter from   'Why do my eyes betray me to you,
the lady to me.   you unfortunate? Why does my mind
      today torture me for you? Why do my
hands write you a letter in spite of myself? Why, against my wish, do my lips name you my lord? Why did my mind and my soul and, with them, my heart pledge themselves that I should never write to you? And again my mind guides me to your messages. And again my heart plays the executioner when I write to you. And when my eyes see your message,*(S940)* straightway my mind is ready and has no other concern than to reply. And since I am tortured by my heart, by my mind, and by all my senses because of you, my hands are writing you, my lord, a letter. I feel sorry for you whom I have grieved with my hostility. I pity you whom I have tortured with my haughtiness. I desire you whom I have made dizzy with my passionate anger. I now take you for my lord, I am enslaved to you. I am sending my eunuch to see you and give you*(S950)* my message and my tidings of love. You will receive news from him and he will explain to you how I shall see you, dear heart, and how I shall meet you. From now, my darling, do not grieve on my account.'

At dawn, when I rose, I found the lady's message. I stood and read it. Imagine, my friend, how I suddenly cast off the anxieties I had previously suffered. A soul gnawed by love sheds the woes it has endured when it receives a sweet word of passion.[118] I thought that I was not walking on the earth, that I was crossing the sky.*(S960)* I shouted, my friend, to my hundred youths and when they had all heard the message and rejoiced greatly, I wrote a letter in reply. Hear it:

Yet another letter from Livistros to the lady.

'Yesterday I was in the abyss. I was walking in Hades because of your boundless anger and your pride. Today, against hope, I have jumped out and risen from the pit and the depths of Hades into this world. Know that I live because of your letter. Only yesterday, because of its terrible distress at your hostility, my soul wanted to drown itself,[(S970)] but today it wants the pain to stay away simply because it has been comforted by your letter. And, in truth, my mind is troubled by your anger with me but *your courtesy in pitying me is enough. Suddenly I again find joy in my grief and woes and forget what I am enduring.*[119] And I give thanks for your discretion, fair lady. I pine for what has made you angry. I want it. I yearn for it since what has made you angry with me[120] has been caused by you, madam;[(S980)] my distress is through love of you and it seems to possess me. If my affliction is caused by my desire for you, then I do not have a pitiless soul and an unfeeling heart, but my soul has sunk into an abyss of emotion. But I know that you, of your own accord, realize when I suffer, that you pity my troubles, and that you share in my suffering.'

I wrote my letter and dispatched it too. The whole day passed. And at sunset, when night was beginning, the eunuch arrived. He had come from Rodamni,[(S990)] as the fair lady had written in her letter of love. He dismounted far from my tent as though in distress. I saw him and went out to meet him, held him by the hand and covered him with endless kisses. With him, my friend, was my man who had won his friendship.

I took the lady's eunuch by the hand and led him to my quarters. We were alone and, while he was in our camp, I treated him as my own soul. I cannot relate what I said to him or his replies[(S1000)] and my great joy. The whole race of eunuchs loves flattery, especially when they are involved in an affair of love. But I shall tell you how the eunuch arranged for me to see and meet her.

He said, 'At dawn the noble lady will go riding with two maids, one squire and myself. Know that we shall go hunting. Rise directly at dawn and when you see us riding through the middle of the meadow,[(S1010)] mount your horse immediately and go[121] to the hill which is planted with countless trees and is in bloom with different flowers. Hide yourself alone in the wood there. The lady will release a falcon with her hands and will pretend to chase it in order to come to the spot where she will find and meet you. But know that you will find me too in the wood. I shall be a solace to you both in that wild place. Farewell, Prince Livistros. It is evening and I go. The castle awaits me so that it can close its gates.'*(S1020)*

How I dispatched him and with what presents would make a long tale and I cannot tell it. In any task every intermediary willingly receives a gift and then does what is required. He bade me farewell and went to the lady, greeted her from me and related all our conversation. And when it was late, about midnight, she came from her room with her two maids who had fair voices. The maids leaned on the battlements*(S1030)* and sang a ditty, my friend. Hear it:

For my comfort the lady   'An excellent youth, unaccustomed to
orders her maids to sing   love, wanders night and day, morning,
a fair song about me.   afternoon and evening. The worthy man
                               is a prey to troubles and he sighs out of
the bitterness of his love. The dawn finds him awake, the night finds him sleepless. He is not experienced in love's woes and when they fall upon him he thinks them very heavy. They cut his heart in two. I see his impatience and I pity his sufferings.*(S1040)* In his troubles I grieve for him lest he should be suffering alone.'

They sang their song and went inside. And I shall tell you this—do not doubt me, my friend—as I hope to see Fortune's face, to learn about the lady, to emerge from my sufferings and not to die in vain: from the pleasure of the song, I stood there like marble. I seemed frozen. I was left without movement. I was fixed to the spot.

At some point I recovered and my senses returned. I was alone, my friend, and I said to myself,*(S1050)* 'Happy the man who wins such love of a noble lady and embraces such a beauty in his arms. If he says he is unfortunate he should be stoned.'

I entered my tent. I fell down and slept. In its anxiety my mind was in suspense and fretted for when, at dawn, the star of love would appear, for when I should see the lady cross the meadow and I should hasten to the tryst of love. Love's cares gave my heart no rest in its fear that it should not see the complete end of such concern.*(S1060)* Finally the morning star came and I saw the sun—it had just started to grow light. I called out to my squire and woke him. He decked out my horse *with a shining saddle and bridle adorned with bright pearls; its mane was dyed with henna. I put on a splendid red garment with a bright fleck and decorated with precious stones and pearls.*[122] From then on I kept watching for the lady to cross.

I saw her!—my mind, my friend, has started to burst as I remember the lady who was born of the sun—I saw her at dawn! She was crossing the meadow, which took on beauty from her countless graces. The horse she rode was as white as snow and its forelock and mane were plaited with tassels[(S1070)] of red silk which blazed like fire. Her dress was in the Latin fashion. Over a red and gold garment she wore a brightly coloured cloak which trailed far back over the ground. In one hand she held a tame parrot, which sat there without constraint and said in a human voice, 'This lady makes slaves of souls not yet possessed by passion, and she shackles hearts still free; she subdues the senses of those reared in the mountains and desolate places.' And I paused from gazing at that wondrous lady[(S1080)] with her rare beauty and indescribable appearance, and marveled at how the bird had been enslaved and was able to tell of its servitude with human voice.

It was dawn when I saw the lady crossing the meadow. I came out of my tent and in my joy I set out. I really seemed to be going on clouds. All rough ground is level in the path of a man whose soul is dreaming of a lady's love. My friend, I seemed to have wings. Quickly, in the very twinkling of an eyelid, I reached the spot[(S1090)] that the lady's eunuch had indicated to me. I found the place and the eunuch was there. I leaned down, I embraced him and got off my horse. He covered my hand with kisses and then my cheek. I embraced and kissed him in turn. He tied my horse to a tree, took my hand and started to tell me about the lady and her cares. After a little while the lady herself came. From a distance she called out, 'Vetanos, speak! Where are you?'[(S1100)]

I heard the fair one, I came out of the woods, and there was a violent battle in my mind as to how I should greet her; what words I should use, how I should address my beloved. A loving heart does not at first know what to say.[123] Still, I came out, I saw her, and the lady looked at me. She gave a sign of confusion and got off her horse. *The eunuch tied it up and went over to her. He took her by the hand and came to me. Full of love's charms, she approached me with dignity. I was struggling in my mind as to how I should greet her. How should I begin our talk of love? The fair one came up and I met her. I lowered my head and bowed. She bowed in return.*

In a distressed manner, I said to her, 'A soul concerned with courting a woman is tormented by the deadly flame of love's passion. Happy the man who trusts in love and does not despair. He acquires a helper and wins his desire. He goes along passion's road without stumbling. But I, despite all my trials and afflictions, despite all I have suffered for my great love of you—after these I have reached my goal and found what I longed for. Now I am happy! Even if I die I care not. I go a happy man!'

*The lady's words to Livistros. *With a smile she replied, | 'The man who despairs in love has Fortune as his ally to fight against Time and the* cruelty of his immutable Fate in the world. But be thankful that I have submitted to you and after your great impetuosity I have come to your will.'*

And why, my friend, should I want to tell the many intervening details? You know what happens when two people in love are united, and so I pass over the greater part.[124]

Ask not how we embraced and with what love, how long we talked and on how many subjects, nor is it fit for me to tell you. I only repeat what she later said to me when she bade me farewell to ride off:

'If the mouth of Love tells you no lie, neither will what he told me in a dream prove false.*(S1120)* Listen to what happened before you paid me court. Some time ago, my father, the king of Silver Castle, announced that the king of Egypt was coming to my country to be given to me as husband. A messenger has arrived with the news that Verderichos, the king of Egypt, is at hand. When he comes, I shall say to my father, "Father, a great desire for Livistros has come upon me. It is death for me to be separated from him. Come, let the two mount their horses and fight.*(S1130)* I shall take the one who conquers by arms. The Latin race loves the brave and especially those who fight for love or fortune." My father has heard of you. He knows both of your wars and of your feats of valor and if he had not[125] announced Verderichos first he would have wished to give you to me as husband.'

I heard this and replied, 'For this, too, I thank you. Love will give his help to show you what sort of person it is who has suffered so much for you.'*(S1140)*

And after she had spoken I covered her with kisses and then I bade farewell to the lady who was born of the sun. She mounted again for the hunt and I rode off to my quarters, afflicted with countless griefs. My heart pondered on the instability of Fortune and how Destiny would decide the course of battle. Why, my friend, why do I draw out my story? Why do I spend time and waste my words?

Verderichos, the king of Egypt, came and set up camp with his army.*(S1150)* They immediately sent a message to King Chrysos, who in turn sent a reply to Verderichos. They sent frequent messages each day and Chrysos came to an agreement with Verderichos. The lady heard but did not consent. She quarreled with her father, who said, 'What is it that you want, Rodamni? What do you want, my darling, light of my eyes? Tell me. Tell me what you are thinking. Tell me your wish.'

The lady replied submissively to her father: 'Father, mighty king, lord, master of the world;*(S1160)* a man mighty and noble who is prince of the land of Livandros has wandered two years for love of me. He has endured fearsome sufferings, he has withstood terrible things. I have seen his anguish and I felt pity for him. I have sworn an oath with him that we shall not part. Now, because of your resolve, father, I am going to suggest something that I think will please you, too. I prefer Livistros; you Verderichos. Tell them to mount their horses and joust. I shall take the one who conquers with his arms.*(S1170)* Combat will decide what is best.'

About the fight between Livistros and Verderichos. An announcement was made to me by the fair lady, and to Verderichos by the king. The news of the contest spread over Silver Castle | and everyone hastened to the spectacle. The king watched from the walls, and the lady with him. There was a combat of foot soldiers and of horsemen, one party on this side and the other on that. The hundred men I had with me were on horseback, as was the force of Verderichos on the other side.(S1180)* They took their places and the joust started.

There was a great concourse of people, a crowd of men and women from the land of Silver Castle. The crowd did battle for me and for him. Some wanted to see the victory go to him and others wanted to see it go to me. The people followed our fight from the further side. At one point king Chrysos gave a sign from above that we should mount and come out into the field. I looked to the lady and she threw me her veil. I tied it to my head, jumped up, mounted my horse*(S1190)* and, taking my javelin, went out into the open. I went up and down so that my horse could prance and I, my friend, could twist my javelin. My mind was troubled about failing. My soul was distressed about the instability of Fate; perhaps Fortune would decree against me and I would be overcome in the battle.

After a short while Verderichos arrived. I shall not conceal the truth. He was a fine man, as far as one could tell, my friend, in body and in courage. He too went up and down in the lists.^(S1200) He too brandished his javelin for a time. At the beginning I was frightened of him. I shall not lie to you, my friend. Anyone who contemplates the possibility of failure is afraid, even if he possesses fearsome courage and daring. Nevertheless, after much time had passed, I went out. I took up a position in the middle of the lists. I sought to hit him, I urged on my black charger and rode down upon him. He did the same. There was a mighty clash. Noise and confusion arose among the onlookers. *His tongue screeched out, 'Swine, now you die!' And I replied, 'Now you die, dog!'*[126] I aimed at the pommel of his saddle and hit him with my lance^(S1210)—do not doubt *what I say*,[127] my friend. He seemed to have never sat on his horse before. I knocked him off, saddle and all. He lay to one side and his horse on the other. The great crowd was looking and, while I stood on the field and claimed the victory, it stopped bickering and shouted in agreement, 'Bravo, Livistros! You win Rodamni!' I was acclaimed king by the whole assembly, which started to shout for Chrysos, the castle's king.^(S1220)

The lady sent me her eunuch who kissed me for her. 'Rejoice,' he said. 'Cast off your former troubles. Banish them. Rejoice, live, leap, thank Fortune. You are without grief, without hindrance, and untroubled by care.'

The great crowd saw the lady's eunuch. They all ran up to me and one by one embraced me. *King Chrysos sent four of his lords*[128] with a hollow shield. They sat me on top of it, raised me up and first cheered the Emperor Chrysos, and then me^(S1230) with the words, 'Long life to King Livistros!' The noise of the acclamation reached the clouds and the land around Silver Castle shook. Nobody then stayed inside the city. All marveled at my victory in the contest. Straightway they opened the castle gates and the crowd, amid its acclamations, carried me in. The king of Silver Castle met me. He gave orders that I should be lowered and he covered me with endless kisses. He began to speak flatteringly to me and in his joy^(S1240) he formally addressed his lords:

'Lords, governors of my land and country, relatives, friends, fellow citizens: you are all well acquainted with my own troubles, my daily woes, all the wars I endured with you for this land until I completely eliminated my adversaries, subdued the world and made free countries tributaries to the land of Silver Castle. Since, friends and relatives, the span^(S1250) of my life is now drawing to a close and I now await my end and our common killer, death, today I am giving you another king in my place, my noble son-in-law, the prince of the land of Livandros, a man of splendid appearance, of incomparable physique, of tried strength, and first in valor, as the land of Silver Castle will bear witness today, together with you, my governors, the first among my relatives.'

They heard and thanked King Chrysos. Next, they applauded and acclaimed him loudly.*(S1260)* Let me pass over the many things then said, the reply each made to the king, the advice, the praises, the flatteries, the plans and opinions of each. My friend, I am drawing the story out. If there is room for expansion, a mind in love is capable of telling its story in great detail.

The king of the land of Silver Castle sat down and wrote out his order to all the land he ruled; to governors, dukes, friends, and relatives. They should all come soon so that the wedding could be performed.*(S1270)* The governors came, the relatives came. The wedding was conducted and I received the lady. A fairer woman than her, my friend, I swear by my worries, by the toil of my soul, by the bitterness of Fortune, our earth has not yet seen. No-one[129] would chance to set his eye on the round outline of her face for fear of being dazzled. You would have thought[130] that the circle of the moon, when completely round, pure and full, resembled the roundness of her countenance.*(S1280)* Her forehead was white as snow or, you might say, the dawn's crystal in bodily form. On it spread out the lady's eyebrows. When you looked at them closely you seemed to see wings flying in the air separate from her body. Nature had adorned her eyes with beauty. Gentle, black and gay, they flashed much when she glanced. In their clarity you could see yourself as in a perfect mirror or a clear river. The hands of the cupids had fashioned her nose*(S1290)* and had placed it to sit in the middle of her face, like a hillock on a level plain, for ornament, for delight, for the heart's refreshment. *Her mouth was small and lovely—enough to suffice for the kiss of a loving heart.*[131] Her lips were red and thin, like a rose when it opens at dawn to receive the dew. Her chin was as round as a circle; her whole face was the same. Such a countenance, friend dear to me as my soul, I swear by my soul's pain and my woe, will never be seen again in the whole world.*(S1300)*

I was proclaimed king of Silver Castle, I accompanied by the surpassingly lovely Rodamni; except that the rank of King Chrysos was maintained until his death, though he was not to rule himself.[132] I was announced as king, openly proclaimed so in all the lands surrounding Silver Castle. I lived, I spent my days in luxury, I rejoiced, I flourished, I spent lavishly, without hindrance, without constraint.

All the other fair and wondrous things in the castle I shall omit, my friend,*(S1310)* but I shall tell you about the pool. Outside the lady's bedchamber was an inner courtyard, a fragment of paradise, the dwelling place of pleasure and spring of sweetness, you would say without dispute. If you had wanted any tree or fair fruit or some lovely scent, you would have found it in that wonderful inner courtyard. And in the middle of it was a pool constructed of glass. Of glass were its floor, sides, edge and its pool-house. Of glass were its pipes and conduits.*(S1320)* However, my friend, the pool's glass was like pure, refined ice. *And in the middle of the pool stood a green pillar with emerald surface. On its top was a ruby-skinned man who held a lovely red bowl in one hand and in the other*[133] a sign with the words: 'Here is a pool, a fountain with water, a fair inner courtyard, the noble mistress of the Graces, Queen Rodamni, and her king, a mighty man from abroad, a prince in his own land. He went into exile because of her, he suffered but he did not fail, he won what he desired.*(S1330)* However, pain and a torment of two years await him after his joy. After that, those separated will be united and love will be without impediment.' I read this writing and noted in my mind, 'These are the verses of the man who is prophet and seer. What he says is about me and I shall suffer again.'

But I wrapped myself up once more in the expanse of my joy and did not trouble at all about grief's bitterness. An hour of joy can drive out a year of woe when the joy is in one's heart and soul.*(S1340)* I shall not, my friend, continue at length, but shall describe the pool. Around it were statues, handsome boys made of glass. Each, *my friend, I shall describe to you.*[134] One stood holding a rod and catching fish from the pool's depths. The next you saw holding a stone—he seemed to be hitting the bottom so that the fish would not be caught. Another was stooping over the water and drinking greedily. Another was undressing to swim. Another, thanks to some mechanism, was playing on his pipe.*(S1350)* Another was walking on the pool's edge and seemed to be frolicking to the pipe's tune. In these you could see the cunning of a skilful craftsman. You would have thought that each figure was alive and that the complexion they had been given was their own. And by the side of the pool on the right there was a vine with roots, it too made of glass, which covered, my friend, the whole width of the pool. And I saw there a strange and wonderful contrivance which the remarkable craftsman had made.*(S1360)*

At the root of the vine, water entered and flowed up into each branch. When there was no water you noticed, my friend, that the fruit on the vine was still quite immature. When there was water you noticed that the vine's fruit was then fully ripe to pick and you conceived a great desire to do so. And on its branches you saw that birds were sitting and that each had a lifelike appearance.[135]

You have heard, my friend, of the remarkable pool.*(S1370)* You have heard of the countless beauties of the inner courtyard. It was amid such loveliness and such beauties that I lived and escaped misfortune's woes. My mind did not remember whether it had suffered any troublesome reversal. For two years, my friend, I lived with the fair lady, free from grief, free from anxiety and from the cares of love. But after the passage of my two years the instability of Fate turned against me. Time's spindle twisted its threads of misfortune and my malicious Fortune came to meet me.*(S1380)*

One day I decided to go hunting with the peerless and lovely Rodamni. I set out from my castle with my squires. I came to a fair meadow and rode through it alone with the lady while my squires went to another part by themselves and hunted. As I was going through the lovely spot I met a merchant in the middle of the field who had many horses and people with him, as well as an old woman, my friend, who was sitting on a camel.*(S1390)* He dismounted, approached me and did obeisance.

I said, 'Who are you, sir, and from where do you come?'

He replied, 'I am a merchant from Babylon.'

'And in what do you deal?' I asked.

'In various things,' he said, 'gold and precious stones, pearls, purple and scarlet cloths, silk.'

'Do you have a precious stone for me to buy, merchant?' I said.

'I have many, and also a fair horse for my lady,' (He quickly pointed to the lady with his finger) 'the like of which has never yet been born on earth. And if you desire, you shall see it and ride it.'

They led out the horse. I saw it and, believe me, my friend, my mind was immediately taken with its beauty. The fair lady wanted to ride it. It was saddled, she mounted and it walked splendidly. The horse rose and fell like running water. It did not know how to remain on the ground.

The merchant said to me, 'Does Your Majesty wish to see the precious stone as well?' I said I did and he produced it. It was in the form of a ring,[136] uncut, natural, red as fire. I saw and desired it. I marveled at its color.[S1400] I put it on my finger and I expired immediately. I fell dead to the ground from my horse.

And, my friend, what then happened to the fair lady and the evil merchant, I do not know. I know only this—I do not know how to say it—after much time my men searched for me and found me lying dead. They saw me, they recognized me. There was a great uproar, which was heard in the castle, and everyone ran out to see me. They carried me and placed me inside the castle like a corpse.[S1410] They took my hand[137] and saw the ring, they removed and examined it and I immediately returned to life. I revived, I jumped up and searched for the lady. I began to mourn. A mighty dirge arose, a great lament and agitation. And how great it was! They told me how they had found me and how I had revived. I asked them for the ring, put it in my purse, and again left to search for the lady. The hundred men I had with me followed. *I took to the road and the tracks*[138] <of the merchant> but, my friend, it split up into a hundred paths.[S1421] I divided my hundred into one for each, and in my misery I kept to the middle way. I ordered them all to wander for two years and at the end of that time to return and wait for me at the beginning of the road. *I farewelled them and went to search the world*[139] to find a person somewhere with whom I could speak. You alone have I found and to you I have related my sufferings[S1430] and lightened the labor of my soul. I was told, my friend, that the king of Egypt had taken Rodamni. I was later informed that in his grief he had left with the words that he would not give up the lady even at the risk of his life.

The third part of the story of love, the heart-rending and tearful account of the woebegone Prince Livistros and Rodamni.

And now we have again come to a town and lodging. Let us concern ourselves with a place to rest[S1440] and tomorrow we shall again take the road together when you will learn anything that was missing from my story.

[*Klitovon resumes the narrative*]

The space of the day came to an end, the whole night passed. Then the east grew bright, and the day rose. We started again to go along the road and the man who had been burnt by desire, who had suffered for love, who had endured countless tortures for longing, started with an oath to speak to me.

'You have heard everything. You have learnt my own woes,*(S1450)* you know my afflictions and my tortures, you have heard the miseries I have suffered in the world, you have learnt the sorrows I have undergone. I have told you all the troubles that occurred to me because of love. Now, if you are a Christian and a good companion, if you have really learnt to pity the miserable, and if you abide by the oath of friendship which you swore with me, you too will relate your story and tell me who you are and of what land, and from where you come. Perhaps if I learn of your troubles,*(S1460)* if you tell me of your sorrows, and if I hear of your woes, my suffering will become somewhat less.'

When I saw that he was using the oath to make me tell him of any troubles that I too had suffered in this world and to relate my sorrows, I began in my distress to speak to him:

'It would have been better for me not to have sworn to die with you, nor to have bound myself to you with an oath, nor for my soul to have entered upon the story of your love. The foundations of my heart hold you within them.*(S1470)* But since Time has caught me up in this, hear, friend, who I am and from what land, and why I wander and search the world. My father, friend, was of the land of Armenia and of the province named Litavia. The parents of my unfortunate self were the rulers there. My father's brother was prince of Armenia. He had a very beautiful daughter, and his son-in-law, her husband, was from the land of Persia. Love for the lady entered my heart*(S1480)* and devoured, mastered, inflamed, and ravaged all my soul, all my senses. A passion which the mind in love conceals can ravage body and heart.

'The Persian was traveling far from Armenia. He happened to be absent for some time. A year passed, and more. I revealed to the lady my soul's passion. I told her of my love, of the desire I suffered. The fair lady heard and pitied me. She felt for my woes, she pitied my afflictions.*(S1490)* She consented to my desire and, succumbing to my passion, she began to love me. And, I shall confess to you, she yielded to my will. Her father, the prince of Armenia heard of the matter, of my love for her and of her passion for me. On the one hand he scolded her as his child, on the other he threatened me as his relative. My heart, friend, held these threats and intimidations, you might say, as nothing at all. There was something it was waiting for, something it was yearning to learn.*(S1500)* I used to say, "If a man who is experienced in the world *does not suffer for love or does not grieve for desire he is no servant of passion and he does not know the world.*"[140]

'Hear and learn what then happened:

'When the prince saw that my passion and the fair lady's love for me could not be separated, he upbraided her and showed his anger. He spoke words of reproof and admonition to the excellent lady as befitted her. He sent for me, apprehended me, clad me in irons with a shackle on my neck and threw me into prison. He kept me there for a year and a half.*(S1510)* At that time, my friend, the Persian arrived back from his journey. He heard the story and learnt everything. From then on he sought an opportune moment to kill me by trickery. I give you this account of my woes and troubles briefly and in summary so as not to distress you further.'

'You have told me everything, my friend,' he replied. 'But you have not mentioned your name and that of the lady.'

'I am called Klitovon and the lady, Myrtani. The names are Armenian and of our country.'*(S1520)*

'You have learnt my story, friend and companion of my journey. You know my pains and anguish. My mind is fixed on Rodamni's kidnapping and whether Verderichos has done this by magic. My mind is all the more set on this idea, my friend, because the prophet told me in a dream, "The trick of a treacherous and evil witch will part you from the lady whom you love desperately." '

'So, since the seer told you this in your dream, let us go on the road which leads to Egypt.'*(S1530)*

We found a spring with water. We were tired and we got off our horses to rest ourselves. When we had eaten bread by the foot of a tree and had drunk water from the spring to quench our thirst we dozed off. I fell asleep leaning on the tree's trunk. As I slept I had a strange dream about my friend. I dreamt I saw a terrible eagle, black as a crow and very large, flying in the clouds. In its talons it held a red partridge*(S1540)* and as it flew to the heavens the partridge made a noise. When I saw it flying up I dreamt that I said to my companion, 'Shoot that eagle and make it drop the partridge!' I dreamt that he quickly loaded his bow and went after the eagle to shoot at it. The eagle, through fear of being hit, let go the partridge, and in my dream it took refuge[141] in Livistros's bosom. I woke up from the confusion of my vision, grabbed Livistros and held him. I said, 'Why are you sleeping?'*(S1550)*

He took me and said, 'Be quiet, you are confused. Surely you had a nasty dream.'

'Yes,' I replied, 'I had a strange dream. I see it as if it were happening. I shall tell it to you.' I sat down and related the dream about my friend which I had seen so clearly. When I had finished, I explained it: 'In my opinion the black eagle means two things: a mighty nobleman who is king of his land (he is the head of a great and populous country*(S1560)* because birds regard the eagle as their lord), and as the eagle was black, I consider the man to be of Egypt, which he governs as sole ruler, because black is, I think, the color of Egyptians. The partridge I consider to be the kidnapped lady, who laments her capture with weeping and shouting. And you gave chase to shoot at the eagle but it, from fear, let go the partridge, which, from the eagle's wing, took refuge in your embrace. This, I consider, means that you are going on your search to find her.*(S1570)* Know that you will find her and that she will again spend her days with you. The partridge is Rodamni and the eagle Verderichos, and up to this time he has done her no harm. This is how I interpret my dream and the result that will ensue. So come now, let us proceed along the road so that we may somewhere find a town and gain information.'

We journeyed on for about twelve days and more. We crossed mountains that approached the clouds.*(S1580)* We passed through gorges unpenetrated by men. And at the end of this time we came out on the sea, on the sea and cliffs, a lonely place on the coast with fearsome crags on the water's edge. This was the end of the road we were on and we searched about to see where we should go. We ran around here and looked there. On one side we saw a crag, on the other a mountain. The only road for us was the one we had taken together.*(S1590)*[142] It was a desolate place with the sea in front of us, on one side cliffs and hills and on the other a precipice. We took counsel as to what the two of us should do: 'Should we turn back? What road should we take? The region with its cliffs is hard to cross and the hills are impassable. So let us wait for a ship to pass so that we can ask for information. Certainly, the road and the path[143] which we took together show human footprints and tracks of horses.'

Amid our deliberations and discussions*(S1600)* I noticed on a fearsome cliff of solid rock, a grass hut big enough for a human being to sleep in. Quickly I said to Livistros, 'Have no worry! I see a grass hut up on the peak. I can also see smoke coming from it as if from a hearth. I think there is someone there. Come and let us find out. The person will know something and give us directions.'

I started off and Livistros with me. We went up to where the hut stood$^{(S1610)}$ and I called out in a loud voice, 'Who's there? Speak to me!'

A miserable old woman, black as a Saracen, naked, completely without clothes, came out and sat on the rock. It was her! The one who had carried out the kidnapping of Rodamni!

'Mother,' I said, 'how are you?'

She replied, 'I cannot describe to you, my children, how I am, living here in this desolate spot on a crag by the sea. But you, how did you come to be on this wild road without a guide?'

'First, mother, tell us who you are, and where you are from,$^{(S1620)}$ and why you are here, living in this lonely place. And when you have told us who you are, then we in turn will tell you about ourselves.'

'Well, my children, dismount, tie up your horses, and come over here to my rock. I shall tell you who I am, how I come to be in this lonely land, and why I pace over this rock where I dwell. But I now put my life in your hands. Do not kill me when I tell you what I have done.'

We got off our horses and tied them to the rock.$^{(S1630)}$ We clambered up, got onto the cliff and sat with the old woman, who started her tale:

'My children, I was born in the land of Egypt, neither of a noble family nor of the lowest class. I learnt to control the heavens, to observe the stars and to foretell the misfortunes of humans by prophecy. Little by little, Time made trial of me and showed me proficient in the art of magic. I used to talk with demons on moonless nights, I used to frequent crossroads by myself to summon them.$^{(S1640)}$ I had such power that, when I wished, I brought the heavens down to earth and milked the stars. Hear, my children, what happened next.

'The king of Egypt, the mighty Verderichos, was still young and had no wife. A certain other king, from Silver Castle, sent him a message that he wished to have Verderichos as son-in-law. The excellent king of Egypt went off with the intention of becoming son-in-law to King Chrysos. He took me with him to watch the days$^{(S1650)}$ and avert troublesome weather.'

I heard the proof and said to my companion, 'You are listening now, my friend?'

'Yes Klitovon, I am listening. Yes, mother, please go on. Do not hide anything from us. Your story is excellent. Go on, do not hesitate.'

'That lady, my children, the daughter of King Chrysos, loved a certain other leading noble. We arrived at Silver Castle and sent a message to King Chrysos. His daughter heard and was angry at the news.*(S1660)* She said to her father, "Let the two fight. I shall take the one who conquers with arms." They fought for a short time and the other was victorious. A hollow shield was brought. He was placed on it and proclaimed son-in-law of King Chrysos.'

'You are listening now, my friend?'

'Yes, Klitovon, I am listening. Yes, mother, please go on. Do not hide anything from me.'

'Verderichos, the king of Egypt, was furious, and with guile and cunning he set about how to kidnap the lady.*(S1670)* He summoned me to ask my advice. He said, "What am I to do? Love for the fair lady overwhelms my heart and I shall not give her up even if I must die here." I said to him, "Calm yourself! I shall show you a way. I shall advise you on how to kidnap her."

'That evening I looked at the sky. I asked the moon and I counted the stars. The reply was this: "If the king undertakes anything he will be successful." And at dawn I joyfully told King Verderichos, "Do not grieve. I shall give you what you desire."*(S1680)*

'In the evening I summoned the demons and separated out the better ones. I bound them by oath and asked them to tell me what I should do. One of them said to me, "Act now. I shall become a horse and another demon a ring and another a camel to carry you. *Let the king give orders to his men: they should all leave*[144] and go back to the country from whence they came. And in their place assemble other demons and let them accompany the king at his command. I shall become a horse which will be beautiful in form and movement.*(S1690)* It will run like a river and be as swift as an arrow. And this demon will become a priceless ruby, uncut, natural, in the shape of a ring." '

'You are listening now, my friend?'

'Yes, Klitovon, I am listening. Yes, mother, please go on. Do not hide anything from us. Your story is excellent. Go on, do not hesitate.'

'Listen, my children, to the words of the demons who advised me, as I have explained.[145] "From that time the king must change his appearance and become a merchant. He should take care to come upon his rival when he is hunting and amusing himself. When the man sees him as a merchant he will ask what he is selling and where he comes from. (And now, my children, listen!) When the man asks him this he should then lead out the horse and show the precious stone.[(S1700)] The lady will see the horse and ask for it. It should be saddled immediately and she should mount it. When the man shows an interest in the shape of the precious stone he will take it to examine it. He will put it on his finger, be sure, and as soon as he does, he will fall to the ground from his horse a lifeless corpse. Verderichos should sit behind the fair lady; he should whip on the horse and return to Egypt."

'In one day, my friend, and one night, I did everything that the demon had told me.[(S1710)] Verderichos became a merchant. He changed his appearance, color and face. We waited, I think, for about two years to find a favorable opportunity and the right time. At the end of this time, my children, Livistros came out and the lady with him. King Verderichos now got on his horse and immediately sat me on the camel. He met Livistros, dismounted, went up to him and did obeisance.

'Livistros asked him,[(S1720)] "Tell me, who are you, sir, and from whence do you come?"

'Verderichos, my children, replied, "I am a merchant from Babylon."

' "And in what do you deal?"

'The other replied, "Pearls, purple cloth, gold and precious stones. *I also have a beautiful horse that would suit my lady." He quickly pointed to her with his finger.*[146]

'The lady wanted to ride the horse. She ordered that they put her saddle on it and she mounted. Livistros put the ring on his finger and immediately fell off his horse dead. Verderichos then sat behind the lady[(S1730)] and in one day and one night reached Egypt. But when we reached this coast he took my camel, made me dismount and continued on alone with the lady to Egypt. He forgot what I had done and how I had helped him. For a year and six months now, my children, I have been sitting on these rocks, suffering countless torments. For food I have the grasses that grow from the earth.

'You have heard, my children, who I am and from where. You have learnt the misery I suffer and endure.*(S1740)* Now I want you to go through your story. Tell me who you are and where you are from. I am sure you will find me a help in your troubles. If you have any sorrows I shall bring you relief.'

'Mother, never mind about who we are, our country, or where we have come from,' I said to her. 'Forget it. I simply tell you this: if you are able to do anything about taking the lady from Verderichos we shall spare your life, give you whatever you want, and, mother, you will come with us to our homes.*(S1750)* But if you do not, be assured by me that I shall inflict every form of pain and distress on you.'

'You, sir, are from the land of Livistros and have come in search of the lady Rodamni?'

'That, mother, is Livistros himself, who has been tortured by his passion for Rodamni. And if you do not believe that, here is the ring which Verderichos had and which killed Livistros.'

Livistros immediately took out the ring and showed it to the old woman. She saw it, was thrown into confusion, and then began*(S1760)* to grovel at our feet. She said in her tears, 'Do not kill me, no, wretch that I am. I shall do what you want.'

And when she began to lament I said to her, 'Do not worry. Sit down, do something to help us take the lady and you will have a life free from trouble and with everything you want.'

Straightway the old woman said to me, 'Good. Let me consult the stars to learn, my children, what has happened to Rodamni. I shall tell you of some trick, some ruse or plan, and advise you on how to see her. And I shall work out a way for you to take her.'*(S1770)*

'Is there a place for us to stay?' I said to her. 'Do you know of one?'

'Stay in my hut. But I give you this command: If you hear any noise, do not come out to see who is talking or what the shouting is.'

I said to Livistros, 'Friend Livistros, have no worry, despite all you have suffered in past years. Now you have reached the end of your misery. Fortune takes away your troubles and Time's web of sorrow now has now released you. You are rid of Fate's evil$^{(S1780)}$, and if we suffer anything let us endure it.'

He replied, 'Yes, let us do that. Let us lie down inside.'

We went and lay down in the old woman's hut. About midnight that evening we heard a great uproar outside and voices talking in an unknown tongue. I cannot tell you what a terrible alarm came over my mind. I shudder to describe it. But I shall omit that and continue. The night passed. About dawn the old woman came and said to us, 'Why are you asleep?$^{(S1790)}$ Wake up! Stop worrying! From now be happy! The lady is distressed on your account and you are not concerned? Her sighs for Livistros are never silent and I see him lying asleep without a care. In order to gather any tidings, the lady has made an arrangement to become an innkeeper for four years—are you still sitting? Get up immediately!'

We got up immediately and quickly grabbed the old woman. 'Mother,' we said, 'give us some comfort!'

'All last night,' she said, 'I consulted the stars.$^{(S1800)}$ I asked the demons for clear information so that I might learn if it is possible for you to take the lady, and what she is doing and where she lives. They told me that it is possible for Livistros, her first husband, to take her and keep her. But she made this compact with Verderichos to become an innkeeper for just four years and after the end of that time to submit to his will; he was to build her a new inn$^{(S1810)}$ and a pool near it for guests to wash.

'I give you these horses, mount them, cross over the sea and the first person you meet, ask him to show you the way. But you, Klitovon, go to the inn first. Call out, "Innkeeper!"[147] and she will come out and hurry you along, "Get off your horse. There's a place for you to stay. You will tell me all the misfortune you have suffered in the world." And when you get acquainted with the lady say to her, "Arrange things so that you do not leave the horse$^{(S1820)}$ which carried you off from Silver Castle." '

I listened to the evil witch's words and took note of her advice and instructions. Immediately the fearsome thought came to my mind that the old woman in her terror had devised some trick with her magic art to drown us. Again and again I saw her on my own, talked with her, and, seemingly in friendship, again asked her, and again she swore a thousand fearsome oaths, 'There is no trick, my children, do not be afraid.'$^{(S1830)}$

What happened next? Was the old woman telling the truth? I turned to Livistros and saw that he was thoughtful. I realized from his appearance that he was troubled in his mind. His soul was in great confusion because of the matter. I said to him, 'Why are you upset? Why are you gripped by fear? Why are you racked by the thought of failure? Why does dread despair plague you? Why has a great panic taken possession of your mind and soul? Have faith in Love's truthfulness, Livistros. Take hope from the words the prophet[148] spoke to you.*(S1840)* If the predictions of his which you tested in the past were not true, give up those about the future and do not trust him at all. But if fear invests your heart and your soul is brooding on the sea's danger, I shall be the vanguard and cross first. I have confidence in[149] the old woman's words. I shall advance boldly and tread upon the sea before you. If anything happens let me perish before my time for your sake. Be assured, my friend, it is fitting that true friends suffer in this way for those they love.*(S1850)* But if, after I cross the sea and step onto dry land, you see me walking on firm ground without trouble, advance upon the sea yourself and without fear, worry or hindrance, come to where you see me. Cast aside, yes, cast aside fear from now on. Come, let us mount. Have confidence in my words.'

I convinced Livistros and he cast aside his fear. Straightway we changed our saddles over to the old woman's horses. We kept to the road by the sea and after we had gone a little way from her hut*(S1860)* the two of us came to the sea's edge. I turned and said, 'Livistros, why are we now standing here? We have found a suitable place for the crossing. *Farewell, and wait till I cross.*[150] And when you see that I am on the further side and standing on firm ground, then advance upon the sea without fear yourself and come without hindrance to where you see me.'

At first Livistros would not hear of staying. 'Let me come with you,' he said, 'and if anything happens to you let it happen to me too so that you will not suffer alone.*(S1870)* You have already suffered much for me, my friend.'

When he saw that my mind was made up he held me, he embraced me, he covered me with endless kisses, and I embraced and kissed him in turn. Together we endlessly lamented our misfortune. But when we had finished I bade him farewell, advanced onto the sea and whipped on my horse. In the twinkling of an eyelid I stepped onto the sand of the shore opposite the old woman's hut. About that horse I can tell you nothing.*(S1880)* I marvel at how it went over the sea. I only know (do not disbelieve me) that I was sitting in the saddle and flying in the clouds. I came off the sea. I stepped onto the sand, then got back on my horse, then dismounted and made sure that I had not been tricked, that I was not still dreaming and that the old woman had told the truth. When I saw that I had really left the sea and was certainly walking on firm land, I signaled to Livistros that he should advance upon the sea and cross. To be brief, he came and joined me.*(S1890)* He came off the sea and stepped onto firm ground.

For a whole day we journeyed along the road. We conversed and talked about our cares, the old woman's success, the passage over the sea, and the horses which she had fashioned with her tricks. *When it was late, towards evening,*[151] we came upon a man. I went up to him, looked at him, stopped and asked if there was anywhere a place where strangers like us could stay. He directed us to the inn that Verderichos had built and Rodamni kept.*(S1900)* We dismissed this man we had found and set off along the road, the road which led to the inn.

I said to Livistros, 'What do you say now? Where will you stay to wait for me?' Some distance off was a river with trees and a meadow blooming with various flowers. I said, 'You see that river with the trees and the meadow ahead of us? You will dismount there, Livistros, and wait for me.'*(S1910)*

He replied, 'Excellent, my friend and my solace! A true man, a true friend is one who knows how to feel for his friend's suffering. And so that you may be more easily recognized, here is the veil, my friend, which the lady threw to me from the castle when I fought Verderichos.'

I took the veil and bade him farewell. I started on the road to the inn and he on the road to the trees and sloping meadow. And in the twilight when the day was completely at an end,*(S1920)* I found the inn.

I entered boldly and said, 'Is there an innkeeper? Mine host! Is there a place for me to stay?'

The fair lady heard, came out and saw me. 'Call for the hostess, not the host, stranger. Nowhere has she an innkeeper.[152] She too is a stranger to the place, to the land you see and to the inn. Her innkeeper has been gone for two years now, dead in another clime, in another land and place.*(S1930)* So call for the hostess, not the host. Stranger, there is a room and a stable. Get off your horse and come in. There is a pool where you can wash. But I shall require you to sit and tell me the story of what you have suffered, what you have seen and heard in this world.'

With every word, with every syllable she sighed. Her mind was in torture from her woes. *Her tears ran like a river. She fainted and fell to the ground as if dead.*[153] I saw how she sighed and I sighed with her. I saw how she sorrowed and I sorrowed with her. I saw how she grieved and I grieved with her.[*(S1940)*] It is natural that a loving heart sorrows with those who are suffering through love and who are gnawed by desire.

I said, 'Lady of the inn, it is good that I have found you and can stay here. Everything I have seen, everything I have suffered in the world, I shall tell you. I shall hide nothing from you.'

I got down from my saddle and handed over my horse. I unfastened my weapons from my waist. The lady of the inn said to me, 'Have no worry. There is food for your horse and for you if you need it.' I heard the lady and remained silent.[*(S1950)*] They stabled my horse and hung up my weapons. The lady said, 'Sit down and have dinner.'

I sat and dined and she then said, 'Stranger, now speak up and tell me what you have suffered in the world, what you have heard and what you have seen.'

'It seems, lady of the inn,' I replied, 'that you desire to increase my affliction, my suffering and my grief even more. If you learn of the misfortunes which I have endured in the world,—I swear by my soul's anguish, if you come to learn them[*(S1960)*] you will become like earth as a result of my countless afflictions. So, lady of the inn, if you wish to know the unbearable hardships which I have suffered, of which I have heard, which I have seen, which I have experienced,[154] tell me first how you happen to be here and of what race and country you are. Your appearance is, to my eyes, very strange beside that of the Egyptians. Come, tell me first where you are from, and in turn I too shall recount my misfortunes to you.'[*(S1970)*]

The lady replied to me, 'Know that over two years I have now lodged I know not how many people and I have never told anyone where I am from. But, since you wish to know this and you ask me, be seated, stranger, and learn where I am from and of what country and how I happen to be here. Learn who I am and of what family. Know that my native place was Silver Castle. My father was Chrysos, the mighty king,[*(S1980)*] and my noble mother had the name Eunostia. They made me the sole successor of their crown, their glory and their fame.'

'Tell me, lady of the inn, tell me and then I shall tell my story.'

'Hear what I have suffered, stranger, and share my pain.[155]

'I was reared in joy and lived free from care. Nothing beautiful or fair was ever lacking. I never had any notion of love. No thought of passion wounded my heart, no recollection of desire affected my soul. The affliction of longing did not torment my mind.[S1990] Then a certain noble person came from abroad, a wealthy ruler, the fearsome prince of the land of Livandros—Livistros was his name, stranger. He was handsome in appearance, young, well-built, and of great bravery. With passion for me the lord of love had deluded him; with love for me the flame of desire had scorched him; with longing for me his soul suffered. My mind was distressed by the love he offered.'

'Tell me, lady of the inn, tell me and then I shall tell my story.'

'Hear what I have suffered, stranger, and share my pain.[S2000]

'He gave up his country and parents, his crown, his relatives, his wealth, his renown, his glory, his splendor. For love of me he renounced his parents. He left his land and his home. He left his land and wandered the world in his search, stranger, to find my country. For two years he wandered. He endured many woes, experienced hardships, suffered misfortunes and troubles. After many miseries he eventually found what he desired.'

'Tell me, lady of the inn, tell me and then I shall tell my story.'[S2010]

'Hear what I have suffered, stranger, and share my pain.

'For another year he waited for my love, for me to fall in love with him. Listen and learn what happened next. My father, the king of Silver Castle, had invited the king of Egypt to come to my country to marry me. In the course of time Verderichos came to my land. He settled and pitched camp outside Silver Castle.[S2020] His party announced itself to my father. He in turn sent a message to Verderichos and they soon reached an agreement about the marriage alliance. But I learnt of my father's plan and did not approve at all of their arrangement.

'My father heard of my stubbornness and angrily said to me, "What do you want, Rodamni?"

'(Listen, stranger, I beg you, to the pangs of my soul.)

'I dutifully replied to him, "Father, mighty king of the land of Silver Castle,$^{(S2030)}$ my soul has been seized by desire for a young man. Love has entered me and holds me in its grip. A mighty man, the noble prince of the land of Livandros left his country and his home through passion and longing for me. His sole purpose was to look for me and he waited another year for my love. I was captivated by him. I pitied him and my mind, till then unbent, bent towards him. To his wish for love I assented.$^{(S2040)}$

' "Now, concerning your own wish, father, I shall propose something of which, I think, even you will approve. Today let the custom of our race be followed. Summon all the Latin races and let a combat of foot soldiers and knights be held. Let all your relatives ride with you, ostensibly for your own recreation. I shall tell Livistros, and you Verderichos, that they will ride and joust and that I shall take the one who is victorious in arms." '$^{(S2050)}$

'Tell me, lady of the inn, tell me and then I shall tell my story.'

'Hear what I have suffered, stranger, and share my pain.[156]

'I said this to my father and he consented. He quickly sent a message to Verderichos who heard and accepted it. He was in complete agreement and the hour of the combat was fixed. And I tell you, my friend, Verderichos was defeated, defeated in a fearsome and noble victory. The fame and renown of Livistros went abroad and he was honored mightily by my father. He was proclaimed king in my land. He was announced as my husband amid great acclamation$^{(S2060)}$ and publicly named the son-in-law of King Chrysos. Glorified and honored beyond all men he was crowned and pronounced king of Silver City. The two of us spent two years of happiness living amid the wonders of the fair castle and enjoying its beauty and charm.

'Listen and learn what happened next. The king of Egypt, the mighty Verderichos, had been beaten, shamed, defeated, and he heard that Livistros had been announced as my husband$^{(S2070)}$ and proclaimed king of Silver Castle. He raged mightily from humiliation. He grew terribly angry and resorted to I know not what guile and cunning. During the two years Livistros spent with me Verderichos was always there waiting to kidnap me.

'Two years passed without trouble. But one day Livistros and I decided to mount our horses and go hunting.$^{(S2080)}$ For our sport and our amusement we intended to release our falcons for partridges. We were completely alone as our squires had gone to another part to hunt.[157] We had not gone a mile from the castle when we found this Verderichos dressed as a merchant together with an old woman, my friend, who was sitting on a camel.

'Livistros saw him, stopped, and asked, "From whence do you come, sir? Who are you and what is your country?"

'He replied, "I am a merchant from Babylon."*(S2090)*

' "And in what do you deal?" he asked.

'The other replied, "Gold, precious stones, pearls, purple cloth, and any fair object you care to name."

'He also had a beautiful horse, stranger, which he showed us. I saw it and mounted.

'Verderichos had a precious stone, my friend, uncut, natural, resembling a ring. He drew it from his bosom and gave it to Livistros. Livistros took it and put it on. He expired immediately and fell down senseless from his horse.*(S2100)*

'As soon as he saw what had happened to Livistros, Verderichos sat himself behind me, whipped the horse and in one day and one night we arrived in Egypt—how, I do not know. The only thing I knew was that I was sitting in the saddle and passing through clouds as I flew in the sky. We first came to a sea; myself, Verderichos, and the old woman with the camel. And when we arrived at the beach he took the camel and left the old woman there alone*(S2110)* in a deserted spot on a cliff by the sea.'

'Tell me, lady of the inn, tell me and then I shall tell my story.'

'Hear what I have suffered, stranger, and now share my pain.

'Verderichos took the old woman's camel and left her sitting there alone on the cliff to worry about what she had suffered in her misery. Again he took me with him and went on. He came to the sea's edge, where we stopped and he said, "Do not grieve. You will be called the mistress of the entire land of Egypt.*(S2120)* I shall give you charge over many possessions and make you mistress of a mighty land. The many rulers of Egypt will do obeisance to you and submit their crowns, my lady, to your will."

With these words he got off the horse and tied me firmly in the saddle so that I would not fall. He mounted again and urged our horse on. How we crossed the sea I do not know.

'We arrived in Egypt and came to his land. Important people who were his relatives, met us.*(S2130)* They dismounted and did obeisance to him and then to me. But why go on at length and make my tale involved? Why draw out the account of my story so much? We came to his land and to his glory. The governors and the leading men learnt the news. His female relatives heard of me and learnt of the boundless sorrow I was suffering, the tears I was shedding for desire of Livistros. The rulers of the land heard and were amazed. At first they started to flatter me*(S2140)* and to say such things as might comfort me. When a person is flattered the harshness of his soul is greatly softened even if he has the nature of a stone. The women, stranger, had confidence in this but they were greatly mistaken and missed their goal completely. I was like a diamond against their flattery.

' "Give up your lament, fair one, be silent, do not grieve. You have wept enough. Your tears give you pleasure. Be assured, the great sorrow you are suffering does not help you. Your noble beauty is wilting, lady,*(S2150)* and the grief of your heart is wasting away your loveliness. They say that if a person's heart is joyful, his face is always blossoming. You were mistress of a great and populous country. But you will rule, madam, the whole of Egypt. You had noble women at your disposal. Noble women you will rule and command again. You were mistress of countless possessions. Now you are the mistress of possessions twice as fair. You had a noble husband who was king of the land.*(S2160)* Today you have a man more handsome than him; the fearsome lord of the entire land of Egypt. You have not sunk in honor at all. You do not have against you the conspiracy of Time or the anger of Fate.[158] If you have been deprived of relatives, acquaintances and friends, today you have us as your relatives, good acquaintances and true friends."

'This was the solace given to me at the very beginning by the leading women of the land of Egypt. But when they saw that my great sorrow could not be moved,*(S2170)* that my tears were unquenchable, and that my grief was something extraordinary, all Verderichos's female relatives stopped, stranger, and after many days went away. They ceased and went, leaving me alone, alone with the memory of Livistros, stranger, to torture and grieve my heart. After that, what stratagem of love did Veredichos not employ, what trick did he not invent to flatter me! I swear in truth's name I am at a loss to list them for you. And when he saw that he could not move me,*(S2180)* or stop my lamentation, or silence my woe, or quench my endless tears, his mind turned from flattery. He began to maltreat me, to trouble me in countless ways and to torture my body every hour. I almost ended by dying of my woes.

'On one occasion I suddenly turned and said to him, "You are not the king of the land. I consider you its executioner. You plunder and lord it over the people you rule. You are now the country's oppressor, not its ruler.*(S2190)* And if, against my will, you come to me as an executioner, not as the country's ruler, then torture me, cut me up, slay me, kill me, chop me up into pieces—I shall take it as pure joy. For me it will be rest, it will be life and nourishment. Know that I shall never satisfy your wish. But if you are lord and king of the land of Egypt, be gentle, do not act as a tyrant, abandon the nature of a bandit, stop maltreating and torturing me, and I shall tell you what I want. If you do it*(S2200)* you will find me disposed towards what you desire." '

'Tell me, lady of the inn, tell me and then I shall tell my story.'

'Hear what I have suffered, stranger, and share my pain.

'When he heard my words he softened a little and replied to me, "Realize this, lady, realize this—be assured of it by me. Love, they say, is capable of terrible madness when unlucky,[159] especially a love for such chaste beauty in a noble woman.[160] Inform me of what you desire. Tell me now what you want*(S2210)* and I swear by my longing for you that I shall quickly fulfil it."

'I heard and replied, "Build me a new inn, with a pool as well, so that by bathing those from abroad I can assuage my sorrow for Livistros. *Let me keep it for four years so that*[161] all those who come from abroad will wash there and tell me what they have suffered and seen in the world. This will lighten my heart's grief. But if, king, you do not do what I have said, then torture me, slay me, cut me up into little pieces. Know that I shall never fulfil your wish."*(S2220)*

'Tell me, lady of the inn, tell me and then I shall tell my story.'

'Hear what I have suffered, stranger, and now share my pain.

'At first, Verderichos would not allow this nor agree in any way to my wish. "For four years," he said, "shall I endure[162] the agony, the flame of Love's furnace which burns with desire? Shall I stand in a sea of so much sweetness but shall I thirst and fear to drink a draught? From love shall I endure a bitterness worse than absinth? Shall I own a lake of honey and not approach it?*(S2230)* Shall I possess a shady tree laden with countless flowers but be burnt in the fire of my desire and fear to draw near its shade? Why do you impose so long a period on me? Do you hope that Livistros will return? You saw how he died. You saw him dead, lifeless, motionless, completely bereft of his senses. But if he did revive, which is utterly impossible, he is separated from Egypt by a journey of two years. How will he come to search for you?*(S2240)* How will he know that you were taken to Egypt? *Who will tell him? How will he find out? Tell me that.* "163

'And I in turn said to him, "Now, Verderichos, torture me, maltreat me, afflict me, burn me, inflict any cruelty on me that a tyrant would. Now I shall never fulfil your wish."

'When he saw that my mind was unyielding in this, he agreed and did what I wanted, fulfilling my desire and my hope. He was obliged to travel and has now been away for half a year I think, stranger.*(S2250)* For the previous time, while he was in his home, harsh torturer that he is and the tyrant who drinks my heart's blood,—day and night—be assured, he did not cease to grieve my heart. This is what my Fortune has made me eat to repletion in this world. This is what unstable Time has made me drink. This is what my Destiny has given me and this is how she has placed me in this inn. You have heard, my friend, the woes I have suffered. You have heard the tortures I have endured.*(S2260)* You have learnt how my fate has inclined to the worse. I have told you of all the agonies I have suffered for love, the many griefs my soul has withstood for desire, the many terrible dangers and trials I have borne.

'Now, stranger, I beseech you endlessly. I conjure you by your weapons, I conjure you by your sword—speak, tell me who you are and from where; what misfortune you have suffered, what you have endured in the world, what you have seen, what you have experienced. Speak, tell me your story.'

In her grief and with many tears and sighs the lady bound me by oath*(S2270)*—and, I swear in truth's name, by my conscience, and by the woes I have endured in the world, if anyone had seen the fair lady when she told of what she had suffered and endured in the world for love, he would have fallen a lifeless corpse and expired. Whenever she spoke of Livistros she immediately fainted. When she recovered a little the lady would cry. When she stopped she would immediately start to sigh. When the lady ceased her sighs$^{(S2280)}$ she began to be racked by countless griefs. She suffered spasms of the soul, failings of the heart, innumerable woes and frequent swoons. I wanted to attend to the lady's story, to comfort her many laments, and to revive her from her fainting. My attention was divided among many tasks and I did not know what to do.

Then, after the lady's long narrative which she related to me with intensity and passion, I began my story$^{(S2290)}$ and I told her what I had suffered, what I had seen, what I had heard and what my Fortune had inflicted on me in the world.

'Hear, lady of the inn,' I then said to her, 'who I am, from where I have come, my native place and the story I heard from my fellow traveler. This I shall tell you. Fair lady, during all the time which you have spent in Egypt, have you heard nothing concerning the Livistros of your story?'

And she said, 'At the end of my first year I received one of his own knights at my inn$^{(S2300)}$—not, stranger, one of the hundred he had, but another from his own land of Livandros—and he said to me, "He is alive and breathes. He is looking for you. He is searching the world for you and weeps for your exile." '

'Hear in turn, my lady of the inn,' I said to her, 'the misfortunes I have suffered in the world. I was born in the land of Armenia, not of a humble[164] family nor of a lowly fortune. My father was noble and likewise my mother; wealthy rulers, feared and of the aristocracy.$^{(S2310)}$ My father's brother was prince of Armenia. He had a beautiful and noble daughter, a lady of lovely figure, remarkable in appearance and of fair sensibility. But the lady had a husband from Persia, a handsome man, feared and first in courage. It happened that he was absent on a journey at that time. Love for the lady entered my mind and I cast desire for her into my heart. My mind was distraught, I was in torture.$^{(S2320)}$ Because of her my soul was suffering terrible pangs. I spent all my time searching for how, lady of the inn, for how I should reveal to her what I was suffering. At one point I found an opportunity. I told the lady of my woes and revealed my passion for her.'

'Tell the lady of the inn what you suffered, stranger.'

'Hear, lady, of the griefs caused by my passion. I told the fair one what I was suffering because of her. She accepted my love and took pity on me. She joined in my sufferings and grief.$^{(S2330)}$ She bent to my love and yielded to my amorous desire. The noble lady's father guessed her passion and in turn learnt of my love. I omit the threats and the harsh words which the prince directed to each of us in turn. To be brief, he ordered for me to be apprehended. He clad me in irons, put manacles on me and threw me into prison where I was held[165] for a year.

'The Persian came back from abroad, lady of the inn.*(S2340)* On returning from his journey he heard the story, learnt everything and constantly sought an opportunity to kill me. The fair one heard of his plan and from then started schemes of all sorts for me to flee the prison, escape death, and go into exile from my country and home. The lady set to work with cleverness. She saw the guards and manipulated them. She gave them money and won them over.*(S2350)* They took off the irons and manacles, opened the prison and showed me the road to leave my country and become a stranger to my home. I left the prison and wandered for a month on difficult tracks and in hidden places. For nourishment I had the woes I was suffering for her and for water I had the tears I constantly shed. For laughter I had sighs, for joy grief, and for companion, my love of the fair one. Such, lady of the inn, is what I have endured.*(S2360)* Such is what I have suffered in the world for love. I have told you of all the woes I have endured for the fair one. I have concealed nothing.

'Now I shall relate to you what a fellow traveller of mine told me during my wanderings.'

'Tell the lady of the inn what you heard, stranger.'

'Hear, lady, his story:

'As I said, I wandered secretly for a month after my escape so that the prince of Armenia would not chase me from my country. And when I had finished this month*(S2370)* I came out onto a side track somewhere in a wild area uninhabited by men. This path I took. For a day or two I went along it and arrived at another road; a fair one which ran through a meadow and was covered with countless trees. On one side was a river and on the other the meadow, and the lovely path stretched out between them. And while I traveled along it I caught up with a man of fair appearance who was going along the path with its countless beauties.*(S2380)* He was mounted on a horse, in his hand was a hawk and behind him a dog followed on a leash. He was girt about with arms and as he went along the road he drenched himself with his tears. He was in torture from his woes. His sighs scorched the path.

'And as I too was suffering countless afflictions from my native land, when I saw such a person sighing constantly, I quickened my pace and sought to learn who he was, where he was from, and the reason for his sighs. And as the young man was grieving and sighing*(S2390)* he did not answer or greet me, but his mind was centred on his tortures and was brooding on the cause of his many sighs. When I saw him, a complete stranger, suffering in such a lonely place in a foreign land, I took him, urged him, and conjured him with fearsome oaths to tell me the cause of his distress and the reason for his sighs. And when I had urged and pressed him much he sorrowfully turned to me and answered.'

'Tell the lady of the inn what you heard, stranger.'*(S2400)*

'Hear, lady, the stranger's story:

' "Sir, if you are a Christian and have suffered in the world, have suffered for love and grieved because of your passion, if you have been tortured through love and a fair lady and have been burnt by the fire of Love's furnace, let me sigh over my woes in solitude. Let me grieve over my countless hardships myself and let me suffer alone what I have suffered on account of my longing. Do not urge me, sir, to tell you why I sigh because, if I tell you the cause of my grief,*(S2410)* you will certainly feel pity for me even if you are more unfeeling than rock. Leave me to suffer alone, to bewail my fate, and to sigh over the oppression of my Destiny. But if you want me to tell you who I am, where I am from, and why I wander and constantly sigh, swear an oath with me that we shall not part, and I shall tell you the misfortunes I have suffered in the world."

'When I heard this I immediately got off my horse, and he with me. The two of us swore*(S2420)* that we would not part even in the face of danger. Hear, lady of the inn, what it was he told me after we had committed ourselves by oath not to separate.'

Then I began to tell her the whole story as Livistros had narrated it to me, except that I concealed his country and his name. The lady sat close by me and attended. She simply sighed, and from her eyes the tears fell silently down like drops. I began the story of Livistros*(S2430)* and told her:

How in the beginning[166] he went out to hunt,
How he hit one dove and the other killed itself,
How he asked his relative about the bird,
How the relative taught him of Love's bonds,
How the relative gave him an emotional account of each aspect of love,

How in his great fear he had a dream that evening,
How the cupids found him and where they took him,
How they spoke to him with advice,
How he entered the courtyard of the lord of love,
How he saw the palace, what he found, what he looked at,*(S2440)*
How he met Love and what Love said to him,
How he swore to Love by his arrow,
How the prophet told him what he would suffer,
How he woke from his dream and to whom he recounted it,
How the following night he had another dream,
How he found Love in the garden,
How Love came holding a beautiful woman,[167]
How Love gave her to him saying, 'Take her,' and how he lost her,
How he again woke up and to whom he told the story,
How he left his country and how long he wandered,
How after many woes, dangers and hardships *and after much distress he*
found what he sought[168]—I told absolutely everything, in detail, to
Rodamni there, the lady of Love's inn.

Then she knew the story[169] and her tears ran down like a channel, her
sighs became louder and more and more frequent. But at the end of my
story I made a mistake—I uttered Livistros's name and country!*(S2470)* The
fair one heard it, fainted and fell to the ground, without spirit or breath,
completely lifeless. I looked at her, I raised her, I held her. I brought water
and refreshed her. She revived a little and I said, 'Do not make a
commotion, be quiet, do not shout. Livistros is here. Have no worry.'
She recovered a little, then fainted and fell in a lifeless swoon close to
insensibility. But why go on at length? She regained her wits, sat up and
said to me:

'Is Livistros alive? Tell me!*(S2480)*
Is he alive, is he alive, the one who was killed by the magic art?
Is he alive, is he alive, the one who was slain by his passion for me?
Is he alive, the one who was rendered lifeless by another's envy of me?
Is he alive, the one on whom my Destiny exhausted her bitterness?
Is he alive, the one whom Fate murdered because of me?
Is he alive? Has he come from Hades? Speak! Tell me!'

I said to her, 'He is alive. Have no worry for him. And here is the veil,
lady, which you gave him when he fought with Verderichos for you.'

She reached over, looked, took the veil and recognized whose it was.*(S2490)*
She said to me, 'Where did you leave Livistros, stranger? How did you

leave him? Alone? As you love him, tell me. Do not deceive me. Tell me this—is Livistros alive? Tell me! Tell me how he revived and came back to life. My doubts are many and my disbelief great. A dead man come back to life—who will believe it? If he is really alive, which I doubt, how has he come to me? Who showed him the way? From where did he learn it? If he has come, which is completely unbelievable,[170] why has he not come to me?'

And again the fair one fainted and fell.*(S2500)* Again her mind lost consciousness and her heart was thrown into confusion. Again her soul was deadened by a swoon and again she revived after much effort on my part. She shed rivers of tears and her breath was fire. Nevertheless, I calmed Rodamni's tears. I said to her, 'Cease your crying. Abandon it! You are putting Livistros and me in great danger. From now be quiet. There is no need of tears now. You have seen how things stand. You know the full story. You have a sure token that Livistros is alive*(S2510)* after being killed by the magic art. Stop your sighs, stop your tears, stop! You will see Livistros here in the evening at dinner-time. You will see him sitting with you, comforting you, telling you how he revived and came back to life, and how he placed himself under me, his friend dear as life. And now I give you this order: take care that you have with you here tomorrow the horse which took you and carried you off from Silver Castle. And, as you see, it is now the hour of midnight.*(S2520)* Let me go to sleep and tomorrow at dinner-time I shall bring Livistros, who has suffered for you.'

The time of the night passed, the beauty of the dawn appeared and the day rose. Again the lady of the inn came, amid many tears, terrible grief, and frequent sighs. She stood by me, woke me and said, 'Awake, your hostess calls you, stranger. Awake, the day has risen. Take the road and leave me by myself to lament my woes.'*(S2530)*

I woke and said to her, 'Have no worry. You have your veil as a token of Livistros.'

She replied, 'Yes.'

And I said, 'You also give me a token so that I shall have a proof to show him that I have found you.'

She straightway took off the ring which he had first sent her with the love letter. She said, 'Here, friend, take this ring. This is the one he sent me with the love letter. I conjure you by the misfortunes you have suffered in

the world, I conjure you by your head and the weapons you bear:^(S2540)
hasten[171] so that he comes quickly, stranger, so that I can see him and my
soul can somewhat escape from its woes.'

I told her, 'As for him, have no worry. Only take care, lady, to have the
horse ready so that you can start with us tonight. Farewell, and do not
grieve. Take comfort as best you can.'

I quickly saddled my horse, donned my arms and immediately mounted. I
bade her farewell and dashed off. I found Livistros and when he saw me he
ran from a distance to meet me.^(S2550) He held me, embraced me and
covered me with endless kisses. His mind lay midway between joy and
grief. His soul trembled constantly for news. He started to ask me if my
journey had gone well, if I had found what I sought, if I had seen the lady,
and if I had discovered the road to her inn. Because of the anxiety that I
saw possessed him—if a soul in the grips of love comes to suffer, it has
the passion of its love as a reminder and is impatient to learn what has
happened to the object of its desire^(S2560)—I said to him, 'Stop, do not be
impatient. I have found what you wanted. I have found the inn and its
lady, and, further, here is her ring which you originally sent to her with
the love letter.'

He held the ring and looked at it in his agony. He recognized it was his,
fainted and fell. His heart trembled, his soul was in a swoon and from his
sudden joy he came close to death. The heart is shaken by something that
happens suddenly, whether of joy or of grief.^(S2570) I saw he was fainting.
I held him and revived him. I said, 'Why faint? Come back to yourself!
Hold your heart firm! Why does your soul tremble? You have suffered so
many misfortunes, you have seen so many hardships, you have withstood
so many trials and other ill treatment and you did not fall in a swoon.
Why faint now when, more than ever, you wish to be rid of the old woes
of an unstable fortune and for a joyous fortune to draw nigh?'

He stood up and recovered from his swoon.^(S2580) After reviving from his
terrible dizziness he said, 'Friend Klitovon, you who share my desires and
my woes, my friend, my dear friend, you who have comforted me in my
toil, strengthened my soul and lightened my grief:

'My friend, dear fellow sufferer, leaf[172] of my soul,
My friend, whom my Fortune has battered with me,
My friend, whom my Destiny has distressed because of me,
My friend, whom Time has afflicted together with me,

My friend, whom I used not to know but whom Time, against hope, has proved my friend—and what a friend!*(S2590)* True, steadfast, a genuine friend to your friends.

'What return shall I give for your friendship? What shall I be able to do as a fair recompense for what you have been through with me and as a requital for your love? And what suffering shall I be able to endure in return for what you have endured with me? What storm of the soul like that you have endured on my behalf? And, friend of my heart, what turmoil of the heart shall I be able to suffer in return for what you have suffered with me? Do I not owe the discovery of the lady to you,*(S2600)* to your true friendship and your esteem? My friend, sit with me, you who have comforted my misery, who have shared my woes and longing from the time when you first suffered griefs with me and we became companions in one camp of sorrow. There we were instructed by the world's miseries which were kneaded by our flooding tears as we moulded the earth with our sighs. Sit down and tell me, friend of my heart, when and how you arrived there, and how you found Rodamni.*(S2610)* What speech did you have with her? What story did you tell her? What reply did she make? How did you make yourself known? How great was the lady's sorrow when she spoke?'

I sat down and told him how I had found the lady, how I had greeted her and what she had replied, how she had begun to relate her sufferings, how I had told her of my own, and, finally, how the lady had caught his name, had fainted and fallen. When I had finished, I gave him instructions.

'If, when we get to the inn,*(S2620)* you see the object of your desire, do not become confused and dismayed like one who has suffered much. Do not sigh and weep and so reveal our discovery of the lady. Put aside everything—shouting, weeping. Refrain from a multitude of questions and tales. *Simply take the lady and kiss her. Then let us ride off immediately and not delay.'* [173]

'Yes, my friend,' he replied. 'I shall do what you bid. Your words and advice are good. And come, let us go and not be late on our journey.'

I took Livistros and we started on the road. He began a dirge with these words:*(S2630)* 'The mountains sigh, the plains suffer for me, the slopes mourn, the meadows thunder, and the trees that I passed, the streams and the gorges, still know my woes and sigh for me. They say, "A knight in pain went by here, young and afire with passion for a fair lady. His tears were rivers, his sighs claps of thunder, his tortured breath was smoke above the mountains. The sun was his witness and, sharing his journey,[174] it covered itself in clouds and grieved for his troubles."*(S2640)* See my woe, the pain of my heart, friend Klitovon. The mountains feel it, things without life suffer in unison!'

I heard Livistros sing his dirge. As he went along the road he cried out mournfully over the fields and my thoughts went to Myrtani. Remembering her, I sang a dirge: 'A much afflicted youth, expelled from his country—the love of a fair lady has put him on the rack and he has gone from his land and from his home. With the steps of an exile he wanders over foreign parts.*(S2650)*[175] He thinks the trees are his woes, the meadows are his afflictions, and his tears rivers and his sighs mountains.[176] If he hears a nightingale sing by the road the beating of his heart and his thunderous sighs stop it from uttering the voice of its heart. This is the misfortune which the knight suffers for his lady. This is his exile—a stranger in a wild land!'

Why go on? Why draw out my story with many words to extend its length? We finally came to the inn*(S2660)* and found the fair lady Rodamni sitting like a guard and watching the road. Her tears were flowing, her sighs were frequent and she was constantly expecting her innkeeper. Livistros was in front and I behind. The lady did not recognize Livistros at once, but he looked at her and recognized her immediately. He rushed up to her, fainted and fell. I grabbed him, held him, lifted him up. I stood and revived him. He came to his senses. The lady looked at him,*(S2670)* her senses failed her and she too fainted in turn. I left him and quickly ran to her. I brought water to refresh her and she recovered a little. I took her inside and put her in the inn. She regained her wits and looked for Livistros, but he had fallen again in a lifeless state. I went back to him and saw him there unconscious. Though without his senses[177] he was constantly quivering and shaking. He was on the point of death, on the way to Hades. I lifted him from the ground, put him on my shoulders*(S2680)* and carried him inside the inn. Even after much trouble I had difficulty in bringing him back to life. I took him in his unconscious state and went to the lady. They looked at each other and revived a little. They took each other, flung out their arms and tightly embraced. They joyously kissed and that kiss was the delight of Love and the concern of Aphrodite. As they kissed[178] and embraced, a noble desire viewed and sweetly enfolded the great joys of their love,*(S2690)* joys bound by a guileless and pure affection. Then they separated, sat down and began to speak words full of love and exiled desire.

'Greetings to the lady of the inn!'

'Greetings to my innkeeper!' she said.

'Greetings to the comfort of my entire heart!' he said.

'Greetings to her whom the magic art removed far from me!

'Greetings to her whom her Fortune afflicted because of me!'

With these words they fainted and fell once more. Again they lost consciousness[179] and their hearts were shaken.[S2700] Again their souls trembled in their swoon. To my astonishment, I witnessed something fearful: Love and Death were fighting one another. He fainted and she recovered, then she fell unconscious and he revived. They were making frequent switches between consciousness and unconsciousness from him[180] to her, from her to him.

I leave this. I pass over in silence what happened then. What would be the point? Everyone knows how much people suffer and the torments they endure when Love the master enters[181] into them in pure and guileless form[S2710] and nothing unforeseen occurs to them in their desire. I leave this, I pass over what they said then.

I said to the lady, 'Madam, Queen Rodamni (I shall not call you lady of the inn now), why are we delaying? The moon has risen (it was evening when we came to the inn) and if the horse is ready, as I instructed you, come, let us be off and not dally.'

The fair one heard and replied,[S2720] 'My excellent Klitovon, friend of Livistros, look, the horse is ready. Come, let us be off.'

And I said to Livistros, 'Why are you delaying now? Why are you wasting time? Hasten to the strait. You and I are foreigners in a foreign land. Let us not talk or the day will appear and be upon us, you will be recognized as Livistros and they will kill us.'

He heard, got up, and put on his weapons. The lady mounted her horse first, then myself and Livistros, and we set out on the road.[S2730] But while we were mounting and on the point of departure, Livistros wrote a message to leave at the inn:

'If tomorrow you seek your lady of the inn, do not shout or make a commotion. Know that her innkeeper, who was abroad, now possesses her. He had suffered countless miseries for her sake and has found her again through the offices of a good friend. He has taken her, departed, and left for his home.'

We went along the road and I said to the lady, 'Fortify your heart and your wits.*(S2740)* Sit well in your saddle. Grip your reins. Keep whipping your horse and, come, let us be off. Hasten, lady, so that we may reach the strait at dawn.'

At dawn we came to the strait and crossed it with ease, as was willed by the demon's art and the old witch's guileful tricks. Once more we saw her hut and as we galloped towards it we shouted for her. The ill-starred old unfortunate came out, saw who we were, and did obeisance on recognizing us,*(S2750)* the lady and Livistros, and myself with them. She beseeched us as best as she could and asked for a recompense and reward for her magic arts.

The fair one saw the old woman and recognized her. She recalled the cruel results caused by her magic, she remembered the separation from Livistros that she had endured. All the misfortunes that she had suffered because of the old woman came to her mind. She remembered, and she conceived a terrible anger against her. With fearsome oaths she addressed Livistros:*(S2760)*

'I conjure you by the misfortunes you have suffered for me, I conjure you by my love and my passion—kill this foul and evil woman. Her magic art exiled me from you and rendered you lifeless.'

Livistros drew his sword and cut off the evil witch's head. 'Today,' he said, 'I free the world of a great evil and I kill a demon in human form.'

With this cry Livistros killed the old woman. He took the fair one and started on the journey*(S2770)* which we had previously made with distressed souls, but which we were now beginning with great joy. And while we were going along the path of gladness the lady gave Livistros an account of their love from the beginning, the first attachment, and how much he had suffered to win her; then how treacherous Fortune had afflicted them and all that Time with its threads of sorrow had done. The lady asked whether he had told his friend about her letters and whether he had ever recited them.*(S2780)* And Livistros began to tell her how many of the fair lady's letters he had repeated to his friend and how many of his own, and how many he had omitted to recite to me. The lady started to recount them from her own mouth.

'Friend Klitovon, listen to the letter which Livistros sent me because of
the grief he suffered on my account: "A shoot of love germinated in my
heart and a tree of woe took root, what a calamity! Love's bush and woe's
tree are flowering.*(S2790)* The latter has fruit but the former has leaves.
From the tree of woe I gather a harvest of bitterness but from the shoot of
love I pick leaves of sweet affection. Love sweetens a little, woe
envenoms more. *Love is small and woe is greater.*[182] *Woe's tree and
love's shoot are the longing for a fair lady and this afflicts me with
countless tortures. I want to pull up the tree of woe but its roots
immediately entwine themselves with those of love's shoot, which has
sent its own roots into my heart and, after taking possession, grows with
it. I am reluctant to pull up love's shoot(N3390) and I say, 'Let the tree of
woe stay with it; love and pain come from you. I suffer pain because of
my love. Grant what I desire so that I am not tortured in vain.'* "

'Hear, friend Klitovon, my letter in reply to the one he had sent:

*' "You say that, on account of me, a sprig of love has taken root in your
heart. You say that a whole tree of woe has come up, that love is small
but woe is greater, and that you ignore the woe because of the love you
desire. Knight, look to what befits you.(N3400) Certainly, love does not
exist without woe. So conceive a love for the woe so that you have the
love as well; or tear up the shoot which love planted so that, for a little
love, you do not get a tree of woe. But if you leave the shoot of love in
your heart, know that the tree of love will grow top." '*

*When Livistros had heard the lady he said, 'I remember, lady, your letter
of love and my letter to you when I was in pain. And listen, friend
Klitovon. I shall recite it to you:(N3410)* "Love, I now deny you and call
you a liar. I break the bond which I made with you. I trample on what I
swore. I renounce my service to you. I shall proclaim that your bow is
idle. I shall tell the world that your torch is without fire and that your
arrow that flies and makes humans captive has struck a rock and has
broken completely. You are not an ally of passion, you are not a friend of
desire. A stubborn lady surpasses you in haughtiness. She breaks your
bow with her arrogance and has extinguished your torch with her pride.
With all her superciliousness she has rendered you*(S2800)* completely
helpless against her beauty. It was through your power and authority that
I became an exile from my own land and went through many a place and
country as an outcast. Because of your promise I suffered terrible woes. I
have come to the lady who was born of the sun and I endure countless
tortures. I had confidence in you but I see that you do not help me. What
road shall I now tread in my exile? What people shall I now approach in

my utter destitution? Whom shall I tell what I have suffered? Whom shall I beseech?$^{(S2810)}$ The sky, the sun, the moon, the three siblings,[183] the earth, trees, mountains, rivers, fountains? I swear in truth's name that I do not know, and my soul's woe bears me, soul and all, off to Hades—ah, the injustice! Let me tell you this, lady, since I am being slain by you and shall, perhaps, again find life in the world through you. I am the one, fair lady, whom passion for you has captured, whom desire for you has tortured in the world. If it is true that you have feelings, you will take pity on me. But if you leave me to go on suffering countless tortures,$^{(S2820)}$ of my own free will I shall seize my sword and cut my heart in two."

'This was the letter I sorrowfully wrote to the lady and she, friend Klitovon, took pity on me: "That was a message from a soul distressed by love. That was a missive from a loving heart plunged into sorrow. That was a letter of distress from an afflicted knight. In turn, my knight, accept my reply, which I write in the grief and the sighs that have come upon me after your letter and its message.$^{(S2830)}$ Tell me why you call Love a liar, stamp on what you swore, resign your service, renounce the vassalage you engaged in, and tell the world that his bow is idle? Why do you suffer for what you desire and sigh for what you love? If it is because of what you say, my knight, be assured by me that what you assert is false and that there is no justice in it. If perchance you suffer because of a passion which you desire, then you will deny the love to which you are enslaved.[184] But if you think that you are sighing on your own$^{(S2840)}$ and that no-one pities you for your sorrow or sighs with you, be informed by me, long-suffering heart, that I am suffering for your suffering, yes, I am grieved at what makes you sad. As for your thinking that you suffer and that no-one pities you, I am suffering twice as much and my sighs are without number. And now, my comfort, my sweet desire, my bachelor knight, my heart, you who are inseparable from me, know that my hands have written this letter with great pain and sent it to you."

'You have heard, friend Klitovon, the lady's message as well.$^{(S2850)}$ You wonder how her loving heart, without experience in affection, came to love, submitted to passion, and wrote such wonderful letters to send to me. However, when a loving mind has entered upon affection, it discovers for itself the impulses of desire and love.'

And after the love-letters which the lady recited to me and, with her, Livistros, we found a sloping meadow, flowering and green, which was full of lovely trees and springs as cold as snow; each tree and each spring$^{(S2860)}$ was a resting place of grace and love, an encampment of charm. We saw the sloping meadow, the trees and springs, and the superbly beautiful flowers which adorned the place. *We directed ourselves to this and made a halt. When we were on the meadow we got off our horses and spied a tree and spring suitable for a camp.*[185] There we stayed to revive ourselves. And because of the charming place with its flowers and the meadow with its countless graces the idea came upon me to sing:

> 'A knight and lady,
> take rest in a meadow.
> Grieved by love,*(S2870)*
> afflicted by passion,
> they take rest in a meadow
> because of its charm.
> For a resting place they have a tree,
> and the lovely field.
> At a fair spring
> they speak of what they have suffered,
> how treacherous fortune
> separated them,
> how many woes *(S2880)*
> were caused by their parting.
> They see the beauty of the place
> and it gives them joy.
> They forget the troubles
> which they both have suffered,
> and they rejoice over their union
> in the lovely meadow.'

And when I had finished this ditty, Livistros started to sing a fair song which had these words:*(S2890)*

'O Moon, you have found together the two whom love has tortured in the world and has filled to satiety with unnumbered woes through the instability of treacherous Fortune. Comfort them, shine your rays on them and send them a message that they have now emerged from the griefs of former years. When they return[186] to their home I shall set up, dear Moon, a memorial to you.'

The time came for us to rest and we slept a little. When we saw the day,*(S2900)* we started again. We took to the road and joyfully began on our way. The lady started to relate to us the verses which she had composed for her lock of hair:

' "Dear knight, here is a lock of hair, a lock of my hair which my hands tore out by the roots and sent for you to keep as a memento. If you wish to see the power it has, tie it on your neck, wind it tightly. You will learn, dear knight, how it will awaken memories,$^{(S2910)}$ and what recollection of my love it will bring back to your mind. Do not tie it to any other part of your body because I tore it out by the roots from my head so that, tied on your neck, it would remind you of our love. Keep this lock of hair as you would me and consider, knight, that you have me with you."

'And hear, friend Klitovon, the letter of Livistros.[187] "Dear heart, the lock of hair, the lock of your hair—I carried out your order and tied it to my neck. And because it was torn out by the roots, it came to life of its own accord inside my heart and embraced me.$^{(S2920)}$ From thinking of you I have not rested a moment. Without you I do not live at all, be assured of that! In return for your lock of hair take, dear heart, a pillow. My love cut leaves from my heart and I sewed them together by myself and filled the pillow with reminders of love and thoughts of desire. When you place your cheek on this, it will, on my behalf, say in your ear, 'Do not cast aside your love for me.' Regard, lovely one, this pillow of mine$^{(S2930)}$ as a part of my feelings, for such it is. Look at it and see in it a reminder of me. Hold it in place of me, kiss it, embrace it. Consider that I am with you, that you are kissing me." '

I am drawing the story out. I am telling it at far too great a length. I now leave off the lady's verses.

At one point we came to the tree and found the spring where I had dreamed about Verderichos. Livistros saw and recognized it, and said to the lady, 'You see this tree? You see this spring?$^{(S2940)}$ When we started off to look for you we were wearied and we dismounted from our horses to rest here by this tree and this lovely fountain. Here my friend Klitovon had a dream which helped us to find you, fair lady.'

He began to tell her the dream and how I interpreted the way in which it would be realized. The beautiful and loving Rodamni marveled at my soul's pure friendship for him.

Days passed and we came to the place$^{(S2950)}$ where I had found the distressed Livistros going by a fair meadow and a delightful river along the narrow path with its countless charms. When Livistros saw it he sighed deeply and turning to Rodamni he said, 'How many of my laments lie in this meadow, how many of my sighs lie on this path, how many tear-drops from my heart lie in this river! If sighs[188] took root and laments sprouted, if tears shed by those in distress were collected,*(S2960)* you would see my sighs as trees, fair one. You would see my laments as plants in the meadow and my tears would supply the river's font. When my Fortune parted you from me, I wandered alone and searched the world for you. The path you see and this meadow with its flowing river received me in my great distress. Here the excellent Klitovon, a friend as dear to me as life, found me with my countless troubles, made me his friend, and swore by my friendship to die with me.'*(S2970)*

The lady turned to him and saw his tears. She said to me, 'Klitovon, most excellent of friends, root and tree of affection, what recompense can I find to give you for your true friendship and your esteem?'

When I saw that her eyes were dropping a tear, I said, 'Hush, lady, be quiet. Do not grieve. We are on the road of joy. You must not sigh. You both must abandon your distress and sing a ditty.'

Immediately Livistros, who had a beautiful voice, one quite out of the ordinary, started to sing:*(S2980)*

'The road I traveled in distress for your sake—now with you, fair lady, I go along it full of joy. Then I had woes with me as traveling companions; now I have happiness once more. Then, in place of laughter, I filled the road with sighs; now, in place of sighs, I fill it with the joys of the world. Then I constantly shed rivers of tears; now, instead, a river of joy flows from me. Then I had with me Fortune's anger;*(S2990)* now I have survived her trials and go on. Happy am I since I suffered for love of a beautiful woman! I shall boast to the world that my sufferings were not in vain!'

Livistros sang his song with great joy and much emotion. I said, 'Why do we delay? Let us dismiss everything. Let us be silent about our many trials and interrupt everything. If you relate old troubles, affliction torments you in double measure. A man must suffer*(S3000)* from what has recently happened to him when he recounts it with emotion.[189] So forget, Livistros, forget, Rodamni, what happened in the past. Hasten along the road, quicken your steps and go to the sight of those who await you. For two years, lady, you have been an exile from your home, and for two years this man has been removed from the world on account of you.'

And what happened then? They set aside everything, their flame, their love, their passion, their desire, the countless misfortunes and innumerable woes,[S3010] the terrible afflictions, the exile. They hastened along the road, quickened their steps and we came to the road's beginning, which was our goal, where there were a hundred paths to many different lands. It was here that Livistros in his misery had dispatched the hundred relatives who accompanied him. He found them there as he had ordered them. The hundred met him, dismounted, and did obeisance. They held him, embraced him, and covered him with endless kisses, the handsome Livistros, and the lovely Rodamni.[S3020] For their sake the hundred had suffered unnumbered woes. Each started to tell Livistros how much of the world he had passed through, how many countries he had seen, how many misfortunes he had witnessed and what had happened to him. This I shall omit. I shall pass over what was then said. I shall strike out this episode too as my story is long. Who could tell in a few words of the joy of that moment? Who could describe it? How could he tell in detail, by word of mouth, the stories of the hundred?[S3030]

When the hundred were assembled, Livistros told them how much of the world he had passed through, how he had acquired me as his dearest friend, and how he had found the lady through what I had done. With these stories and talks we spent six days there. And at the end of these six days Livistros addressed me with these words:

'Excellent friend Klitovon, worthy companion, pillar possessed of life,[S3040] faithful friend to your friends and true to those you love, I have attained my wish through your actions, your steadfast mind, your esteem, your excellent counsel and your wisdom. I want now to make some recompense, some return for your friendship and sound judgement. You too have been afflicted by love's desire. Affection's flame has lit your heart too. Passion's hailstorm has lashed your soul from within and you have been wounded by Love's bow.[S3050] The fury of an amorous attachment has subdued your mind. Since you have suffered in the world from the same cause as myself, I wish to make a return to you and suffer with you in what you have suffered with me. Come, let us take the road to Armenia, and when we come to the city of Litavia I shall be able, friend Klitovon, to do you the same service as you have done me. Today I am handing the lady over to my hundred men for them to take her to Silver Castle.[S3060] Alone, with no companion, we shall take the road to Armenia.'

With an afflicted air, sad appearance, and countless sighs I replied, 'Friend Livistros, prince of the land of Livandros, I have told you of the woes I suffered through Fortune. You know the pangs I have endured in the world. It is impossible to undertake the matter of my amorous attachment and set it right. It is not possible for us alone, without helper or guide, to go resolutely over such a distance,*(S3070)* spy out the land, conduct a search, and then find and meet the queen of a mighty and populous country. Alone without guides we cannot! I have done what befitted me, my friend. I have fulfilled the bond of my friendship and carried out love's duty fully. Now I shall bid you farewell, my friend, and go to dwell in another world under another sky.'

When Livistros heard this he became angry.*(S3080)* He sighed from his heart, his tears streamed down. He was suffering terrible grief and he said, 'Friend Klitovon, hear again the beginning of woe, the beginning of bitterness and pain for me if you exile yourself from me, my dear friend. I conjure you by what you suffered and endured on my behalf. I implore you by the bitterness you have experienced at Fortune's hands. But you know that you swore to die with me. And again I conjure and beseech you by your sword: do not go away, do not exile yourself, do not leave me.*(S3090)* I shall share my power equally with you and I shall make you my brother-in law. The lovely Rodamni has a sister like her, who resembles her in every way. Give up all this, cast it aside, abandon it and come with me, Klitovon, to Silver Castle and enjoy with me the fair charms of the castle and its surroundings. If perchance you do not consent to this, friend Klitovon, know that with you I shall share my life, my sufferings,*(S3100)* my hardships, the pangs of exile and death to see if Fortune changes from the hostility she now shows towards you. But give up all this and take my advice. What you have suffered in former years is enough. Rejoice, spend the rest of your life in joy, in comfort and prosperity. Do not wait for the trials of treacherous Fortune. Do not endure the misfortunes sent by insane Destiny. You see the time which <Fortune's> wheel[190] has now allocated to you.*(S3110)* She has changed from maltreating you. Take courage from her goodwill and live. Exile yourself from past misfortunes.'

I heard, I was swayed and I consented. I softened a little through faintheartedness. I gave up my stubbornness and adopted a different attitude. I yielded to Livistros's advice and wish. I judged it better to live than to die and I picked the best of the evils at hand. I said in reply, 'Livistros, ruler of the land,*(S3120)* I agree to your wish and I obey. I shall go to your country to die there with you.'

Why should I tell in detail what I said, what Livistros said, and the charming words of the lady and of the hundred men? I pass over everything in silence.[191] We started again along the road, the path which led to the land of Silver Castle. And who will describe the joy, the happiness and the pleasure witnessed on the fair road? But most I shall omit. I shall only record the lines which Livistros[S3130] composed on the way.

'I went over the whole earth. I followed the sun. Alone, in two years, I traversed as much of the world as he does in one day. I sought to find and meet a fair lady whom Time had unseasonably exiled from my love. My heart suffered countless woes. I withstood terrible miseries, hardships beyond nature. Sorrows shook my inner soul. And at one point I found a friend, one who shared the grief of my love,[S3140] who chose to endure my woes with me. He was my companion, prepared to join me in death. This he swore. He made an oath that we would not part.

'I found the one I sought. I won her whom treacherous Fortune had taken from me. I took her and I am returning to my home. As my companion I have also the friend of my heart, the one whom I had amidst my sorrows to share the grief of my love.'

So we went along the road with its fair charms. And when the lovely Rodamni with her countless graces[S3150] saw that I was now named as her brother-in-law, she showed I cannot say how much love for me, how much affection, warmth and sincere feeling. But I omit the details up to our arrival at the castle. If I were to think back and recall how many fair and pleasant diversions we enjoyed on the road when Misfortune and the madness of Fate had finally left us, you would say that I was still witnessing and enjoying them. Since there are many things which I cannot relate[S3160] I shall pass over the many intervening details and say this: we came to Silver Castle.

All the many inhabitants of Silver Castle came out to meet Queen Rodamni. They used much ornament and decorated much of the road with pearls and silk, gold and precious stones. There was a great commotion which reached the clouds—musical instruments, sistrums, tambourines, horns, every type which adorned the great land of Silver Castle. They came out to meet Queen Rodamni[S3170] and immediately shouted this eulogy:

'To Livistros, all-prosperous and great king of all the famous and glorious land of Silver Castle and prince of the land of Livandros, with the fair Rodamni, our glorious and supremely prosperous queen, many happy years free of all care!'

Three times they sang it amid shouting and noise. There was such a commotion that you would have said that the whole earth was shaking, tottering and moving.

What happened next? We entered the castle*(S3180)* and the splendid palace with its fair inner courtyard. We saw it and disported ourselves there for not a few days. Then Livistros assembled all his governors, chiefs, dukes, and his relatives. He sat in royal state and addressed them:

'Dear relatives, governors, dukes, by virtue of your judgement and wish I was made king of the land of Silver Castle with Rodamni, who was born your queen. You all are fully aware of what happened to me and Rodamni.*(S3190)* You all know the story. My friend Klitovon, given to me by Fortune as a comfort in my many misfortunes, has come today with me to my country, a complete and unhappy exile. But if it had not been for him with his good counsel and firm mind I would still not have seen Queen Rodamni. Since my most excellent friend Klitovon, the fairest nephew of the prince of Armenia, put his life into danger for me,*(S3200)* went through countless lands, and shared my woes and sufferings, so, if you approve, dear relatives, I take him as husband for the sister of Queen Rodamni and name him my brother-in-law.'

The sister's name was Melanthia. The leading men of the land and the governors heard, united in approval and did obeisance to us. A second time they pronounced a eulogy, with these words: 'To Klitovon, the brother-in-law of the all-prosperous Livistros,*(S3210)* the mighty king of the land of Silver Castle, and to the noble queens Rodamni and Melanthia, many happy years free of all care!'

I was made king with Melanthia. (I abridge the story and speak concisely. From now I shall tell what happened in broad outline.) I lived a number of years with Melanthia. I was happy, I forgot the past years, the difficult threads of unstable Fortune. My mind had no care—or if it did, it forgot.*(S3220)* Again the will of unjust Fortune changed, the wheel of Time turned against me and Death sharpened his sword. Like a robber, Charos took the lady Melanthia. Death killed the comfort of my soul and Hades unjustly seized my source of sweetness and delight. I alone was made the servant of misfortune. In my dominion of woe I suffered[192] my miserable Fortune. Again I was an exile in a foreign world, an exile in the joyous land of Silver Castle*(S3230)* even though[193] I had the glory of a crown and a worldly kingdom. Again my heart turned to thinking, pondering and deliberation, to recollection, care and reflection—I had to leave. Alone, I had to go to my own country if there was a road and if I was able to find it.[194]

So I mounted my horse, donned my weapons, and went in search of my native land. And after six months I arrived here and found you, my relatives and friends of the land of Litavia. And you, lovely Queen Myrtani,[(S3240)] I found a widow. With you I shall live, with you I shall die. With you I shall share death and suffering. Together we shall enjoy our ancestral dominion. For you I left a populous land, and I suffered all the misfortunes which I have related to you. I endured all the woes, lady Myrtani, which I recounted and which you have heard.

I have told you, lovely Queen Myrtani, of my friend's woes which he suffered by himself and with me.[(S3250)] But the troubles which I suffered in the world, who will describe them? What other person will tell of my hardships, who will speak of my afflictions, who will write of my woes, who will set forth my sorrows in detail? But a man whose soul is so inclined will pity those who suffer, will learn from their sorrow, and will tell their story to other sufferers. *If someone, after inquiry and scrutiny, writes down <my story> in detail,*[195] even though he cannot tell everything, he will compose an account of most of what I say.[(S3260)] But if perchance some lover wishes to describe it, he will refashion it according to his wish and fancy.

The story of Livistros is now, by the grace of the Almighty, finished. Praise be to God!

Notes

N.B. Emendations suggested in Lambert's critical apparatus have in most cases been adopted without comment.

1 The manuscript S also contains a second version (designated as Σ) of about 270 lines of its text. This can be ignored for present purposes.

2 The only two editions, both published last century, were based on insufficient evidence.

3 The suggestions of Hatziyiakoumis (pp.161f.) on the use of the manuscripts have been followed.

4 See bibliography. This book, which is of paramount importance for the study of the romance, is not an edition in any normal sense of the word. It is an edited transcript of N (up to *l*.979), S and E.

5 The Greek compound, ἐρωτοπαιδευμένος, which occurs three times in the first twenty lines, can mean either *schooled in, versed in, love* or *tortured by, persecuted by, love*. The latter meaning seems to be emphasized in the third instance, the former in the first two.

6 Following the text of Hatziyiakoumis (p.147) in N22, N24.

7 P13 (Λατῖνος ἦταν...).

8 P30 (τὸ ἐκράτει...).

9 P56 (συνοδοιπόρε...).

10 Reading τά for τό and τα for το (twice) in N81 and inserting after it E50f. with the emendations σύντομα and κίνδυνον.

11 Substituting E58f. for N85.

12 Substituting E67-71 for N92 and reading κίνδυνος for εἰς κίνδυνον in E70 (cf. S2421) and with Lambert's changes in E68.

13 Another form of Charon (cf. *Kallimachos l.*235, p.41 above and note). The meaning of this sentence appears to be that Livistros's weapons have reduced him to this state because, as we learn later, they were of no use in preventing Rodamni's abduction.

14 Following the text of Hatziyiakoumis (p.148) in N110.

15 The river god Alpheios from the west Peloponnese pursued the nymph Arethusa across the Ionian Sea. When she was changed into a spring at Syracuse in eastern Sicily, he consummated his love by mingling his water with hers. This and the other examples of non-human love formed a regular topos in the rhetorical tradition inherited from antiquity.

16 Dropping ἄνθρωπος from N199 (on the syntax cf. S402) and emending χαί to κἄν in N201.

17 Following the text of Hatziyiakoumis (p.148) in N226.

18 Emending οὐκ to την in N235.
19 This sentence is the version in E (*l*.242) with Lambert's correction.
20 Reading τροπικῆς τοῦ στέγους/ ἡ κρίση in P278f. (καὶ εἶχεν...).
21 Following the text of Hatziyiakoumis (p.148) in P283 (νὰ στέκουν...).
22 Following the text of Hatziyiakoumis (p.148) in P306 (καὶ ἡ ἄλλη...).
23 P338 (ῥοῦχον λατινοκόκοπον...).
24 Substituting E327f. for N466.
25 Reading δικάζει in N427 (cf. P373 ἃς ἔλθῃ...) and του at the end of the next line.
26 In N430 taking ἀπ᾽ from P376 (ἐμεταστάθην...) and in N431 reading κρυφοφιλοῦνται from P377.
27 In N361 reading ἀπὸ μαρμάρον from V.
28 In N389 reading νὰ εἶπες from E395.
29 Following the text of Hatziyiakoumis (p.149) in N391.
30 In N288 reading αὐτούς from P421 (σεβαίνω ἀπέσω...).
31 In N295 reading τρυφερόν from P428 (ἀπαλοσάρκιν...)
32 In N318 reading αἰσθητῶν from P453 (τῶν ἀναισθήτων...).
33 In this passage, P470 (ἐπροσηκώθην ἐκ...) to P558, various readings have been taken from E without comment.
34 Reading στομάτων for τὸ στόμα in P474 (καὶ ἤκουες...).
35 Reading τῆς καθεμίας for της τῆς μίας in P483 (ὁλόλαμπρα ἦν...).
36 Deleting εἰς in P485 (τῶν δύο...).
37 Reading ὀμνεῖ τὸν Ἔρωτά μου in P490 (λέγουν την...) and ψευσθῇ τό in P491 (ἵνα μὴ...); the latter reading is from E481.
38 Replacing the latter half of P508 (τὸ ἐγγυτικόν...) with the latter half of E498.
39 Following the text of Hatziyiakoumis (p.149) in P533 (σύζιοι νὰ...).
40 Following the text of Hatziyiakoumis (p.149) in P539 (θεωρεῖτε το...).
41 The last clause has been taken from E538.
42 Following the text of Hatziyiakoumis (pp.149f.) in P556 (πολλῶν πραγμάτων...).
43 These two clauses are from E (*l*.544). Also, in both P and E the prophet uses the third person to refer to Livistros but this has been changed to conform with the second person used in N.
44 Following the text of Hatziyiakoumis (p.150) in N477.
45 P599 (νομίζω ἔνι ...), E593, P600-601.
46 P618 (καὶ ἔπεσα...).

47   From P623 (τὸ ἐκόσμει...).
48   In N521 reading ῥαγῆς from P640 (μὴ τώρα...).
49   P646-648 (ἔναν πρᾶγμα...).
50   P659-668 (καὶ πάλιν...).
51   In N560 reading αὐγὴν νὰ μὴ ἀνεντρανίζω from E685.
52   N578 here calls Livistros *king* (βασιλεύς) which must be a corruption because elsewhere he is *prince* (ῥῆγας) *of the land of Livandros*. P707 (χώρας Λιβάνδρου...) contains a vestige of the true reading.
53   Following the emendation in Kriaras *s.v.* ἐδουλοκαταδούλευτα.
54   P728f. (...νὰ μὲ συγκακοπαθήσῃ / εὐχαριστῶ τον καὶ ἃς ἔλθῃ).
55   In N601 reading συνέριζεν from P732 (καὶ πρὸς...).
56   The last three words of N619 are corrupt and have been omitted.
57   E764.
58   Following the text of Hatziyiakoumis (p.150) in N702.
59   P835f. (ἐβγαίνω εἰς...).
60   From E845.
61   This passage from P (from the middle of *l.*847 (...καὶ πρέπει ν' ἀσχολῆται...) to *l.*855) has been supplemented (after P851) with E853, and in P854 the reading πρώτου has been adopted from E856.
62   P877 (καὶ πῶς...).
63   This rubric is misplaced in the original and occurs eleven lines earlier.
64   P884f. (τί περιμένεις...) and reading λέγε in P885.
65   In N759 reading εἶπα τους from P892 (εἶπα τους...).
66   In N794 reading ὁ μὲν νὰ παίζῃ μουσικὴν καὶ ἄλλος νὰ παίζῃ λύραν; cf. E931 and P918 (ὁ μὲν νὰ...).
67   In N797 reading πνοήν from P920 (ἄκουε πῶς...).
68   Supplied from E (*ll.*940-942) with Hatziyiakoumis's correction (p.150).
69   In N813 reading πρὸς τὸ τέλος from P937 (καὶ πρὸς...).
70   P939f. (...καὶ τὸ ἔναν της τὸ χέριν / εἶχε χαρτὶν...).
71   In N818 reading ἀνδρείας from P943 (καὶ δίχα...).
72   P949 (καὶ Πίστις...).
73   Following the text of Hatziyiakoumis (p.151) in N834.
74   The Greek Ἀγάπη is translated by *Affection* in the context of the Twelve Virtues and the Twelve Cupids. Elsewhere it is usually translated by *desire* by way of making a distinction, albeit small, between it and ἔρως *(sexual) love*.
75   P973 (ἡ Ἀγάπη...) with the emendations in Kriaras *Lexicon, s.v.* ἰχνάδι.
76   Following the text of Hatziyiakoumis (p.151) in N876.

77 There are also rubrics which simply give the name of the month. These have been omitted (and also one giving the name *Justice* in the previous section).

78 E1024f.

79 E1061.

80 See Lambert's note on E1062.

81 In N924 reading οἶνον μὴ ἀναθέτουν (see Lambert p.37).

82 P1049ff. (εἰς τὸ ἔναν...) but reading νὰ κρατῇ κλουβὶν μετὰ πουλία from E1074.

83 E1087-1091 with the final line as given in Lambert's note but reading συνέκλυσεν (see Kriaras *Lexicon, s.v.* ἀποκλείω II).

84 P1069 (πᾶς κυνηγὸς...).

85 P1072 (ἄνθρωπον ὅλον...).

86 E1114f. with παραμελῆται from P1087 (καὶ θέλει...). However, the two lines are probably corrupt.

87 E 1126f.

88 The remainder of the translation from this point is based on the manuscript *Codex Scaligeranus.*

89 In S53 Livistros is made to refer to himself by name; this has been eliminated.

90 E1192.

91 In S89 reading τὴν πανεξαίρετον from E1217.

92 In S174 reading βραδύνει νὰ πολεμεῖ; cf. P1255 (βραδύνει, οὐδέν...).

93 Reading τινὰ νὰ τὰ ἐγκαλέσω; cf. P1256 (καὶ ἐγὼ...).

94 In S202 reading ῥήγας from E1325.

95 In S217 reading νέον from P1282 (λέγει με...).

96 In S222 reading τὸ βραδύ from E1345.

97 In S225 reading ὁρμεῖ from P1290 (ἦλθε, δοξάριν...).

98 E1372f. (reading τον for το in E1373).

99 In S284 reading θαρρῇ (cf. E1407).

100 In S290 reading ἂν μή; cf. P1333 (εἰ μὴ...).

101 Following the text of Hatziyiakoumis (p.152) in S351.

102 Emending πόντος to πόνους in S358.

103 Omitting μή in S465; cf. E1583 and P1444 (καὶ διά...).

104 E1600f.

105 Following the text of Hatziyiakoumis (pp.152f.) in S524.

106 E1630 (see Hatziyiakoumis pp.152f.).

107 Following the text of Hatziyiakoumis (p.153) in S537.

108 Taking ὑπέμεινε εἰς διάκρισιν from E1652.

109 Emending οὐρανόπλαγον to οὐρανόπλαστος in S610 (cf. E1717).

110 Line 614 has been omitted.

111 E1754f. (from μὴν ἀπὲ...).
112 S697 has been omitted.
113 Supplying πόσῳ δὲ μᾶλλον ἄνθρωπος νὰ δέχεται πιττάκι after S711; cf. E1812, N1623 (πόσα δὲ...) and Kriaras *Lexicon* s.v. εὐυπόληπτος.
114 Emending μου to σου in S734 (cf. E1830).
115 This rubric occurs in two places, here and five lines earlier where it was written by mistake.
116 E1981.
117 Emending βλέπω to βλέπει in S906 (cf. S909) and εἶμαι to εἶναι (Lambert).
118 Reading πόθου (E2037) for λόγου in S959.
119 Replacing S975-977 with N1809-1811 (ἀλλὰ τοῦ σπλάγχους...) but keeping πάλιν εἰς μίαν τά from S977.
120 Emending ὀργίζομαι ἀπ᾽ ἐσέν in S980 to ὀργίζεσαι εἰς ἐμέν; cf. N1813 (ποθῶ τα...).
121 Reading ἀνέβα (E2085) in S1011.
122 P1734-1737 (λαμπρὸν σελοχαλίνωτον...).
123 Text corrupt.
124 For this passage, of which only vestiges exist in S, I have taken E2187-2194, N1949 (ψυχὴ ὁποὺ...), E2196-2204, N1958 (καὶ ἐκείνη...), E2205-2213 with minor changes; the text of Hatziyiamoumis (p.155) in E2212 has been adopted.
125 Reading εἰ μὴ... (the text of N) in S1136 as suggested by Lambert.
126 E2312f.
127 Replacing the latter half of S1211 with the latter half of N2060 (μὴ μὲ...); the text here is very doubtful.
128 P1877 (πέμπει Χρυσὸς...).
129 Reading κανείς (E2407) in S1276.
130 Reading παρείκαζες in S1278 from N2128 (παρείκαζες ἀνθόμοιον...).
131 P1915f. (στόμα μικρόν,...).
132 Following the text of Hatziyiakoumis (p.156) in S1304.
133 P1936-1939 (καὶ μέσα...) with ἀνάγων from E2459.
134 E2485 (note that the texts of S and E do not run exactly parallel at this point and the last three words of S1343 are repeated in E2485).
135 Text doubtful.
136 Substituting P1997-2008 (ἔχω πολλὰ...) for S1398.
137 Reading πιάνουσιν τὸ χέριν μου in the first half of S1411; cf. P2021 (πιάνουσιν τὸ...).
138 Substituting P2026 (ἐπίασα στράταν...) for S1420.
139 Replacing S1427f. with E2576 (with ἐγώ for εἰς μίον).

140 P2097f. (ἐὰν οὐ...) with Hatziyiakoumis's reconstruction of the passage (p.156).
141 Following the text of Hatziyiakoumis (p.157) in S1548.
142 Following the text of Hatziyiakoumis (p.157) in S1590.
143 Emending σκοπός to κοπός in S1598; cf. N2451 (τὴ στράτα...).
144 E2836.
145 E2845-2849.
146 E2882f.
147 N2678 (ὦ ξενοδόχε...).
148 Following the reading in E, N and V.
149 Following the text of Hatziyiakoumis (p.157) in S1846.
150 Replacing S1864 with E3021.
151 Replacing S1896 with N2749 (συναπαντάμε ἄνθρωπον...).
152 Adopting Lambert's correction ἔχει; πούπετε has the sense of *anywhere*, cf. S1578, S1898 etc.
153 N2789f. (ἐτρέχασι τὰ...).
154 Following the text of Hatziyiakoumis (p.160) in S1964 (this is mistakenly called 2964).
155 This line, which is half of the refrain occurring below, is missing here in S but occurs in E and N.
156 The refrain occurs at this point in both E and P.
157 Reading καὶ τὰ παιδόπουλά μας in S2083; cf. N2914 (εἴμεσταν ὁλομόναχοι...).
158 Following the text of Hatziyiakoumis (p.157) in S2164.
159 Following the text of Hatziyiakoumis (p.158) in S2207.
160 S2208 has been omitted.
161 This essential part of Rodamni's request is missing from E, N, P and S although it is the first thing that Verderichos mentions in his reply; it has been supplied it from V2961.
162 Reading νὰ ὑπομένω in S2225 with Agapitos (p.318) and adopting his punctuation.
163 N3064 (τίς νὰ...).
164 Emending εὐγενοῦς to ἀγενοῦς in S2308.
165 Following the text of Hatziyiakoumis (p.158) in S2339.
166 Emending ἀργά to ἀρχήν in S2431; cf. P2639 (καὶ εἶπα...).
167 From this point Klitovon's summary as given in S does not agree with what we have been told in the original narrative. To bring it into line I have substituted E3624-3627 for S2444 and omitted S2448-2462; the latter passage is garbled and repetitious and has no equivalent in the other mss. In E3626 μεσοκῆπιν has beeen changed to περιβόλιν; cf. S2451.
168 P2648 (καὶ μετὰ...).
169 The corrupt εἰς τίνα (S2466) must conceal something like ὅλα.

170 Following the text of Hatziyiakoumis (pp.158f.) in S2499.
171 Following the text of Hatziyiakoumis (p.159) in S2541.
172 Following the text of Hatziyiakoumis (p.159) in S2585.
173 E3791f.
174 Text doubtful.
175 Reading περιπατεῖ καί (E3818) for καὶ οὐρανοῦ in S2650.
176 This bizarre hyperbole (if the text is correct) seems to pick up, and elaborate upon, what Livistros has just said (*his tears were rivers*).
177 Following the text of Hatziyiakoumis (p.159) in S2678.
178 Reading καταφιλήματα (E3853) for τὰ ἀφηγήματα in S2688.
179 Following the text of Hatziyiakoumis (p.159) in S2700.
180 Reading ἀπ᾽ αὐτόν for εἰς αὐτόν in S2706 (cf. P2751) and adopting the reading αἰσθητοαναισθησίας of P2752 (νὰ συχνομεταπίπτουσιν...) in S2707 as suggested by Lambert.
181 Text doubtful.
182 The gap which occurs here in S has been filled with N3383-3415 (καὶ ἔναι...) with some readings from P, viz μυριοτυραννεῖ με (from P2817 κόρης ὡραίας...) in N3385; τοῦ πόθου τὸ κλαδὶν ἐλεῶ (from P2821) in N3390; τὸ δένδρον τοῦ πόνου (from P2822) in N3391: and πλήρωσέ το τὸ ποθῶ (from P2824) in N3393. Ἔρως at the beginning of N3411 is Lambert's emendation (at E3978).
183 This may be a constellation (Lambert).
184 The meaning appears to be: *In saying that Love is powerless you are denying that he can have had any effect on you, which is clearly not the case.*
185 E4051-4053.
186 Following the text of Hatziyiakoumis (p.160) in S2897.
187 E4089.
188 Reading στεναγμοί in S2959 from E4129 and N3496 (οἱ στεναγμοὶ...)
189 Emending the final τον to το in S3001 (Agapitos p.64).
190 The wheel may be that of Time, as below at S3222.
191 Omitting the corrupt λαλῶ τα in S3125.
192 Reading ὑποφέρω for συμφέρω in S3228.
193 Reading κἄν for καί at the beginning of S3231 (cf. E4373).
194 Emending both occurrences of ὡς in S3235 to ἄν (cf. E4376).
195 Replacing S3258 with E4396, and in S3259 emending ὡς πάντων to τὰ πάντα οὐ (cf. E4397 ἀπ᾽ αὐτὰ οὐ).

GARLAND LIBRARY OF MEDIEVAL LITERATURE

JAMES J. WILHELM
AND LOWRY NELSON, JR.
General Editors

Series A (Texts and Translations)
Series B (Translations Only)

BRUNETTO LATINI
Il Tesoretto (The Little Treasure)
Edited and translated by
  Julia Bolton Holloway
Series A

*THE POETRY OF WILLIAM VII,
COUNT OF POITIERS, IX DUKE
OF AQUITAINE*
Edited and translated by Gerald A. Bond;
  music edited by Hendrik van der Werf
Series A

BARTHAR SAGA
Edited and translated by Jon Skaptason
  and Phillip Pulsiano
Series A

GUILLAUME DE MACHAUT
*Judgment of the King of Bohemia (Le
Jugement dou Roy de Behaingne)*
Edited and translated by R. Barton Palmer
Series A

WALTHARIUS AND RUODLIEB
Edited and translated by Dennis M. Kratz
Series A

*THE RISE OF GAWAIN, NEPHEW OF
ARTHUR (DE ORTU WALUUANII
NEPOTIS ARTURI)*
Edited and translated by
  Mildred Leake Day
Series A

THE POETRY OF CINO DA PISTOIA
Edited and translated by
  Christopher Kleinhenz
Series A

*FIVE MIDDLE ENGLISH
ARTHURIAN ROMANCES*
Translated by Valerie Krishna
Series B

*THE ONE HUNDRED NEW TALES
(LES CENT NOUVELLES NOUVELLES)*
Translated by Judith Bruskin Diner
Series B

*L'ART D'AMOURS (THE ART
OF LOVE)*
Translated by Lawrence Blonquist
Series B

BÉROUL
The Romance of Tristran
Edited and translated by
  Norris J. Lacy
Series A

GRAELENT AND GUINGAMOR
Two Breton Lays
Edited and translated by
  Russell Weingartner
Series A

GIOVANNI BOCCACCIO
*Life of Dante (Trattatello in
Laude di Dante)*
Translated by Vincenzo Zin Bollettino
Series B

*THE LYRICS OF THIBAUT DE
CHAMPAGNE*
Edited and translated by
  Kathleen J. Brahney
Series A

THE POETRY OF SORDELLO
Edited and translated by James J. Wilhelm
Series A

GIOVANNI BOCCACCIO
Il Filocolo
Translated by Donald S. Cheney with
  the collaboration of Thomas G. Bergin
Series B

GUILLAUME DE MACHAUT
*The Judgment of the King of Navarre
(Le Jugement dou Roy de Navarre)*
Translated and edited by R. Barton Palmer
Series A

*THE STORY OF MERIADOC, KING OF
CAMBRIA (HISTORIA MERIADOCI,
REGIS CAMBRIAE)*
Edited and translated by
  Mildred Leake Day
Series A

*THE PLAYS OF HROTSVIT
OF GANDERSHEIM*
Translated by Katharina Wilson
Series B

GUILLAUME DE MACHAUT
The Fountain of Love (La Fonteinne Amoureuse), and Two Other Love Vision Poems
Edited and translated by
R. Barton Palmer
Series A

DER STRICKER
Daniel of the Blossoming Valley
Translated by Michael Resler
Series B

THE MARVELS OF RIGOMER
Translated by Thomas E. Vesce
Series B

CHRÉTIEN DE TROYES
The Story of the Grail (Li Contes del Graal), or *Perceval*
Edited by Rupert T. Pickens and translated by William W. Kibler
Series A

HELDRIS DE CORNUÄLLE
The Story of Silence (Le Roman de Silence)
Translated by Regina Psaki
Series B

ROMANCES OF ALEXANDER
Translated by Dennis M. Kratz
Series B

THE CAMBRIDGE SONGS
(CARMINA CANTABRIGIENSA)
Edited and translated by
Jan M. Ziolkowski
Series A

GUILLAUME DE MACHAUT
Le Confort d'Ami (Comfort for a Friend)
Edited and translated by
R. Barton Palmer
Series A

CHRISTINE DE PIZAN
Christine's Vision
Translated by Glenda K. McLeod
Series B

MORIZ VON CRAÛN
Edited and translated by
Stephanie Cain Van D'Elden
Series A

THE ACTS OF ANDREW IN THE COUNTRY OF THE CANNIBALS
Translated by Robert Boenig
Series B

RAZOS AND TROUBADOUR SONGS
Translated by William E. Burgwinkle
Series B

MECHTHILD VON MAGDEBURG
Flowing Light of the Divinity
Translated by Christiane Mesch Galvani; edited, with an introduction, by Susan Clark
Series B

ROBERT DE BORON
The Grail Trilogy
Translated by George Diller
Series B

TILL EULENSPIEGEL
His Adventures
Translated, with introduction and notes, by Paul Oppenheimer
Series B

FRANCESCO PETRARCH
Rime Disperse
Edited and translated by Joseph Barber
Series A

GUILLAUME DE DEGUILEVILLE
The Pilgrimage of Human Life (Le Pèlerinage de la vie humaine)
Translated by Eugene Clasby
Series B

RENAUT DE BÂGÉ
Le Bel Inconnu (Li Biaus Descouneüs; The Fair Unknown)
Edited by Karen Fresco; translated by Colleen P. Donagher; music edited by Margaret P. Hasselman
Series A

THOMAS OF BRITAIN
Tristran
Edited and translated by Stewart Gregory
Series A

KUDRUN
Translated by Marion E. Gibbs and Sidney M. Johnson
Series B

PENNINC AND PIETER VOSTAERT
Roman van Walewein
Edited and translated by David F. Johnson
Series A

MEDIEVAL LITERATURE OF POLAND
An Anthology
Translated by Michael J. Miko
Series B

HELYAS OR LOHENGRIN
Late Medieval Transformations of the Swan Knight Legend
Edited and translated by
Salvatore Calomino
Series A